ADMINISTRATIVE AND COMPLIANCE COSTS OF TAXATION

Other Books by CEDRIC SANDFORD

Hidden Costs of Taxation, Institute for Fiscal Studies, 1973.

An Accessions Tax (with J. R. M. Willis and D. J. Ironside), Institute for Fiscal Studies, 1973.

An Annual Wealth Tax (with J. R. M. Willis and D. J. Ironside), IFS/Heinemann, 1975.

Costs and Benefits of VAT (with M. Godwin, P. Hardwick and I. Butterworth), Heinemann Educational Books, 1981.

Tax Policy-Making in the United Kingdom (with Ann Robinson), Heinemann Educational Books, 1983.

The Irish Wealth Tax: A Study in Economics and Politics (with Oliver Morrissey), Economic and Social Research Institute, Dublin, 1985.

Case Studies in Economics (joint editor and part author with M. S. Bradbury), Longman, 1985.

Economics of Public Finance, Pergamon, 4th edition due 1990.

ADMINISTRATIVE

AND

COMPLIANCE COSTS

OF TAXATION

Cedric Sandford
Michael Godwin
Peter Hardwick

with an appendix by

David Collard

FISCAL PUBLICATIONS
1989

British Library Cataloguing in Publication Data

Sandford, Cedric, *1924-*
    Administrative and compliance costs of taxation.
    1. Great Britain. Taxation. Compliance. Costs
    I. Title II. Godwin, Michael III. Hardwick, Peter
    336.2

    ISBN 0—9515157—0—5 Hardback

Printed in Great Britain by
Redwood Burn Ltd,
Yeoman Way, Trowbridge, Wiltshire.

Published by Fiscal Publications,
Old Coach House, Fersfield, Perrymead,
BATH BA2 5AR.

CONTENTS

PART I

Meaning and Measurement

PART II

Administrative and Compliance Costs of the United Kingdom Tax System 1986-87 with International Comparisons

PART III

Policy Issues

ACKNOWLEDGEMENTS

First and foremost, the thanks of the authors are due to the Economic and Social Research Council and its predecessor, the Social Science Research Council, for finding almost all the finance to fund the studies over a series of years. Funding for one small part of the study was provided by a Nuffield small research grant in the social sciences, for which the authors are likewise most grateful.

The study would have been impossible without the unstinting help of Inland Revenue and Customs and Excise. Many officers of both services could not have been more generous of their time and expertise; whilst they were not slow to correct our errors they fully respected our independence, even when that led us to make comments which they found unpalatable. Our thanks are also due to the Department of Social Security.

We gratefully acknowledge our debt to members of an advisory panel whose expert comments on an earlier draft of the book led to substantial changes. Besides senior representatives of Inland Revenue and Customs and Excise, the advisory committee members comprised John Avery-Jones, Ken Etherington, Malcolm Gammie, Michael Holland, Professor Jim Ilersic, Donald Ironside, Peter Kempton, Jonathan Langdon and Alan Willingale. All busy men, they yet found time to write comments and attend an all day meeting at Bath. The authors are most grateful to them. Peter Dean acted as a consultant to the study and made many useful suggestions at different stages of the work and Professor Francois Vaillancourt of the University of Montreal and Jeff Pope of the University of Western Australia, both of whom were engaged on studies of compliance costs in their respective countries, also provided valuable comments on the draft.

The number of individuals in the private sector who assisted by submitting to interviews is too numerous to mention and there is always the danger that an attempt to single out some for special mention does injustice to others. Reference will therefore only be made to those who, in their official position, helped to gather information for the study - i.e. Paul Chisnall, of the British Bankers' Association, Christopher French, of the Building Societies Association, Bill Nicolle, Chairman of the United Kingdom Oil Industry Taxation Committee, Colin Miles, Secretary of the Oil Industry Indirect Taxation Committee, Charles H. Clarke, formerly Director-General of the National Association of Warehouse Keepers and Members and Officers of the Tobacco Advisory Council. Whether specifically mentioned or not we thank all our interviewees most sincerely. Without their help and that of the thousands of respondents who carefully completed our questionnaires, we could have done nothing.

Finally our sincere thanks are due to Julia Howard for turning our poor script into immaculate type and whose speed and accuracy remains a source of continual wonder to us.

There remains only the essential disclaimer. The views expressed herein and any errors are the sole responsibility of the authors.

Cedric Sandford   Centre for Fiscal Studies
Michael Godwin   University of Bath
Peter Hardwick   June 1989

GLOSSARY OF TECHNICAL TERMS

Administrative costs: public sector costs incurred in administering an existing tax code (including advice on its modification).

Cash flow benefit: the benefit which accrues (i) to a third party in the process of collecting tax from the final taxpayer and withholding the money until the date on which it becomes payable to the tax authorities; or (ii) to a taxpayer who is legally permitted to withhold tax for a period after the completion of the economic transaction giving rise to the tax liability.

Commencement costs: once and for all costs (administrative or compliance) incurred at the inception of a new feature of the tax system.

Composite rate tax (CRT): a rate of income tax paid by banks and building societies to the Inland Revenue in respect of the interest due to depositors, who receive their interest net of basic rate tax.

Compliance costs: costs incurred by taxpayers or third parties, notably businesses, in meeting the requirements laid on them by a given tax structure (excluding the payment of the tax itself and any distortion costs arising from it).

Discriminant function analysis (DIF): a technique developed by the United States Internal Revenue Service and designed to identify the tax returns most likely to yield revenue from an audit.

Enforcement costs: public sector costs to ensure compliance; part of administrative costs.

Excess burden (or dead weight loss) of taxation: welfare losses arising because firms and individuals change the pattern of their behaviour and activities because of taxation.

Financial Management Initiative (FMI): a programme to improve financial management in United Kingdom government departments.

Horizontal equity: the equal tax treatment of persons with the same taxable capacity.

Marginal cost: the cost of supplying an additional unit.

Marginal revenue: the revenue obtained from applying an additional unit.

Net compliance costs: compliance costs minus offsetting benefits, in particular, cash flow benefits.

Operating costs of taxation: administrative plus compliance costs plus other Exchequer costs.

Opportunity cost: the sacrifice of using resources in one particular way rather than in the best alternative use.

Other Exchequer costs: public sector costs additional to administrative costs in operating a tax, notably the (opportunity) cost incurred by the Exchequer arising from the existence of a lag in tax payment.

Psychic (psychological) costs: costs of the burden of anxiety imposed by the requirement of tax compliance.

Regular costs: administrative and compliance costs arising from the continuing operation of a tax, excluding temporary costs.

Social costs (benefits): costs (benefits) experienced by the community as a whole which arise from the operation of a tax.

Temporary costs: administrative and compliance costs arising from unfamiliarity with a tax.

GLOSSARY OF ABBREVIATIONS

ACT	Advance corporation tax
APRT	Advance petroleum revenue tax
CAB	Citizens Advice Bureau
CIPFA	Chartered Institute of Public Finance and Accounting
CGT	Capital gains tax
CRT	Composite rate tax
CT	Corporation tax
CTF	Canadian Tax Foundation
DIF	Discriminant function analysis
DTI	Department of Trade and Industry
EO	Executive officer
FEU	Federal Union of Employers (Ireland)
FMI	Financial Management Initiative
GST	Goods and services tax (New Zealand)
HEO	Higher executive officer
IFA	International Fiscal Association
IFS	Institute for Fiscal Studies
IHT	Inheritance tax
IRS	Internal Revenue Service
MC	Marginal cost
MIRAS	Mortgage interest relief at source
MR	Marginal revenue
MRP	Maximum revenue potential
NAWK	National Association of Warehouse Keepers
NES	New Earnings Survey
NI	National insurance
OECD	Organisation for Economic Co-operation and Development
PAYE	Pay-As-You-Earn (survey 1981-82)
PET	Potentially exempt transfer
PIT	Personal income tax (survey 1983-84)
PRSI	Pay related social insurance (Ireland)
PRT	Petroleum revenue tax
RPI	Retail price index
SEO	Senior executive officer
SERPS	State earnings related pension scheme
SPI	Survey of personal incomes
TPD	Tobacco products duty
TR	Total revenue
VAT	Value added tax
VAT 1	Value added tax survey 1977-78
VAT 2	Value added tax survey 1986-87

INTRODUCTION

This book analyses in some detail the nature of administrative (public sector) and compliance (private sector) costs of operating a tax system and the problems of measuring them. It also records the findings of research to measure those costs for the United Kingdom tax system in 1986-87.

Whilst policy objectives in respect of administrative costs are discussed and analysed, the prime purpose of the book is to stress the importance of compliance costs.

Compliance costs are important for their sheer size, which makes them the equivalent of a large industry and offers considerable scope for resource saving, but, even more important, for the way in which they are distributed. They are frequently inequitable in their incidence and, in particular, the compliance costs of business taxes fall with disproportionate severity on particular sectors of the economy, but especially on small firms. Compliance costs tend to be particularly resented by some small businessmen and are thus a seedbed for tax evasion. Because they are less visible than administrative costs and because there is a degree of transferability between administrative and compliance costs, there is a real danger that a cost-cutting government will cut public sector costs at the expense of private sector costs. Finally compliance costs are important to every aspect of tax policy-making - the choice of a new tax, tax structure, administrative methods or changes to the whole balance of taxation. Consideration of compliance costs should form part of every tax policy-making debate.

The United Kingdom has moved a long way towards this objective and has, in various recent documents, recognised the need to take careful account of compliance costs. However, its deeds do not always match its words.

Few other countries have come as far as the United Kingdom in recognising the importance of compliance costs, at least partly because less research on compliance costs has been undertaken in other countries. A feature of the book is a review of the history of attempts to measure compliance costs and extensive reference to other studies.

Part I of the book is concerned with definitions and concepts, with the historical aspects of the subject and with some of the particular problems associated with measuring compliance costs. Although illustrations are drawn more frequently from the United Kingdom than elsewhere, the matter considered is equally applicable to any tax system.

Part II is, in effect, a major case study. It describes the methodology and the findings of research undertaken at the Centre for Fiscal Studies, University of Bath, to measure the administrative and compliance costs of the United Kingdom tax system in 1986-87. Although centred on the United Kingdom, the methodology used has a wider applicability and, whenever relevant, the findings of research in other countries are compared with those of the United Kingdom study.

Part III draws out the policy implications. As the conclusions flow primarily from the findings of Part II, they have an especial relevance to the United Kingdom; but most of the conclusions can be applied with equal relevance to tax policy elsewhere.

Finally there are a series of Appendices. One Appendix summarises the methods and findings of earlier studies published in English on compliance costs; three Appendices chart some of the more technical aspects of the study for the interested specialist; whilst an Appendix, written by Professor David Collard, relates compliance costs to the more theoretical tax literature on the 'excess burden' of taxation.

Administrative and Compliance Costs of Taxation

PART I

Meaning and Measurement

CHAPTER 1

DEFINITIONS AND CONCEPTS

Costs of various kinds arise from the existence of individual taxes and of the tax system as a whole. In this chapter we seek to identify and define these costs, clarify their nature and consider, in particular, those on which this book will be concentrating. However, it must be recognised at the outset that complexities and inter-relationships make it difficult if not impossible to define the various costs with absolute precision or in a neat, mutually exclusive, way; moreover operational definitions need to be geared to the data available.

The starting point of the analysis is a broad distinction between public and private sector costs. Let us begin with public sector costs as covering the more familiar ground.

Public Sector Costs

In principle, total public sector costs of a particular tax can be thought of as constituting those costs which would not have been incurred if the tax had never been introduced; or alternatively the public sector costs which would be saved if the tax were abolished. On a short-run view these two measures will not be identical: there are temporary costs associated with a new tax; and the abolition of an existing tax may not save, in cash terms, all the costs incurred because equipment may need to be written off or redundancy payments made. In the long run, however, the two measures converge.

The most obvious public sector costs are those incurred by the revenue departments in bringing in the tax revenue: wages and salaries of revenue staff, accommodation and the like, which we examine more fully below. Such items should clearly be classed as administrative costs. But they are not the total of public sector costs; and the borderline between what should be classed as 'administrative costs' and what constitute 'other exchequer costs' is a hazy one.

If we seek to establish the total public sector costs of the tax system we must take account of the costs of introducing a tax or making major

3

modifications to it, which fall outside the cost structure of the revenue departments. Thus, it is normal for the Treasury or Finance Ministry to play a part in planning and preparing a new tax or a major tax change. The advice of other government departments, whose activities or whose clients may be affected, may be sought and a government body (such as the Property Services Agency in the United Kingdom) may be called on to provide accommodation. Parliamentary Counsel draft the necessary legislation. Government ministers are the prime determiners of policy and ministers and the legislature spend much time turning proposals into law. Once legislation is enacted, government law officers may be called on to interpret the law and judges, whose salary is paid from the public purse, will be required to adjudicate on cases brought before them. Moreover the courts will be invoked in the recovery of tax in default. In addition, special courts, such as, in the United Kingdom, the General and Special Commissioners in respect of income tax and the VAT tribunal, all incur costs. The list can be extended almost indefinitely — from the costs of the court-house itself, and the salaries of the officers required to ensure the functioning of the courts dealing with tax cases, to the cleaners who clean the court rooms.

A very different kind of public sector cost arises from the existence of what are, in effect, interest-free loans to businesses and individuals. With many taxes, taxpayers or third parties, notably businesses, are legally allowed to hold tax revenue for a period. Such a provision does not take the form of an explicit outlay by the Exchequer, but it is a very real and important opportunity cost. This is clear if we postulate a change in administrative practice. For example, with value added tax (VAT) there is always a specified 'collection period' — during which the tax is being collected by a business on behalf of the revenue authorities, and a specified 'grace period' — during which the business is allowed to retain the tax before passing it over to the revenue authorities. In the United Kingdom the standard collection period is three months and the grace period is one month. Other countries have different periods; for example the collection period in Ireland is two months and the grace period nineteen days; in Sweden the periods are, respectively, two months and one month plus five days (OECD 1988). If a government changed the law to reduce the length of either or both the collection and grace periods, the effect would be to generate a once-and-for-all cash flow benefit to public funds which would (other things being equal) reduce the public borrowing needs and bring an annual saving in debt interest. Changes to reduce the collection and grace periods for tax withheld from employees, or to bring forward the date of payment of corporation tax, or of income tax on the self-employed, would have similar effects.

What Should Count as Administrative Costs?

How far should these kinds of costs — costs associated with new taxes, legal costs and interest costs — be regarded as *administrative* costs? The precise borderline is unclear. Consider new legislation; staff of the revenue departments invariably advise ministers on tax policy with respect to new taxes and amendments to the tax system, as do staff of the Finance Ministry. In the United Kingdom, Inland Revenue, Customs and Excise and the Treasury all have solicitors' offices. The staff of the revenue departments continuously advise ministers whilst legislation is going through Parliament. Revenue departments invariably are the source of considerable secondary legislation, by means of statutory orders. Such activities might reasonably be regarded as part of administrative costs, as might the costs of the special courts such as the VAT tribunal in the United Kingdom. However, there is a much stronger case for excluding the time parliamentarians take in enacting tax legislation. As to the costs of that part of the legal system which relate to tax, it would seem reasonable that the costs incurred directly by the revenue departments in themselves bringing cases before the courts should count as part of the costs of administration, but not the general costs of running that part of the legal system associated with interpreting and enforcing the tax statutes in the courts.

The main argument for excluding from administrative costs the costs of interest-free loans to the private sector is that such an element of cost is not really under the control of the administrators. There is more of a case for including as administrative costs any 'interest-free loans' to firms and individuals who have failed to comply with the law by not paying tax on the due date; but, in principle, penalties might be expected to offset that cost. Perhaps the most satisfactory procedure is to define administrative costs as the public sector costs incurred in administering an existing tax code (including advice on its modification). Then the bulk of the costs of new legislation and of law interpretation would fall outside the definition*, as would the cost of legal interest-free loans. In that case we are left with a structure of public sector costs as in Figure 1.

---

* It might be noted that Vaillancourt, in his study of the personal income tax in Canada, found court costs to be very small (Vaillancourt 1988)

Figure 1

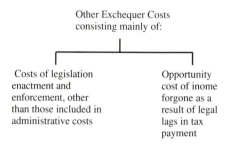

Administrative Costs (costs of administering an existing tax code, including advice on its modification)

Other Exchequer Costs consisting mainly of:

Costs of legislation enactment and enforcement, other than those included in administrative costs

Opportunity cost of inome forgone as a result of legal lags in tax payment

Public Sector Costs

This definition of administrative costs has the advantage of according closely with the costs attributed to the revenue departments in the United Kingdom (with which we are concerned in Part II), after the deduction of the costs of services they undertake for other departments; although, as we shall see in the next section, the method of calculating administrative costs does not always produce the correct opportunity cost. In what follows we shall have little to say about the other Exchequer costs in relation to legislation but a lot to say about the value of lagged tax payments, mainly from the standpoint of the taxpayer, for whom they constitute an important offset to the costs of compliance.

The Composition of Administrative Costs

Administrative costs obviously include salaries and wages of staff at all levels, including national insurance contributions and superannuation costs; accommodation costs (including rents, rates, heating, lighting and cleaning); postage, telephone, printing, stationery; travel; computing and other equipment costs.

An important problem which arises in studying administrative costs is the limitations on available information. Many countries do not, as a matter of routine, record the detailed components of expenditure or allocate that expenditure to particular taxes (IFA 1989). In this respect the United States (to which we refer more fully in the final chapter) and the United Kingdom are notable for the amount of detailed information which is analysed and available.

In the United Kingdom as part of the so-called Financial Management Initiative (FMI) which was formally introduced in May 1982 to build on work already done in improving financial management in government departments, Inland Revenue and Customs and Excise now undertake a much more detailed breakdown of costs than was formerly the case. The FMI works best in those government departments which are functional, providing a direct service with a more easily measured output, than in those which are primarily stimulative, like education and health, where the output is provided by other agents (Robinson and Sandford, 1987). The revenue departments are functional departments and FMI has proceeded a long way and become part of their basic management structure. The object of the FMI is to provide more effective allocation and control of resources through a system of management planning and budgeting. Each revenue department has a corporate plan, linked to the Public Expenditure Survey, which is endorsed by ministers at the start of each financial year. The plan sets out priorities, aims and objectives and the resources for each work area. Considerable authority including a large degree of control over budgets is delegated to lower management levels within the departments. A series of specific objectives and targets, framed in quantitative terms, are developed and outcomes monitored.

One result of this process has been a detailed breakdown of costs. The revenue departments in the United Kingdom now allocate costs both to specific aspects of the service (e.g. the investigative activities of Inland Revenue) and to individual taxes and groups of taxes, so that the costs can be related to out-turn wherever possible. Where services to an activity area (which might be the collection of revenue from a particular tax) are provided jointly with services to other activity areas, a *pro rata* allocation of costs is made. Details of costs are published in the annual reports of the Commissioners. Whilst the United Kingdom has gone much further in such analysis than most other countries, the breakdown of costs has not yet proceeded as far as might be wished; for example, Customs and Excise provide costs for administering the duties on alcoholic drinks (which can be set against the revenue out-turn) but do not provide a separate breakdown of costs for each of wines, spirits and beer, although these duties are each quite distinct in structure.

A second general problem arises about the nature of government costings, both as to their amount and their allocation over time. The ideal would be the opportunity cost of the resources used (their value in the best alternative use) with the cost of a resource being spread over the period during which it contributes to output. Staff costs may be taken as reasonable reflection of opportunity costs at the time they are incurred, but problems arise under other heads*.

Thus, with accommodation charges a true opportunity cost would reflect the rent the accommodation would fetch in the open market. In the United Kingdom, whilst the policy may be in the process of changing, the Property Services Agency, which is responsible for providing accommodation for all government services, charges a department an average cost of accommodation determined on an area basis rather than the actual accommodation costs; and where departments occupy buildings on long leases in desirable areas, the lease may well understate the market value — in other words the accommodation could be sub-let at a figure above the actual rental paid. In such a case the costs recorded against the services provided are lower than the true economic cost.

The issue of the appropriate spread of costs over time arises in relation to capital expenditures. The accounts of revenue departments are often, as in the United Kingdom, on a cash basis, when, in principle, the costs should be allocated over the life of the equipment by an appropriate depreciation charge. Thus there is some distortion of the true economic costs where there are significant variations in capital expenditure between years. For example, if there is a major expenditure on computerisation, all the cost is attributed to the year of purchase.

A query also arises about how training costs should be treated. In principle there is a case for training costs to be dealt with on lines similar to those appropriate for capital costs (as an investment in human capital); an increase in the training budget would then be spread over the period during which the benefit might be expected. However, it is by no means certain how long that period would be, both because some part of training may be rendered obsolete by changes in methods or taxes and because of staff losses to the private sector. So it is only realistic to allocate training costs to the year in which they occur, which is the practice followed in the United Kingdom and generally elsewhere. Nevertheless, this procedure does mean that, where there is a heavy training expenditure in a particular year (for example, because of the introduction of a major new tax, like VAT) a false impression of the costs appropriate to that year could be given.

Whilst it is impossible to make any judgements affecting countries as a whole, in the United Kingdom these divergencies from true economic cost in the costing procedures of the revenue departments are unlikely to

---

* For a fuller treatment of some of these issues, see Goode, 1981, to which the authors acknowledge their indebtedness.

be significant, at least in their aggregate effect; the costs of the revenue departments are overwhelmingly staff-related costs (over 70 per cent) and the divergencies in respect of accommodation and equipment would not, on the face of things, appear to be unduly large.

Various categories of administrative costs can be distinguished, which are common also to compliance costs. It is therefore convenient to examine the two together later in the chapter.

Private Sector Costs

The imposition of a tax generates a variety of costs for the private sector. There is the most obvious cost for the taxpayer of the sacrifice of purchasing power which paying the tax entails, which has its counterpart in the corresponding government expenditure. There are also welfare costs arising from the distortions that a tax generates. Thus an income tax distorts the choice between work and leisure, whilst a tax on goods or services distorts the consumption pattern of the consumer and the production pattern, generating inefficiencies in the allocation of resources. (These costs are often referred to as the 'excess burden' of taxation, a subject explored in Appendix E).

Thirdly, there are costs which taxpayers and third parties, notably businesses, incur in meeting the legal requirements of the tax system — completing tax returns, compiling and keeping the necessary accounts and records and the like.

The borderline between distortion costs and the costs of formal compliance is itself somewhat hazy. Thus distortion costs are not only a function of the existence of a tax but also of the manner in which it is imposed. Thus, for an equal revenue yield, a turnover tax on all transactions with no credit for inputs (a cascade tax) distorts industrial structure (e.g. by encouraging vertical integration) which a turnover tax with input credit (a VAT) does not. A tax on goods levied at the manufacturer's level creates more distortions than one imposed on the same goods at the retail level because, for example, businesses will seek to re-arrange their activities so as to minimise manufacturing prices (on which tax is based) by transferring some expenditures, like advertising and transport, beyond the tax point. Again, given the economic stage at which the tax is imposed, the effect and the degree of distortion may differ according to whether tax is paid on the raw material as it goes into the factory or on the finished product as it leaves the factory; and again, on whether the tax takes the form of a specific duty, an ad valorem duty or combination of the two. (The significance of some of these features is dramatically brought out by the changes in the form of taxing the British tobacco manufacturers, briefly described in Chapter 10, below). Moreover, where compliance costs are incurred by business, the question of their effective incidence arises: who ultimately pays them? The manner in which they are met may generate welfare costs similar to those resulting from the tax itself (see Chapter 12).

What Should Count as Compliance Costs?

In this study we are not concerned with the costs of distortion which are inherent in the imposition of a tax — costs which cannot be avoided once it has been decided to tax income at a certain level, or to impose a particular level of tax on a good or service. Our prime concern is with the costs incurred by taxpayers and third parties in meeting the requirements laid upon them in complying with a given structure and level of tax. We are also concerned to explore the implications of compliance costs — their effective incidence and features in the tax structure (such as a multi-rate scale) which may generate additional costs.

The term 'compliance costs' is itself ambiguous; it could equally well, in logic, refer to the costs incurred by the authorities in *securing* compliance (in which case it would be a public sector cost and a part of administrative costs) or the costs incurred by taxpayers (including third parties) in complying, in which case it is a private sector cost. In this study we follow the practice of the literature and confine the term to the costs of the taxpayer. Public sector costs of ensuring compliance can be called enforcement costs.

To sum up: compliance costs are defined as those costs incurred by taxpayers, or third parties such as businesses, in meeting the requirements laid upon them in complying with a given tax structure. They thus include, for individuals, the costs of acquiring sufficient knowledge to meet their legal requirements; of compiling the necessary receipts and other data and of completing tax returns; payments to professional advisers for tax advice; and incidental costs of postage, telephone and travel in order to communicate with tax advisers or the tax office. For a business, the compliance costs include the cost of collecting, remitting and accounting for tax on the products or profits of the business and on the wages and salaries of its employees together with the costs of acquiring the knowledge to enable this work to be done including knowledge of their legal obligations and penalties. These costs include associated

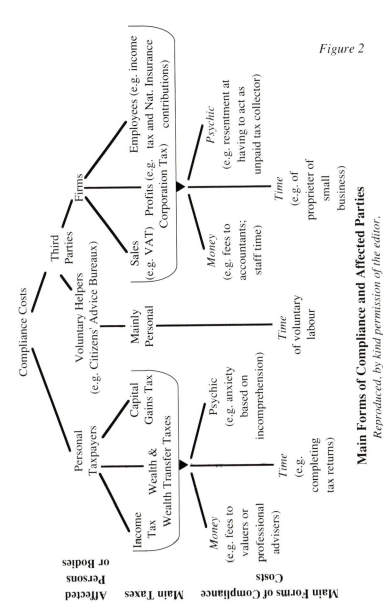

Figure 2

Main Forms of Compliance and Affected Parties
Reproduced, by kind permission of the editor,
from an article in the British Tax Review by one of the authors of the present study

overhead costs including the costs of storing records as required by the tax authorities. The existence of uncertainty about the meaning of some aspect of the tax legislation will generate additional compliance costs. It is also appropriate to include as compliance costs those costs incurred by representative bodies (paid for by their members) in making presentations and lobbying for tax changes. A summary of the main forms of compliance cost and affected parties is set out in Figure 2.

However, this definition still leaves some matters requiring further discussion.

The Costs of Tax Planning

In the limited literature on compliance costs, a distinction, stemming from Johnston (1961), has been made between unavoidable (mandatory) and avoidable (voluntary or discretionary) compliance costs. Unavoidable costs are those necessarily incurred if the taxpayer is to meet the legal requirements laid upon him, whilst avoidable costs are tax planning costs he chose to undertake in order to minimise his tax bill. It has been argued that as the avoidable costs were voluntary, they should not be included as part of compliance cost. On the other hand, it has also been responded that even the discretionary costs should be included because they were a product of the existence of the tax; remove the tax and they would disappear.

The unavoidable/avoidable distinction has flaws. For example, all income taxes have a number of allowances, which may include child allowance, housekeeper allowance for the disabled, allowances for insurance premiums and the like. A taxpayer does not *have* to claim these allowances, even though he is fully entitled to them. Thus the compiling of any records and the completion of the tax return in respect of such allowances is a voluntary act. Yet in common sense it can hardly be regarded as anything other than an essential part of complying with the tax. Perhaps rather than 'unavoidable' costs, we need a concept such as that of the lawyer: 'the costs which a reasonable man would incur'.

If we consider business costs, it is sometimes possible to separate tax planning from the purely computational aspects of tax compliance, but such a separation has little value. The timing of investment, or arranging cash flows to maximise benefit from tax provisions, are the kind of measures which we would expect from 'a reasonable man'. The compliance costs associated with them, whilst avoidable in the literal sense, are the outcome of matters no reasonable businessman can afford to ignore.

With big commercial transactions, such as mergers, or the transfer between countries of assets of a multi-national company, there is, of necessity, a large input of tax planning. In the literal sense it is avoidable, but any company which ignored it could find itself in serious trouble. Such tax planning, which consists of a detailed examination of the implications of a transaction and the choice of a method which minimises tax, is an essential cost of compliance, a necessary ingredient of commercial activity. As some interviewees expressed it, it is 'defensive' rather than 'offensive'; seeking to avoid tax traps in a genuine commercial transaction rather than setting out, as a specific exercise, to engage in tax minimising activities.

If a distinction has to be drawn perhaps the best is that between tax planning which is a concomitant of a genuine commercial transaction and tax planning which involves purely artificial transactions. But costs of this purely artificial kind are likely to be very small in relation to compliance costs as a whole (though they may be large for a few taxpayers, both individuals and companies); compliance cost data rarely allows them to be distinguished; and even these costs are costs which would not arise but for the existence of the tax.

Offsets to Compliance Costs

The compliance effects of a tax may not be entirely detrimental; there may be benefits from compliance which constitute an offset to the tax. Thus an individual, in completing an annual tax return and carefully filing the documentation to do so, may at the same time be stimulated to review his investments and be prompted to a more efficient management of his financial affairs. More significantly, businesses may receive benefits. Stringent record-keeping to comply with the requirements of the tax system may enforce a businessman to introduce a more efficient financial information system which can bring managerial advantages. The introduction of VAT generated some gains of this kind. Moreover, with some taxes there are distinct cash flow advantages where businesses have the use of tax revenues for a period before they must be handed over to the revenue authorities. The whole question of cash flow detriments and benefits is considered at some length in Chapter 3 and we have already noted their existence in the context of other Exchequer costs. Where there are offsets to compliance costs it may be useful to talk of *net compliance costs* which are compliance costs after deducting the value of benefits. Where 'compliance costs' is used without an accompanying adjective it can be taken to mean 'gross' compliance costs. Because of the difficulty of valuing other benefits, net compliance costs are generally compliance costs minus the value of the cash flow benefit.

The pattern of private sector costs and benefits from taxation is summarised in Figure 3.

Problems in Measuring Compliance Costs

As with administrative costs, in measuring compliance costs we are concerned with opportunity costs — the value of the next best use to which the resources might be put. Moreover, we are seeking to establish what costs are incurred specifically because of the existence of the tax — or alternatively what costs would be saved if the tax were abolished. These measures are often difficult to obtain.

For example, a taxpayer who employs an accountant may receive an unitemised bill for unravelling all his financial affairs including taxation. Clearly some proportion of this bill represents a tax compliance cost, but the amount to be allocated is a matter of judgement. It may be that non-corporate taxpayers would not produce accounts at all if they were not considered to be necessary for tax purposes. On the other hand, a company is required to publish annual accounts for the benefit of its shareholders and may in any case collect the information required for management purposes.

There is also a problem in isolating the marginal addition to costs caused by the imposition of a particular tax. Where a company has a tax department, it may be argued that the marginal cost of an additional tax is zero if the specialist tax staff can take the extra work in their stride. Alternatively the marginal cost is simply the extra labour cost incurred in cases where that labour can be accommodated within the existing office space. This line of argument may then be pursued for each separate tax which the department operates. However, clearly the costs of the department (or the overhead costs) would not have been incurred if the tax system as a whole had not existed.

There has been considerable discussion, particularly by Yocum (1961), of this problem of allocating overheads. The issue hinges on whether compliance work simply results in a more intensive use of existing facilities. If a business has to rent, heat and light additional offices solely for its tax department, the costs of such offices are clearll

Figure 3

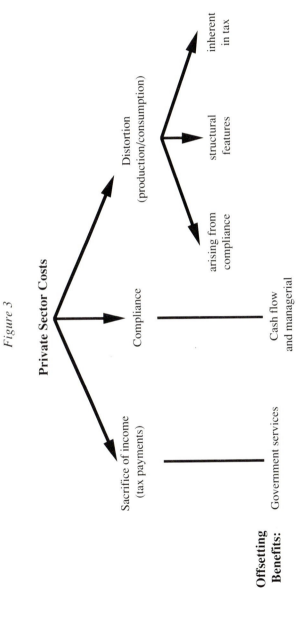

Private Sector Costs and Benefits from Taxation

compliance costs. However, in many cases tax work is done within an accounting department which would continue to be needed if there were no taxation. In this case it may be argued that the overhead expenditure is independent of tax compliance, and the overhead compliance cost is zero. It seems probable that the percentage of overhead expenditure allocable to tax compliance work increases with the size of firm and the complexity of tax duties performed. The sole proprietor who spends extra time at work every month to update his tax accounts and returns will incur minimal extra costs in heating and lighting, together with some cost in storing the obligatory records. A larger firm may find it efficient to set up a separate accounts department, renting additional space which will be devoted to tax work for part of the time. The largest businesses may have offices maintained exclusively for tax accounting purposes.

Much of the costs of compliance consists of time costs. Where the time is that of paid employees to the firm the cost is evident — it is the addition to the wage or salary bill. But where the cost is additional work undertaken out of working hours by the proprietor of a business or his family, the value to put on that time is more problematical. We consider this issue at some length in Chapter 3.

Categories of Administrative and Compliance Costs

A number of cost categories can be distinguished which are common to both compliance and administrative costs.

Costs of Change and Regular Costs

Commencement costs arise with the introduction of a new tax or a major change in a tax. In principle some commencement costs, like the administrative or compliance cost of a new computer system to operate a new tax or the administrative or compliance costs of training new tax officers or, on the private side, new book-keepers to deal with tax, should, strictly speaking, be spread over a period rather than be considered a cost solely at the time incurred, but it is difficult to put the principle into effect.

Temporary costs are the additional costs for both the revenue and the tax compliers, whilst learning is taking place for both revenue officers and taxpayers.

Regular costs are the continuing costs of running a tax or tax system, without the additional temporary elements of tax change. In practice, if governments change the tax system very frequently, there will always be, at any time, some element of temporary costs.

A problem may arise in distinguishing between temporary, regular and once-only costs of administration or compliance. An observer may well over-estimate the level of costs if he investigates them during a period when a new tax has just been introduced, for costs will fall as the tax becomes familiar.

Considerable care is needed in allocating costs to the correct category. Where a single business has incurred large legal fees in a tax dispute, this will usually be categorised as an isolated case of high costs. If, however, it emerges that, due perhaps to ill-conceived legislation, a large percentage of taxpayers are regularly in dispute with the authorities, then taking taxpayers as a whole such expenditures may be considered a regular cost of administration or/and compliance.

The categories of regular, temporary and commencement costs are illustrated diagramatically in Figure 4, which depicts a model of the pattern of costs following the introduction of a new tax. With a new tax there is likely to be a build-up of compliance costs before the tax is implemented; with a change in an existing tax there may be very little build-up depending on the magnitude of the change and whether an announcement preceded implementation. With administrative costs the pattern will be an earlier build-up both before the start of a tax and before a change.

Figure 4

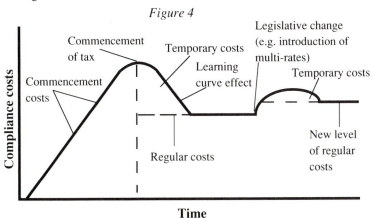

Time
Model of Changes in Administrative and Compliance Costs with a New Tax

It is clear from the diagram that there are compliance costs of change. But if there are major changes in a tax structure or in the form in which a particular tax is levied, the costs may be more than is indicated in the diagram; the change may necessitate the write-off of equipment or personal skills acquired over many years.

Psychic (or Psychological) Costs

Psychic or psychological costs, whilst difficult or impossible to measure satisfactorily are an important component of compliance costs. Many people experience considerable anxiety and frustration in dealing with their tax affairs; some employ a professional adviser primarily to reduce this burden of worry. In so far as this has the desired effect, the psychic cost then becomes a monetary cost.

Psychic costs are particularly felt by the old and retired: they may have been used to obtaining advice from the accounts department of an employer (responsible for deducting income tax); their retirement income may come from several sources; they meet new and somewhat complicated age allowances; and have much difficulty in comprehending tax literature (James, Lewis, Allison, 1987). Moreover, not all of them find tax offices congenial places from which to seek enlightenment. If they cannot afford professional help, they often seek help from the tax advice services of newspapers or from Citizens Advice Bureaux (Sandford and Lewis, 1986). Psychic costs are particularly acute for widows (or divorced and separated women) who (because of the UK system in which husbands are responsible for their wife's tax return*) have never been used to dealing with any tax matters.

Another source of psychic costs is the anxiety which may be generated, even for the most honest taxpayers, by a tax investigation. Besides tangible costs, such an investigation may generate very substantial stress for the taxpayer, especially if not conducted with sensitivity.

There may also be psychic *administrative* costs if the revenue staff in contact with the public find their job particularly stressful.

Psychic costs are extremely difficult, if not impossible, to measure and do not figure in the estimations of compliance cost in Part II; but they are considered in more detail in Chapter 13.

---

* This situation will change as from 1990, see Chapter 13.

Social Costs and Benefits

The operation of a tax may generate social costs and/or benefits over and above private costs and benefits. Thus, if, in order to reduce compliance costs, a retailer withdraws a particular line of products which carried a different rate of tax from the standard rate (as happened with the UK VAT during the period of the higher rate) then some consumers will lose their most convenient source of supply and the reduced number of suppliers will diminish competition which may lead to higher prices. On the benefit side, the data required for compliance with one tax may make it easier for the authorities to check evasion of another.

Similarly, the administration of a tax may generate additional costs and/or benefits. Heavy-handed administration may increase compliance costs. On the other hand there are external benefits where trainees of revenue departments move to the private sector to use their acquired skills; where the administration of one tax, by facilitating cross-checking, improves administration of another; and where tax administration generates data which is used to improve understanding and control of the economy or to answer social questions (e.g. on the distribution of income or wealth).

Costs as a Percentage of Revenue or Liability

It is common practice to present figures of administrative cost as a proportion of revenue, both for an individual tax and for the tax system as a whole and, indeed, this is a procedure often followed in this book. However, a cautionary word should be offered at this stage about this cost:revenue percentage. It has value as indicating the relationship between input and output; but it needs to be interpreted with care and is particularly suspect if used as a measure of the efficiency of the revenue department in general or its efficiency in administering a particular tax.

First, and most obviously, the ratio is heavily dependent on the rate of tax. Other things being equal, if the rate (or rates) of a tax was doubled we would expect the cost:revenue ratio to be halved, or nearly so. (The inverse relationship might not hold exactly because the higher tax rate might generate changes in behaviour, e.g. disincentive effects, demand changes, more evasion and avoidance. Then either the revenue would not rise in proportion, or additional administrative cost would need to be incurred to secure a revenue increase proportional to the tax increase.) A clear example of such a change was the increase in standard rate of the United Kingdom VAT from 8 to 15 per cent in 1979. Following this change, over the next few years the cost:revenue ratio in the collection of VAT fell from 2 per cent to one per cent mainly, though not solely, because of the increase in rate.

Secondly, a change in tax structure may affect the ratio. Thus a removal of complications in the tax system, or an increase in the tax threshold, may reduce administrative costs as a proportion of revenue.

Thirdly, an increase in national income or in the consumption of a taxed commodity may generate additional revenue which reduces the cost:revenue ratio. In such cases changes in the ratio tell us nothing about the efficiency of administration.

Whilst these factors can often be allowed for in any time series which seeks to examine revenue efficiency, there is another and more fundamental factor: it relates to the proportion of revenue potential which is collected. This point can be demonstrated by a somewhat over-simplified diagrammatic representation. Figure 5. shows the relationship between revenue and administrative costs for a particular tax (or it could be a group of taxes or the tax system as a whole). The line A-B represents the maximum revenue potential. Some administrative costs in the form of overheads are incurred before any revenue is generated, hence the curve showing the relationship between costs and revenue begins part way along the horizontal axis. (It should be noted that the scales of each axis are different: the horizontal axis might have a scale of one hundredth of that of the vertical axis). The curve rises sharply at first, as additional administrative expenditure yields substantial revenue; but after a while additional administrative costs generate a diminishing proportion of revenue; the nearer the curve moves to the AB line the more cost is needed to produce an additional unit of revenue (i.e. marginal cost rises relatively to marginal revenue). The difference between the curve and the line AB represents the shortfall on maximum potential revenue or the degree of evasion, both deliberate and unintentional. A comparison of cost:revenue ratios as a measure of changes in efficiency over time is only meaningful in relation to the same proportion of maximum potential revenue.The argument can be illustrated by reference to points X, Y and Z on the curve. For convenience let us assume that the maximum potential revenue is £100m., so that points on the tax revenue axis represent both receipts in £ millions and percentages of the maximum revenue potential. At point X, 40 per cent of maximum revenue potential is raised at a cost of OP. At point Y, 80 per cent of revenue potential is raised at a cost of

Figure 5

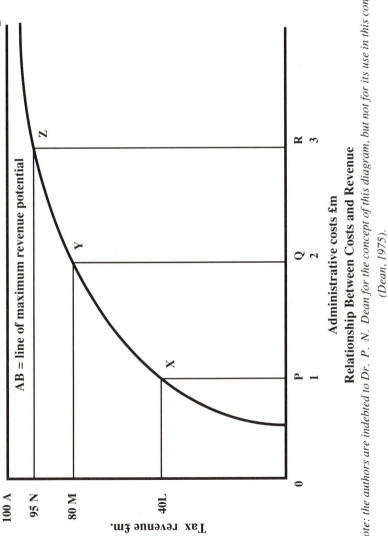

Relationship Between Costs and Revenue

Administrative costs £m

Note: the authors are indebted to Dr. P. N. Dean for the concept of this diagram, but not for its use in this context

(Dean, 1975).

OQ which is twice OP. Thus the ratio of cost to revenue is the same in both cases but at cost OQ, twice the revenue is collected. Finally, point Z represents a situation in which 95 per cent of potential revenue is collected at cost OR. The cost:revenue ratio OR/ON>OQ/OM but it is by no means clear that Y should represent a preferred point to Z. Indeed, there may be points to the right of Z where the cost:revenue ratio is higher still, which might be regarded as preferable, and indeed as representing higher administrative efficiency, because the revenue yield is larger.

In the final chapter on policy some of these issues are pursued. At the moment it is necessary simply to register a caution about the meaning and use of cost:revenue ratios.

There is still another complication about the cost:revenue ratio for a particular tax. Some taxes have the effect of protecting and hence increasing the revenue of other taxes. Thus a gift tax may protect a death duty and a capital gains tax (CGT) may protect an income tax. Thus, for example, the introduction of a CGT may induce taxpayers to seek an income return on an investment rather than a capital gain. Then, in effect, part of the revenue yield of the CGT appears in the income tax figures. A cost:revenue ratio for CGT should, in principle, include such revenue and the ratio for income tax exclude it. To do so is hardly feasible; but not to do so means that the ratio is too high for CGT and too low for income tax. Whilst this effect will make little difference to the ratio of the high revenue-yielding income tax, the effect of the omission on the cost:revenue ratio of CGT may be significant.

Whilst the question of revenue potential relates exclusively to administrative costs, the other caveats about cost:revenue ratios apply also to the ratio of compliance cost to tax liabilities or revenue collected. Changes in tax rates, in incomes or in the general level of prices may alter the ratios without affecting (or without much affecting) absolute compliance costs. Such ratios are useful for comparing with administrative costs and with similar ratios for other taxes; but their validity is restricted to a particular tax at a particular time. The caveats about cost:revenue ratios are particularly important to bear in mind when making international comparisons.

Relationship of Public and Private Costs

The public and private costs taken together may be referred to as tax *operating costs*. The link between the cash flow benefit to the private sector and the Exchequer cost of interest-free loans has already been indicated. If we take public and private costs together — that is, consider total operating costs — these two cancel out; the gain in cash flow to one sector is exactly offset by the loss to the other sector. (However, it might be noted that whilst the total cash flows cancel, the benefits and detriments may not precisely cancel because of the different terms on which public and private sectors can borrow and lend).

There are other links. A measure simplifying a tax may reduce both administrative and compliance costs. On the other hand, there may often be an element of transferability between compliance costs and administrative costs. A government may put responsibilities for aspects of tax collecting either on businesses or on its own administration. Similarly with personal taxes; thus income tax may be wholly or partly self-assessed or it may be revenue-assessed. For this reason it is important that both administrative and compliance costs be considered together.

Finally, it should not be thought that the existence of administrative and compliance costs necessarily constitutes an argument against the public sector. There are costs in the private sector of obtaining information and managing one's affairs which are to some extent a counterpart of the compliance and administrative costs of taxation. The prime object of this study is to highlight the differences between taxes in terms of administrative and compliance costs; to identify areas of high compliance costs; to indicate to policy-makers the importance of administrative and especially compliance costs, and to provide tax policy-makers with guidelines on how the costs of operating the tax system might be minimised, within the constraints imposed by other objectives.

CHAPTER 2

TAX OPERATING COSTS IN THE HISTORY OF ECONOMICS

Adam Smith

The first systematic study of the functions and objectives of taxation was made by Adam Smith in his *Inquiry into the Nature and Causes of the Wealth of Nations* (1776), Book 5, Chapter 2, Part 2 'Of Taxes', in which he sets out his four famous maxims (or 'canons') of good tax practice, usually referred to respectively as the principles of Equity, Certainty, Convenience and Economy.

I   'The subjects of every state ought to contribute towards the support of the government, as nearly as possible, in proportion to their respective abilities.'

II   'The tax which each individual is bound to pay ought to be certain, and not arbitrary. The time of payment, the manner of payment, the quantity to be paid, ought all to be clear and plain to the contributor, and to every other person. Where it is otherwise 'the taxpayer' is put more or less in the hands of the tax gatherer.'

III 'Every tax ought to be levied at the time, or in the manner, in which it is most convenient for the contributor to pay it.'

IV   'Every tax ought to be so contrived as both to take out and to keep out of the pockets of the people as little as possible over and above what it brings into the public treasury of the state. A tax may either take out or keep out of the pockets of the people a great deal more than it brings into the public treasury in the four following ways. First, the levying of it may require a great number of officers, whose salaries may eat up the greater part of the produce of the tax, and whose perquisites may impose another additional tax upon the people. Secondly, it may obstruct the industry of the people, and discourage them from applying to certain branches of business which

24

might give maintenance and employment..... Thirdly, by the forfeitures and other penalties which those unfortunate individuals incur who attempt unsuccessfully to evade the tax, it may frequently ruin them and thereby put an end to the benefit which the community might have received from the employment of their capitals. An injudicious tax offers a great temptation to smuggling..... Fourthly, by subjecting the people to the frequent visits and the odious examination of the tax gatherers, it may expose them to much unnecessary trouble, vexation and oppression; and though vexation is not, strictly speaking, expense, it is certainly equivalent to the expense at which every man would be willing to redeem himself from it. It is in some one or other of these four ways that taxes are frequently so much more burdensome to the people than they are beneficial to the sovereign.'

Although Adam Smith's maxims have continued to be referred to with reverence and respect, it is not often appreciated that two of the four are concerned wholly with compliance costs, whilst a third includes both compliance and administrative costs. The fourth reason under the fourth maxim represents a vivid statement of the psychic costs of tax compliance.

Nineteenth Century Economists

The general attitude of the early nineteenth century economists was to quote Smith with approval but then largely to ignore all but the first of his four principles. John Stuart Mill typifies this attitude:

'The qualities desirable, economically speaking, in a system of taxation, have been embodied by Adam Smith in four maxims or principles, which have been generally concurred in by subsequent writers, may be said to have become classical.......... The last three of these four maxims require little other explanation or illustration than is contained in the passage itself. How far any given tax conforms to or conflicts with them is a matter to be considered in the discussion of particular taxes. But the first of the four points, equality of taxation, requires to be more fully examined.' (Mill, 1848)

An exception was J. R. McCulloch, in what his biographer describes as 'the first really full length and systematic work in English in the field of public finance', (O'Brien, 1975). McCulloch's *Treatise on Taxation* was first published in 1845; in it McCulloch, whilst not disagreeing in principle with Adam Smith's first maxim, and interpreting equity as proportional taxation, considered it impracticable. Rather, he emphasised that 'no tax, whether it be proportioned to their means or otherwise, can be a good tax unless it correspond pretty closely with the last three maxims of Smith.' He went on to give examples of taxes in France and Turkey which seriously contravened these principles.

Perhaps because the burden of taxation became less, both because of the fall in tax as a proportion of national income and because many of the iniquities of customs and excise duties, which had incensed Smith, were swept away with the abandonment of Mercantilism and the moves to free trade, tax operating costs drop out of the main stream of economic thinking. There were few significant works on public finance in the latter half of the nineteenth century and in so far as the utilitarians concerned themselves with the subject, their interest took a very different form from investigating tax operating costs.

The neglect of compliance costs continued into the twentieth century. A. C. Pigou's *Public Finance*, the first edition of which was published in 1928, contained but one sentence on the costs of administration, including compliance costs.

At least until very recent times, discussion of the two principles, equity and efficiency (in terms of the allocation of resources) has almost completely dominated the main stream of economic literature. Thus a recent encyclopaedia entry on 'Taxation', referring to Smith's maxims, states:

> 'Today only the first of these canons is considered of prime importance. The other three have been overshadowed... The costs of assessing, collecting and controlling taxes should be kept to the lowest level consistent with other goals of taxation.... (but) This principle is of secondary importance; obviously equity and economic rationality should not be sacrificed to cost considerations'
> (*New Encyclopaedia Britannica*, (1986), Vol 28, pp.410- 411)

However, if costs of complying with tax laws fall *inequitably* on different taxpayers, then costs considerations are being 'sacrificed' without attaining the goal of equity. And much of the research on compliance costs provides evidence that such inequities are widespread. Moreover, the implication in the quoted passage that cost considerations are not in themselves part of economic rationality is extraordinary.

Attempts at Measurement

The public sector costs of the revenue authorities have been subject to official measurement of a more or less accurate and sophisticated kind, from the earliest days of taxation. The more governments spent on tax administration, the less they had to spend on other programmes, or the heavier the taxes they had to levy — and taxes are generally unpopular. Moreover the development of estimates and audit procedures and parliamentary scrutiny all helped to keep expenditure on tax administration under some measure of surveillance, however imperfect.

Compliance costs, on the other hand, are not subject to such automatic measurement; and, unlike administrative costs, there is no central agency or agencies concerned with their collection. Rather they take diverse forms and are dispersed through the economy. The remainder of this chapter is concerned with attempts to measure compliance costs.*

North American Research, 1930s to 1960s

American management scientists were the first academic group to become interested in the costs of operating tax systems. In 1933, the Taxation Committee of the American Management Association, chaired by J. W. Oliver, proposed 'the elimination of wastes incident to the simultaneous use by federal and state authorities of the same type of taxes'. The 'pioneering expedition into this unexplored territory' was undertaken by Professor R. M. Haig (1935).

Haig published few details of his questionnaire to corporate members of the American Management Association and his conclusions must be regarded as suspect because of a low response rate and a bias towards large corporations; but he raises an interesting issue of the trade-off between administrative and compliance costs, hypothesising that a tax with high administrative costs had low compliance costs and vice versa.

Haig's conclusions were subsequently examined by Martin (1944) who supplemented Haig's survey by case studies and interviews. Although on a very limited scale, many of Martin's conclusions have been borne out by later research, in particular that 'there is evidence of considerable cost which does not vary significantly with the size of the tax bill'. Martin

---

* No attempt is made in this chapter to refer to all the compliance cost studies, many of the earlier of which are methodologically very weak. A review of the studies published in English is given in Appendix A.

also stressed the compliance costs of changes in the tax system and the importance and difficulty of defining compliance costs accurately and separating them from ordinary business expenses.

A characteristic of the work of Haig, Martin and a number of the earlier studies of compliance costs of businesses, was an attempt to measure the 'total compliance burden'. In 1962 the Neeld Committee was highly critical of this approach: 'It is not believed that meaningful results can be had by searching for *overall* tax compliance cost figures.... to be of real help in the effort to ease such costs [studies] must be developed tax by tax in order to point up those areas of taxation where compliance burdens are excessive.' (Neeld, 1962)

A more rigorous approach to the measurement of compliance costs on a tax by tax basis was adopted in a series of studies from the Ohio State University Bureau of Business Studies, (Oster and Lynn, 1953, Oster, 1957, Johnston, 1961 and Yocum, 1961). Of these the study by Yocum is the most thorough.

Yocum identified two types of sales tax compliance cost: sales clerk costs (the time taken to add on retail sales taxes at the point of sale — the common pattern in North America); and 'administrative' costs (the costs to businesses of tax associated paper work, e.g. billing customers for tax, compiling records of tax taken, making tax returns). With the aid of 25 graduate accountants he examined sales clerk costs by time studies and 'administrative' costs by field interviews in 520 stores in 1959. The stores were selected in a probability sample of stores with gross sales of $50,000 or more ($500,000 or more for department stores).

Yocum concluded that 'differences in sales tax collection costs by kind of business are in general associated with differences in scale of operations (size of store), in size of average taxable transaction, and in the ratio of taxable sales to gross sales... sales tax collection costs as a per cent of tax liability are generally higher for smaller stores, lower for larger stores. This variation by store size is probably associated with the fact of certain fixed elements in collection costs, and economies of scale in store operations'.

In the same year as Yocum's study the first Canadian study appeared, by M. H. Bryden (1961), sponsored by the Canadian Tax Foundation. Like the earliest of the studies in the USA it was an attempt to measure all the tax compliance costs of corporate taxpayers and was in many ways akin to Haig's study, except that Bryden secured a much better response rate. The main conclusions were that compliance costs were highly variable even between similar firms; they were proportionately higher for small firms; and the costs of minor taxes were very high compared to liability.

Up to the 1960s virtually all compliance cost research had been concerned with corporate taxpayers; even the studies of the retail sales tax had concentrated on multiple and chain stores. However, factors such as the regressiveness which had been discovered in many studies, and increasing interest in the processes promoting the birth and development of new businesses, led to an extension of research to unincorporated businesses and individual taxpayers.

F. J. Muller (1963) provides an important early study of the tax collection costs incurred by small businessmen. Muller was clearly aware of the methodological weaknesses of earlier studies, and made positive efforts to ensure that his own research was more soundly based. Rather than rely exclusively on one method of collecting data, Muller employed (1) a questionnaire to 250 firms; (2) follow-up interviews and time studies with 100 of these firms; and (3) supplementary interviews with tax officials and accountants. An exceptionally high response rate of nearly 80 per cent was obtained to the questionnaire.

Muller found that most records maintained by small businessmen were kept primarily for tax purposes; that they would not employ outside accountants were it not for tax requirements; and that they did not use these accounting records and statements in the operation of the firm. Few questionnaire respondents had any idea of the total time or money spent on compliance, other than that it was 'too much'. Estimates of the costs were made during the follow-ups; average time spent on tax compliance for withholding income tax from employees was estimated at 9.3 hours p.a.; administration of sales tax paperwork averaged 8.1 hours p.a.; and sales clerk time spent on sales tax computation averaged 15-20 seconds per sale.

Confirming earlier views, Muller noted that costs were disproportionately high for smaller firms: 'There is little difference between the costs to prepare a return with a tax liability of $500 and one of $10'. He concludes that the 'small businessman, pressed into the role of tax collector, is troubled about the uncertainty of his legal tax requirement, the multiplicity of reporting and other requirements of the tax authorities, investment in clerical and accountancy services, and the time and emotional tension required for tax compliance. The problem is a very real one, and in some states the small businessman feels that the choice is between compliance and failure or non-compliance and survival. Time and again the investigators were told that the interviewee had no objection to paying taxes, but the methods of record-keeping and reporting had become so complicated that it grew into an unreasonable burden.'

This principal period of compliance cost research activity in the USA ends with three studies by J. H. Wicks (1965, 1966 and jointly with M. N. Killworth, 1967). They are notable as the first attempts to measure the compliance costs of personal taxation; but the costs relate only to the State of Montana and all three suffer from severe methodological limitations.

After the work of Wicks we have to wait until the 1980s before any further studies emerge from North America. Despite the very considerable deficiencies of these early American studies, they have two important merits. They raise many of the conceptual and definitional questions which need to be answered in any attempt to measure compliance costs. They also establish certain consistent findings, which can be summarised as follows:

1)   Compliance costs are not directly proportional to liability or taxable income.
2)   Compliance costs are regressive; economies of scale are likely to occur.
3)   Compliance costs are related to occupation; the self-employed incur high costs.
4)   Compliance costs are variable, and are especially likely to increase when taxable activities cannot be predicted and made routine.
5)   Multi-state operation is associated with high costs, especially where the states use different definitions of the tax base and of tax borderlines.
6)   *Ceteris paribus*, sales tax costs also vary with the number of transactions undertaken.
7)   Costs of change will be high.
8)   Costs of operating low-yield taxes are high (in ratio terms).
9)   There may be scope for trade-offs between taxpayer compliance costs and administrative costs.

European Research 1960s and early 1970s

About the time that interest in compliance cost research seemed to be waning in North America, it was beginning in Europe.

The first European study took place in West Germany, by B. Strümpel (1966). It was restricted to a representative cross-section of small businesses. Strümpel employed a commercial market research organisation, the German Gallup Poll Institute, to ask four questions covering the time the respondent, his family and his employees spent on tax affairs and how much the respondent paid his tax consultant. Strümpel estimated that time spent by the proprietor and his family averaged 18 hours per month, plus 4 hours per month by employees: fees to advisers averaged 60 DM per month (then equivalent to just over £5 or about $15).

In Strümpel's view, three-quarters of this cost was attributable to personal and business income taxes. He emphasised the conflict of this burden with the equity objective of tax policy. One group of the population, the self-employed and professionals, were being forced to put in substantial amounts of their own time and money for the purpose of complying with their tax duties. Strümpel also observed economies of scale in compliance costs. 'The burden... is basically of a regressive nature; its revealed incidence is inconsistent with the goals of progressive income taxation.' He makes no attempt to distinguish between avoidable and unavoidable compliance costs — indeed he criticises the term 'compliance costs' as unduly narrow, and uses 'disguised tax burden' instead, to emphasise the fact that he is drawing a somewhat wider definition than the American researchers. He concedes that in certain respects the self-employed enjoy a privileged position: they can vary their hours of work readily, and they have greater opportunities for tax planning, avoidance and evasion than employees. However, he also emphasises the possibly dysfunctional psychological consequences of placing an inequitable tax burden on one group of taxpayers: 'Those psychologically most oppressed by their tax burden may lessen their anger by searching diligently for... loopholes and opportunities for evasion'. However Strümpel made no attempt to validate these speculations.

The early 1970s saw the beginnings of the compliance cost studies in the United Kingdom, at the Centre for Fiscal Studies, University of Bath.

Two publications, Sandford and Dean (1971/2) and Sandford (1973) were the outcome of a project on the compliance costs of the personal direct taxes in the United Kingdom. The material for the study was derived from complementary surveys of personal taxpayers, of accountants and of banks giving tax advice and an analysis of tax enquiries to press bureaux and Citizens Advice Bureaux. The personal taxpayers' survey was a two-stage enquiry. A small number of questions was 'bought in' to one of the regular surveys of a national polling organisation (NOP Market Research Ltd), and followed up by a mailed questionnaire to those respondents categorised as having high compliance costs (defined as spending 8 hours or more per annum on tax affairs or/and employing a tax adviser). A 78 per cent response rate was obtained for the interviews, yielding 2773 respondents; and a 41 per cent response (137 respondents) for the follow-up. The accountants' survey was conducted by mail questionnaire followed by interview and a short supplementary questionnaire. Eighty-two firms responded from a sample of 219 (a response rate of 37 per cent).

Findings from the study included that the self-employed incurred the heaviest costs; that tax compliance costs tended to be inequitable and regressive; that compliance costs were particularly high for capital gains tax; and that psychic costs, even though they might not be measurable, were an important consideration, especially for the retired, for divorced persons and for widows.

Work at Bath in the later 1970s (e.g. Godwin, 1976) merges into the programme of studies of the 1980s of which this book is the culmination.

Growing International Interest

The past decade has seen a growth of interest in compliance costs which is world-wide.

In the United Kingdom a series of compliance cost studies have been undertaken at Bath University with the co-operation of Customs and Excise and Inland Revenue. The major studies have been a large-scale survey of VAT (Sandford *et al*, 1981); a study on the costs to employers of collecting income tax withheld from employees (PAYE) and national insurance contributions (Godwin *et al*, 1983); a survey of the costs of personal income tax and capital gains tax relating to 1983-84; and a survey relating to 1986-87 of VAT traders, with some questions on PAYE income tax, national insurance contributions and corporation tax.

Much of the income tax study and all the findings of the most recent survey are published for the first time in this book. As well as updating the earlier work the present study extends to the whole of the operating costs of the United Kingdom tax system for the year 1986-87. The methodology of these studies is set out in detail in Chapter 4 and the studies form the core of Part II.

Also the work in the United Kingdom, at Bath, has included a consideration of the comprehensibility and readability of Inland Revenue literature and in particular the problems of the elderly in dealing with their tax affairs (James *et al*, 1987).

The influence of the United Kingdom spread across to the Republic of Ireland, where two studies of administrative and compliance costs have taken place. One is by Bath University researchers (Sandford and Morrissey, 1985) on the Irish wealth tax. The other is an unpublished thesis by R. J. Leonard of Trinity College, Dublin, on the costs to employers of collecting income tax and PRSI (social security contributions) in 1983. Details of these studies are included in Part II when their findings are compared with those for the United Kingdom.

Two small-scale studies on VAT have also been undertaken in Europe: a study of 286 firms in the Netherlands (Snijder, 1981) which has not been published in English, and a comparison of the compliance costs of VAT for small businesses in the United Kingdom and the Federal Republic of Germany (Bannock and Albach, 1987). We refer to this study in Chapter 8.

In North America interest has also quickened. Two detailed studies of retail sales tax compliance costs in seven states have been carried out by Peat Marwick (1985) for (1) the American Retail Federation and (2) the Small Business Administration, both of which utilised a computer model in developing the cost estimates.

Peat Marwick found that the extent of exemptions, and the rate of tax, affect the cost of compliance as a percentage of sales significantly. For all cases except those where small firms made less frequent returns, costs for small retailers were more than twice the costs for medium retailers, and more than three times the cost for large retailers. Filing returns represented over 28 per cent of compliance costs for small firms, but less than 3 per cent of large firm compliance costs. Peat Marwick conclude that reduced filing and remittance frequency, and more generous collection credits for small retailers offer the most scope for reducing cost inequities.

As well as sales taxation there have been notable attempts to measure the compliance cost of the United States income tax (Slemrod and Sorum, 1984 and Arthur D. Little, 1988), which we consider in Chapter 5. Professor Slemrod, from the School of Business Administration, University of Michigan, is continuing his investigations of tax compliance costs with a study of the compliance cost of itemising deductions in the United States income tax (Pitt and Slemrod, 1988).

In Canada two (unpublished) studies were undertaken by Arthur Andersen for the Federal Government Department of Finance, on the Federal Manufacturing Sales Tax and the Retail Sales Tax System of Ontario. Also, under the auspices of the Canadian Tax Foundation,

Professor Vaillancourt, of the University of Montreal, has undertaken a major study on the administrative and compliance costs of personal income taxes and payroll taxes in Canada in 1986 (Vaillancourt, 1989) with which we compare our own findings in Chapters 5, 6 and 7.

Finally, although no results are yet available, a study of compliance costs of both personal and corporate taxation is taking place at the Economic Research Centre, University of Western Australia, sponsored by the Australian Tax Research Foundation.

A further indication of the international interest in compliance is the decision of the International Fiscal Association to make administrative and compliance costs one of the two main subjects for their congress in Rio de Janeiro in 1989. The published cahier includes reference to other studies (e.g. in Sweden and Germany) which have not been published in English.

It is tempting to speculate on why interest in this subject has grown so much in the past decade. One reason may be the increase in the overall weight of taxation as public expenditure has increased during the past two decades. Another is that, in their attempts to control or cut back public spending, governments may have reduced public sector costs at the expense of private sector costs. Further, VAT has been the tax most widely adopted in recent years; whilst it has many merits it is also a tax regarded as having particularly high compliance costs; this was certainly one reason that the large-scale study of VAT compliance costs was undertaken in the United Kingdom. Finally, perhaps, governments, however inconsistently they approach it, in a time of high unemployment, have sought to encourage small businesses — and it is these businesses which are hit hardest by the costs of compliance.

CHAPTER 3

TIME VALUATION — OF LABOUR AND OF CASH

Although the earlier literature, described in the previous chapter, raises many of the fundamental conceptual issues which need to be faced in research on compliance costs, on two major matters it is markedly deficient. There is little by way of depth analysis of the value to be accorded to time spent on tax compliance; and there is virtually nothing on the timing of tax payments, which may generate benefits or detriments to the taxpayer. It is with these two issues that this chapter is concerned. Both are aspects of the value of time: in the one case, labour time spent on tax compliance work; in the other case, the value of holding cash for a period of time.

Value of Labour Time

A major part of the compliance cost of taxation is a labour cost, the time taken by people to do the compliance work. Four main and different situations can be distinguished: (1) the time of professional advisers; (2) the time of employees doing tax compliance work for an employer; (3) the time of the self-employed doing tax compliance work in connection with their own businesses; (4) the time of individuals doing their own personal tax work in what would otherwise be leisure time.

(1) Professional Advisers' Time

The time of professional advisers raises no conceptual problems. It is included, together with overheads, in the fee charged to clients. That fee represents both the cost to the client and the resource cost to the economy. (However, where the fee comprehends other services as well as tax work, there may be a practical problem of separating the cost of the tax work from the cost of the other services).

35

(2) Employees' Time

Similarly, the value of the time of employees is relatively straightforward. There has been some discussion in the literature of tax compliance (e.g. Yocum, 1961) about the possibility that tax work can represent a small additional burden that can be carried by an existing staff within existing hours of work; in which case the marginal cost is zero. But, whilst this may sometimes be the case, it is equally true that, because labour is imperfectly divisible, tax compliance work may create the necessity to take on an additional clerk even though he may be less than fully employed. There is a general consensus that the appropriate valuation of the time taken by an employee is the employee's wage rate including any other inescapable payments associated with employing labour, such as national insurance and pension contributions. Again, this is both the cost to the employer and the resource cost to the economy.

(3) Time of the Self-employed

In principle the value of the time of the self-employed engaged on tax compliance work in the business is the opportunity cost to the business, i.e. the return which could have been gained for the business if the director/partner/proprietor had devoted the time to other business matters. An approximation to this figure is probably the average rate of remuneration received by the individual; but it could be argued that his charge-out rate, which may well include an element of profit, is an equally valid measure. Either figure rests on the assumption that additional work would have been available to the business.

If this assumption is valid there remains a problem in ascertaining the appropriate figure. With the employee, a defined market normally exists for his particular skill of labour; and any valuation given in a survey can be cross-checked for accuracy against official statistics on wage and salary rates. With the self-employed there is no such direct check. If the occupation of the self-employed person is known, then a cross-check can be made with comparable occupations for employees; but the comparison is imperfect.

(4) Leisure Time

The biggest difficulty arises with the valuation of time which, but for the tax compliance work, would have been own leisure time, e.g. time an individual spends doing his personal tax work; or time that the wife of a small business proprietor spends on VAT returns at the weekend. Arguments can be deduced for valuing leisure time in any of the following ways. (a) At the individual's wage rate or what he or she could have received had they chosen to work; this is particularly appropriate if extra work is on offer so that the wage rate is the opportunity cost. (b) At the individual wage rate less income tax, on the grounds that this is the cost to the individual. Whilst the deduction of tax is valid from that viewpoint, the full cost of the wage rate without the tax deduction is the cost to the economy. (c) At a value which is a proportion of the wage rate, on the grounds that many will not have the option of working extra hours at their wage rate; in other words, the opportunity cost is less than the wage rate. The view that the value used should be less than the wage rate is reinforced by the argument that, within limits, the individual can choose *when* he does the tax work; he is not as constrained in the timing as he would be if he undertook an extra hour of paid work. (d) A value which is a multiple of the wage rate because this reflects an overtime rate; and that a higher value is appropriate for an activity which is often intensely disliked.

In this situation it is apposite to seek guidance from other parts of the economic literature; and much has been said on the value of leisure time in the literature on the economics of transport, where the relationship between costs and benefits in many transport schemes depends crucially on the value assigned to time saved. On work-time saved the conclusion from the transport studies is in line with our conclusions above. But much of the time-saving of a transport scheme is in travel to and from work and on pleasure trips. How are these time-savings valued?

Various ingenious studies have been undertaken to try to measure the value people put on time, e.g. the comparison of different routes or modes of travel (slower and cheaper with faster and dearer) to give a trade-off between time and cost, (e.g. the study by Earp *et al* of hovercraft and ferry travel, 1974); or the trade-off between house prices and distance from work (Wabe, 1971). The outcome of these studies has been variable; whilst some have come up with a figure of the value of time spent commuting which is as low as 25 per cent of the average wage rate, others have concluded that the appropriate figure is in excess of the average wage rate.

For all their real or apparent inconsistency, the transport studies offer two valuable lessons. The first is that the value of time is a function of how you are constrained to spend it. As Tipping (1968) argued in a paper commenting on some of the earlier transport studies, time is not divisible from an accompanying activity. Thus, studies which derive a value for time by observing the behaviour of people who choose a faster but more expensive route in place of a slower and cheaper take no account of the fact that travelling may be more or less comfortable; can be compatible with pleasurable reading or listening to the car radio on the one hand, or unpleasant strap-hanging on the other; and that it may or may not be associated with changes or waits on draughty stations; and so on. A recent Australian study (Hensher and Troung, 1985) found that people put nearly three times the value on out-of-vehicle time saved (walking and waiting) compared with in-vehicle time.

In other words, if we are to place a value on a given period of time/activity, this value will not only be a function of time for a particular person but also a function of the (dis)utility attached to the activity.

The second lesson from the transport studies is that people are by no means uniform in their attitudes. It has been pointed out about the method of analysing costs by trade-offs between modes of travel that the travellers divide into two groups and 'There are good reasons for not treating these two groups as homogeneous since one group prefers time to money whilst the other group prefers the opposite' (Department of Environment, 1970).

Applying the first lesson, it is clear that time spent on tax compliance should be accorded a higher value than that of time saved in most transport studies, both because doing tax work is not compatible with other pleasurable activities and because of the disutility associated with it. In an earlier study at Bath (Sandford, 1973) a sample of high compliance cost income tax payers was asked to express their attitude towards attending to their tax affairs by saying which of five categories best described it. 'Of the 135 respondents... one person enjoyed attending to his tax affairs; no-one enjoyed it very much; 67 neither enjoyed nor disliked it; 33 disliked it and 34 disliked it very much. Thus, in round terms, respondents divided almost equally between neutrality and dislike, with half of the latter disliking very much.'

The different attitudes which taxpayers have to time spent on tax compliance work argues for using each individual's own valuation as the best measure of time values in this particular activity.* On the other hand,

---

* An alternative approach would be to ask taxpayers what they would be willing to pay to avoid all the paperwork and inconvenience associated with attending to their tax affairs. This approach was attempted by Sandford (1973) but this hypothetical question did not lead to very satisfactory answers.

if that value is above the opportunity cost (i.e. what the taxpayer would be paid if he applied the time to the best paid alternative use) it must be regarded as a welfare valuation rather than as a measure of the resource cost to the community.

Constraints and Procedures

Whatever the theoretical ideal, in practice constraints are imposed by the data available. In the four major surveys which form the core of this book, the time taken on tax compliance work has been given by respondents and also the value they put on that time. These valuations form the consistent basis on which time is valued throughout the study. However, as detailed in the next chapter, such valuations have been checked for reasonableness against external data, such as that from the *New Earnings Survey*.

Further, of these four studies, the value of leisure time represents the biggest component in the one which estimates the compliance costs of personal income tax and capital gains tax; and, for this study, we also have data on the annual earnings of each taxpaying unit. Thus, it is possible to make an estimate of the hourly rate of wage or salary of the taxpayer to compare with their own time valuation. The estimate is imperfect, for we have no case by case data of the number of hours worked to enable us to reduce the annual earnings to an accurate hourly rate and the hours worked have therefore had to be assumed from national data; but, for full-time employees, this estimate does provide both a check on own valuations and an alternative set of valuations.

Leads and Lags in Tax Payments

Chapter 1 already indicated some of the issues which arise where tax is collected by third parties (mainly businesses) who have the legal obligation to pay it to the Revenue and where there is a time difference between collection and payment. The result is the equivalent of an interest-free loan by the Exchequer to the business or by the business to the Exchequer. In the former case the payment arrangements represent an offset to the compliance costs; in the latter case an addition to those costs. We decided that the costs to the Exchequer from such 'loans' should not be designated an administrative cost but put into a category of 'other

Exchequer cost', because once the structure of a tax is in place, such costs are outside the control of the revenue departments. Similarly, where there is an advance payment, this is an Exchequer benefit which is not regarded as an offset to, or reduction of, administration costs, as we have defined them.

This section elaborates on the issues raised by such 'lags' and 'leads' in tax payments and further explores their implications.

The starting point is to establish a datum line from which to measure a lead or lag. Let us distinguish taxes which are *directly paid* by the intended taxpayer (the person or organisation the government wishes to tax) and those which are *paid indirectly* through a third party, usually a business, which has imposed on it the duty of collecting tax on its products (where the intended taxpayer is the consumer), its employees (PAYE income tax and national insurance contributions) and its profits (where the intended taxpayer is less clear, but may be taken as a shareholder).

The relationship between this distinction, of direct and indirect payment of taxes, and the usual direct/indirect classification of taxes, needs some clarification. First it should be recognised that in much popular literature the terms are used loosely, with 'direct' being employed for taxes on income and capital and 'indirect' being used for taxes on expenditure on goods and services. However, in origin and principle, the distinction is an administrative one, indicating whether the intended taxpayer is being approached directly or through a third party. In general the administrative distinction coincides with the income/expenditure distinction, but not invariably, e.g. a vehicle licence is essentially a tax on the use of a good, but it is paid directly; it is possible to have a direct expenditure tax. The distinction we are making is akin to the administrative distinction, but not identical to it. Because our distinction is based specifically on methods of *payment*, it differs from the usual administrative distinction. Income tax paid by employees counts as a direct tax (under the usual distinction) because the employee is being directly *assessed*; however, because *payment* is indirect, in our classification it becomes indirect.

Taxes Paid Indirectly

Let us first of all consider the taxes paid indirectly. In some cases, as with VAT, the extent of a lag is relatively clear cut. The organisation which is responsible for paying tax to the revenue authorities on the basis of a specified time schedule is also responsible for collecting that tax in relation to a specified time period. Thus, in the United Kingdom, the trader who is not entitled to regular repayments, collects VAT from his customers over a three-month period (the collection period), pays VAT on his purchases over the same period, and then holds the difference between the two for a (legal) maximum period of one month (the 'grace' period) before handing it over to Customs and Excise. Assuming a smooth flow of payments and receipts, his average holding of tax is two-and-a-half months' VAT or 5/24 of the annual VAT payment (one-and-a-half months for the collection period and one month for the grace period — for details see Chapter 8). This is the lag in payment and the extent of the interest-free loan from the Exchequer. In other cases, e.g. the United Kingdom tobacco tax, the situation is less clear cut. The manufacturer pays tax to Customs and Excise according to a specified time schedule (not later than the fifteenth day of the month after the product leaves the registered premises); but the time taken to recover that tax from the wholesaler, who in turn recovers it from the retailer, who in turn recovers it from the consumer, is not precisely defined; indeed, it will vary, not only at different times of the year (e.g. quickening up before a Budget in anticipation of a price increase) but according to the nature of the business; e.g. for cigarettes the average period before sale is usually much shorter in a supermarket than in a tobacconist's shop.

It would seem logical to take as our datum line a (hypothetical) situation in which the revenue department(s) receive tax the same day as it is paid by the intended taxpayer, i.e. the person on whom the government intended the formal incidence* to lie as distinct from the legal incidence which, with taxes on goods and services, rests with the designated supplier. In other words the datum line assumes an instantaneous transfer from intended taxpayer to the revenue department(s). In such a case there would be neither advance nor deferred payments, no leads and no lags, no 'loans' in either direction. Thus, to take the case of the United Kingdom tobacco tax, if the customer (the smoker) buys the product and thus pays the tax on average on the fifteenth day of the month after it left the

---

* In this study we use the term legal incidence to indicate where the legal liability to payment lies; formal incidence to indicate the intended taxpayer (eg with tobacco tax, the smoker); and effective incidence as the answer to the question 'Who really pays the tax?' In principle the effective incidence includes all the consequences arising from the existence of the tax (eg that, following the increase of tobacco tax, smokers might substitute sweets for cigarettes). We consider the effective incidence of compliance costs in Chapter 12.

registered premises of the manufacturer, there would be no lead or lagged payment. If the customer paid before that date there would be a cash flow benefit (an interest-free loan) to the private sector; if he paid after that date there would be an advance payment, a loan from the private sector to the Exchequer. Within the private sector the distribution of the cash flow benefit or detriment would depend on the credit terms existing on payments between retailers, wholesalers and manufacturers.

Taxes Paid Directly

Where taxes are paid directly, the appropriate datum line would appear to be the economic transaction or event giving rise to the liability. With income tax the appropriate point is, in principle, the receipt of the income — this is the point of payment for the economic transaction giving rise to the liability. If, for a period, a person has the use of that part of the income which constitutes the tax liability, then there is an interest-free loan from the Exchequer. The employed taxpayer pays at the time the income is received; but in fact payment is indirect, through the employer, who does get a cash flow benefit arising from a collection and a grace period (as outlined in Chapter 6 for the United Kingdom). The self-employed taxpayer, however, pays direct and in arrears and therefore obtains a cash flow benefit, which, for United Kingdom taxpayers, is usually approximately six months (see Chapter 5 and Appendix B for details). Capital gains tax in the United Kingdom is another tax paid directly by individuals in arrears. With a death duty (or gift tax) the appropriate datum point is date of death (or of gift). With corporation tax again the position is complicated (see Chapter 9 for the United Kingdom) but, in principle, it must be when the profit is earned, even though it may be a long time after that before the shareholder gets his hands on the money.

So far we have referred only to payments which are legally deferred. Where taxpayers fail to pay on the due date they may obtain an additional deferment or loan of an illegitimate nature. However, in so acting they may become liable to penalties which, in principle, should at least wipe out the gain.

A Zero Sum Game

The implication of what we have said about legitimate payment leads and lags is that (as indicated in Chapter 1), taking the economy as a whole, they cancel out — they constitute a zero sum game. If a business or individual gains an interest-free loan from deferred tax payment, then the Exchequer (i.e. the community as a whole) suffers as the lender. Taking the economy as a whole, there are no real resources to be gained by altering tax payment provisions to increase or reduce leads and lags (except in so far as such a change may enable tax payments to be made at a more convenient time, e.g. to coincide with a business accounting period). However, to the beneficiary, the benefit of deferred payment, with the implied increase in cash flow, is real. To the loser the cost is equally real. Thus, there may well be important policy decisions to be made about the distribution of the benefits and detriments both between the public and the private sectors and within the private sector.

A number of specific points require further examination. First is the question of measuring the value of the cash flow benefit and its sensitivity to the rate of interest and to the rate of inflation. This leads on to the question of cash flow benefits and horizontal equity. Finally, we consider what rate of interest is most appropriate for measuring cash flow benefits.

Rate of Interest and Rate of Inflation

Clearly, the value as distinct from the size of the cash flow benefit depends crucially on the rate of interest — indeed, changes in the value of the benefit are directly proportional to changes in that rate, other things being equal. There is something of a paradox (of a kind not uncommon in economic affairs) that a change in a variable will make people worse off in one way but better off in another. A rise in real interest rates is generally detrimental to business, but, where the business gets a cash flow benefit from tax collecting, the increase in interest rate reduces net compliance costs and may, in some instances, render them negative.

The inflation rate exercises a potent influence on the rate of interest. If the degree of inflation is fully anticipated it will be reflected in the market rate of interest. If it is not fully anticipated, then the value of a loan to the debtor increases with its length; the longer tax payment is deferred, the less the value of the tax payment to the Revenue, because it is being made in a depreciated currency; conversely, the beneficiary is getting the use of the money at a time when its value is greater. This is a simple application of the principle that, when there is unanticipated inflation, debtors gain and creditors lose. Where there are advance payments of tax, of course, the Revenue correspondingly gains. A marked effect of inflation on cash flow benefits occurs in relation to the self- employed. For example, when the income of the self-employed (Schedule D) taxpayer in the United Kingdom is steady the taxpayer obtains a deferment of tax of up to six months. When money income is rising there is an additional deferment on the increase, because tax in year 't' is levied on the earnings of year (t-1) or even (t-2). Thus, in times of inflation additional deferment is obtained even if income in real terms remains unchanged.

Horizontal Equity Issues

The distribution of cash flow benefits raises some important issues of horizontal equity: the equal treatment of taxpayers in similar circumstances. The treatment of the employed and the self-employed in the United Kingdom is an obvious case in point; the employed taxpayer obtains no cash flow benefit, whilst the self-employed obtains a benefit equal to the interest on half his annual tax payment plus an additional benefit if his income is rising in money terms. The reasons for this difference are, of course, that, until the accounts of the year are completed, the income of the self-employed is not known. But this would not prevent the self-employed from making (say) monthly tax payments on account, based on their income in the previous tax year. On the other hand, the compliance costs of the self-employed are a larger proportion of income than those of the employed (see Chapter 5); moreover, whereas the employee's income is available as cash, the profits of the self-employed are often tied up in the financing of stock, debtors etc. and therefore are not available for the payment of tax. Thus it is perhaps not unreasonable that they should benefit from an offset, although the self-employed in the United Kingdom are also more favourably treated with regard to expenses rules and enjoy lower national insurance contributions.

The different treatment of employees (Schedule E) and the self-employed (Schedule D) taxpayers in the United Kingdom in respect of deferred tax payments raises the question of horizontal equity in the treatment by the public sector of one section of taxpayers as compared with another section of taxpayers in similar circumstances. Other questions of horizontal equity are raised where the private sector is uniformly treated by the public sector, but the cash flow benefits of lagged payments are unevenly dispersed within the private sector. For example, in 1986-87, in the United Kingdom the tax point for most VAT registered traders who were not selling for cash was the date on the invoice. Thus, when such a trader issued an invoice to a customer he became liable for tax from that date and when he received an invoice from a supplier he could offset the VAT on that invoice (i.e. deduct input tax) from that date. It follows that if the traders' customers were slow in paying or/and his suppliers required early payment, that trader suffered a reduced cash flow benefit. In other words, the distribution of cash flow benefit from VAT payments depended on commercial credit arrangements and these would be affected by market power. The more powerful businesses were in a position to maximise their cash flow benefits at the expense of the less powerful. In general, market power is a function of size. It is because small businesses were liable to lose out in this way that the United Kingdom government made proposals in 1987 for a cash payment option for smaller firms.

Analysing the distribution of the cash flow benefit within the private sector is, in fact, a very difficult exercise, because it merges with the whole complex of ways in which firms can compete in markets. Thus, in the United Kingdom tobacco industry, some manufacturers are prepared to forgo cash flow benefits by offering longer credit terms as a competitive inducement, whilst others seek to maximise cash flow benefit by requiring prompt payment. At the extreme, where, as with the United Kingdom petroleum revenue tax, the sums involved for individual firms may be huge, arrangements for tax payment, with their cash flow implications, may figure in discussions between the industry and government as a part of the total tax burden on the industry.

What Rate of Interest?

If small firms lose out because they have little market power to prevent their cash flow benefits being squeezed, do they also lose out in the value of such benefits as they retain? If collected tax payments are lent out on short-term by businesses before they must be handed over to the Revenue, the larger businesses can be expected to get a better return both because larger loans carry a higher rate of interest than small and because the transaction costs of investment are proportionately less for large loans. But this is not the whole story. If a business uses the extra cash arising from tax collection to reduce its bank debt, rather than to lend, the benefit may be proportionately more for small than for large firms, simply because small firms often have to pay a higher rate of interest on their bank overdrafts; they therefore save more if the cash from tax collection keeps their overdraft down. Whether small firms lose or gain, compared with large, from the value of the cash flow benefit, thus depends on their credit situation and is not susceptible to generalisation.

So far we have spoken of *the* rate of interest; but there are, of course, many different rates depending on length of loan, risk of default and risk of capital loss in the event of early withdrawal. In calculating the value of cash flow benefits, what rate of interest should be used? It is clear that tax payments temporarily in the keeping of firms or individuals should not be used for speculative investments; nor, given that the money will always be required within a relatively short period, are investments where risk of capital loss from early withdrawal (such as medium- or long-term government securities) appropriate.* What we are mainly talking about, therefore, are the rates on short-term loans (of a gilt-edged variety) on the money market or (from the point of view of interest saving) the rate businesses pay on their overdrafts. In 1986-87 the relevant annual average rates of interest in the United Kingdom were as in Table 3.1.

Table 3.1 United Kingdom Average Interest Rates 1986-87

Type of Loan	Rate of Interest per cent
7 day	6.33
3 month inter-bank	10.5
Base rate	10.5
Overdraft rates	13-15

There is clearly an argument for relating the interest rate to the period of deferred tax payment — and using a higher rate to calculate the benefit when the collection and grace periods are longer. On the other hand, there is an argument for uniformity of treatment, especially as there is in fact no clear-cut rate in any situation, the actual value of the cash flow benefit varying according to the credit/debit position of the individual or trader and the size of their deferred payments. Moreover, a too sophisticated treatment might mislead; interest rates for the same kind of loan vary considerably within a year and between years. Our purpose in

---

* In the United Kingdom, in practice, for weekly paid employees, there will always be a hard core of tax and national insurance contributions in the hands of the employer for which the interest rate for longer term loans would be appropriate.

calculating the value of the cash flow benefit is to give some general idea of the extent of the offset to compliance costs (or, in the case of advance payments, the additions to them). In the United Kingdom bank base rate occupies an intermediate position in the schedule of rates set out above. The fact that it is several percentage points lower than overdraft rates is not a disadvantage when it is recalled that, in some instances (e.g. the collection period under VAT) the additional cash available from tax payment fluctuates and only gradually builds up — making it more difficult to invest at the most favourable terms. In all these circumstances there is much to be said for taking a single, uniform and easily accessible rate — and we have therefore used bank base rate throughout the calculations in Part II.

Administrative and Compliance
Costs of Taxation

PART II

Administrative and Compliance Costs of
the United Kingdom Tax System 1986-87,
with International Comparisons

CHAPTER 4

METHODOLOGY

Introduction

In this chapter, after a brief glance at the source of data for administrative costs, we review the methods which have been used to try to estimate compliance costs and then examine the methodology of the four main surveys in the United Kingdom which form the core of this book. Reference is made to the other sources of data on compliance costs used in this study and the structure of the rest of Part II of the book is outlined.

Administrative Costs

In this study (as in most others) the source of data on the administrative costs of central government taxes consists primarily of published data by the revenue departments — in the United Kingdom Customs and Excise and Inland Revenue. In particular the data come from annual reports of these two revenue departments which, following the Financial Management Initiative (FMI) provide a fairly detailed breakdown of costs. Other official publications have helped to refine the data on administrative costs (e.g. *Review of Value Added Tax*, Cmnd. 7415, 1978) as have interviews with senior officials. Furthermore, the comments of respondents to mail questionnaires and discussions with interviewees, respondents and professional advisers provide further data on the way taxes are administered or are perceived to be administered.

With the local authority rates, data on the costs of valuation come from the Inland Revenue, whilst the collection costs of local authorities are derived from several sources, but principally data compiled and published by the Chartered Institute of Public Finance and Accounting (CIPFA).

Compliance Costs

In principle, any of the methods used in social research can be applied to studying tax compliance costs, and indeed have been. These methods include:

(1)   Highly structured questionnaires/interview schedules.
(2)   Semi-structured or unstructured interviews.
(3)   Time and motion studies.
(4)   Participant observation/action research.
(5)   Other types of case study, e.g. studies of the comprehensibility of tax forms.
(6)   Archive research, using records held by government departments, tax advisers, etc.
(7)   Simulation or modelling exercises.

In addition to these basic categories, there are alternative methods of administering a project. For instance, structured schedules may be administered by mail, telephone, or face to face.

In practice, the majority of studies have been either large-scale mail questionnaire studies or in-depth time and motion studies; both of these approaches have often been supplemented by face to face or/and telephone interviews. Two of the more recent studies (Sandford, 1973 and Vaillancourt, 1988) have used a large interview sample with a small number of questions 'bought in' from a commercial polling organisation.

The main advantage of the time-study method of investigation is that time spent on compliance can be measured precisely, and a uniform definition of compliance costs can be specified and applied consistently. The main disadvantage is that it is very labour intensive, hence usually only small samples can be drawn, and there is consequently no means of telling how typical the studied sample is of the whole population of taxpayers.

In contrast the big advantage of mail questionnaires is their relative cheapness. Large samples become feasible, with the possibility of improvement in statistical reliability. However, with a mail survey the response rate is usually lower than with interviews; respondents may be interpreting the questions differently; they may be answering questions on a sound basis, or on the basis of mere guesswork — the researcher cannot tell at first glance. But although some individual responses may be of doubtful reliability, a well-designed questionnaire should minimise such replies; reliable responses will be identifiable because of their similarities; the few unreliable responses will appear 'out of line', and can be investigated further and/or rejected. External checks can also be used to test the reliability of responses. Mail questionnaires also have the advantage over interviews (unless the interviewee has been pre-warned) that the respondent has the opportunity to consult his files, or indeed his colleagues, before responding. In some opinion surveys the possibility of such consultation may be a disadvantage; but not on the factual aspects of compliance costs.

The face to face interview carried out by researchers knowledgeable in the subject area is often the best way to get the most accurate and meaningful responses from the individual respondent; but such interviews are extremely expensive and can therefore only be undertaken on a small scale, which limits their representativeness. The large interview sample becomes feasible on grounds of cost if questions are 'bought in' on one of the surveys of a commercial organisation engaged in regular national polls. Even so, on cost grounds the number of questions has to be minimised. Moreover, the enumerators administering the questionnaire must keep to a rigid script. They are not the researchers and have neither the knowledge nor the time to follow up interesting leads which may emerge at interview. Furthermore the rigidity of the procedure means that interviews of this kind carry the same dangers as the mail questionnaire that questions may be misinterpreted or differently interpreted by respondents. Such interviews are thus, individually, much less fruitful than in-depth interviews by members of the research team.

Telephone interviews are a convenient and relatively cheap way of checking out one or two points on which the respondent can be expected to have a ready answer; but, even if the respondent has been forewarned, they are unsuitable for lengthy in-depth interviews.

The big advantage of archival or documentary evidence is that it provides a reliable factual base. However, the circumstances in which it can be used as the sole or main method of compliance cost research are very limited. The one instance of such research known to the writers is the study of the Irish wealth tax (Sandford and Morrissey, 1985), a tax with a small number of taxpayers, employing professional advisers whose fees constituted the predominant component of compliance costs; such data on fees was obtained from file records (see Chapter 11).

After the early studies of compliance costs, in which mail questionnaires were used and very low response rates obtained, it has become common practice to combine several methods of research, to try to get the best of all worlds, or at least to minimise the disadvantages of the main research method. Thus, a mail questionnaire may be supplemented by a small number of face to face interviews or/and some telephone interviews with some of the respondents.

Methodology of the Main Bath Surveys

Four surveys provide the bulk of the empirical data for this study:

(1)   a survey of the compliance costs of value added tax relating to the financial year 1977-78 (referred to as VAT 1);

(2)   a study of the costs to employers of administering the system for deducting income tax from the wages and salaries of their employees, known as the Pay-As-You-Earn (PAYE) system and also the cost of deducting the national insurance contributions of employers and employees relating to the year 1981-82 (all referred to as the PAYE study);

(3)   a survey of the costs to taxpayers of personal income tax and capital gains tax, relating to the year 1983-84 (referred to as the PIT study);

(4)   a further survey of the compliance costs of VAT, which included a small number of questions specifically addressed to VAT traders who were also employers and to VAT traders who were incorporated. This study is referred to as VAT 2 and relates to 1986-87.

Full details of the methodology of these studies are given in the Appendices together with reproductions of the questionnaires of the PAYE, PIT and VAT 2 studies. The VAT 1 questionnaire has already been published (Sandford *et al*, 1981) and the VAT 2 questionnaire (apart from the questions to employers and companies) is mainly an abbreviated version of VAT 1. In this chapter we concentrate on the essential features of the methodology and also seek to answer some of the main issues about the validity of the findings.

All four studies have certain features in common. All were undertaken with the co-operation of the appropriate revenue department, under conditions which safeguarded the identity of the respondent. All were mail surveys, with two reminders being despatched at 2-3 week intervals, the second reminder containing a further copy of the questionnaire.

The first three surveys were all preceded by pilot surveys to test out the questionnaires and the method of analysis. With VAT 2 there were bigger time constraints and also a pilot was less necessary because the larger part of the questionnaire replicated the VAT 1 questionnaire, but the contents were fully discussed with Customs and Excise, Inland Revenue and some independent accountants.

Table 4.1 summarises vital features of the studies. Particular points call for comment. It will be seen that supplementary interviews are recorded against all the surveys except PIT.

Before the completion of the PIT study it was known that the research team would be following up with a further study to update the earlier work to 1986-87, and extend its scope to the whole United Kingdom tax system. The interviews with accountants and others that had been planned as part of the PIT study were therefore included with the later study.

In order to obtain figures pertaining to the total population the survey responses have to be 'grossed up' in a way which reflects the composition of the sample and differential response rates. Thus, with the PIT study, it was known that, under the United Kingdom system (outlined in Chapter 5), the large majority of employees with low income have nil or virtually nil compliance costs. The sample was therefore stratified to include only a small number of such cases, with a much higher sampling fraction of the self-employed and of the higher income groups, whether employed or self-employed, than in other groups. The grossed-up figures are derived by multiplying the reciprocal of the response rate in each category by the numbers in the category. With VAT the grossing up has been by reference to the numbers and response rate in each size/economic category; and with the PAYE data, the grossing up has related to each of the categories in which the data is held by the Inland Revenue, which is primarily in groups by size of payment.

The variability in the response rates as between the different questionnaires calls for some explanation. With a national sample earlier experience suggests a response rate of 30 per cent is rather better than par for the course on a mail questionnaire dealing with this subject matter. The VAT 1 and PAYE studies are very much in line with this figure. The PIT figure is well above it. This may partly be due to the structure of the

Table 4.1   Main Surveys by Mail Questionnaire

Mail survey and date	Coverage		Approx. population size	Sample size	Usable response[1]		Supplementary methods used
	Taxes	Date			Number	Rate %	
VAT 1 Sept-Dec 1978	VAT	1977-78	1,274,000	9,094	2,799	31	220 telephone interviews with respondents, 44 face to face interviews with respondents, small no. of interviews with professional VAT advisers.
PAYE[2] Pilot: Sept-Dec '81 Main: July-Sept '82	Costs to Employers of PAYE and N.I. contributions	1981-82	1,013,000	3,039	783	29	17 face to face interviews with respondents.
PIT Oct-Dec 1984	Personal income tax Capital gains tax	1983-84	24,700,000	4,241	1,776	43	
VAT 2 Oct-Dec 1987	VAT PAYE Corporation tax	1986-87	1,526,000	3,000 unknown unknown	680 318 139	24	Some 50 face to face interviews with tax advisers, heads of tax depts, revenue officials. Small no. of interviews with respondents.

[1] The usable response rate has been calculated by deleting from the sample size those known to be out of frame (e.g. gone away; ceased to trade).
[2] The PAYE Pilot sample was drawn by the same method and at the same time as the Main sample. For some purposes Pilot and Main survey responses were combined and they have been combined in this table.

sample, which included a higher proportion of 'middle class' who might be expected to respond more readily; but it is probably largely because the PIT questionnaire was the shortest and simplest of the questionnaires and did not include sensitive questions about incomes. The Inland Revenue was able to supply additional data about the respondents without identifying them by name to the researchers, so that fewer questions in total needed to be asked and the sensitive questions could be omitted.

Conversely the VAT 2 study had a poor response rate, some 7 percentage points down on VAT 1. Possible reasons were that the VAT 2 questionnaire was probably longer and certainly more complex, in that it also included questions on two other taxes; that for reasons outside the control of the researchers there was insufficient time to do preliminary work, such as writing to trade associations for their support, as had been done with VAT 1; and that the VAT 2 questionnaire, again for reasons outside the control of the researchers, was not despatched until mid-October, later than VAT 1, and hence ran into the very busy pre-Christmas period for many potential respondents.

The Validity of the Findings on VAT and Income Tax

In assessing the validity of the findings from these surveys, there are three main questions to be asked: (1) How representative was the usable response? (2) How appropriate were the questions? (3) How accurate were the responses?

(1) The samples for VAT, PAYE and PIT were drawn from the best source, respectively the Customs and Excise VAT register, the Inland Revenue list of employers and the Inland Revenue representative sample of personal taxpayers which is used for the official survey of personal incomes. Both the VAT 1 and the VAT 2 samples were drawn to ensure an appropriate distribution among firms of different sizes and economic activities. The PAYE sample was chosen to ensure an appropriate distribution amongst employers in different payment categories and the PIT sample, as described above, was stratified to ensure a full representation of the most relevant categories.

The main exception relates to the questions on corporation tax and PAYE in VAT 2. Because many organisations were exempt or outside the scope of VAT, the VAT register was not ideal as a sample frame of employers; for similar reasons, (though the deficiency is nothing like as big) it did not provide a complete coverage of companies. This was, of course, realised; but to attach a few questions on PAYE and corporation tax was an economical way of obtaining data which would not otherwise have been available.

A second limitation is that in VAT 2, the sample of registered VAT traders is much smaller than in VAT 1. VAT 2 was intended primarily as an update of the earlier work and the cost of a larger sample could not be justified. As a result some size/economic categories in VAT 2 are too small to serve as a basis for generalisation. However, a high degree of confidence can be placed in the broad picture which the findings portray. The response rate in all the surveys is not too far out from what was anticipated. As described above, the reliability is much increased if the response rate is known for each of a series of relevant categories, and the grossing up can proceed in relation to these categories. For example, if for the VAT survey the response rate for primary producers in the 20,000-50,000 turnover band is below the average response rate, then, since the size of that particular population is known, the multiple for grossing up (which is the reciprocal of the response rate) can be used to estimate the true figure. Nevertheless, the reliability of this method depends on the extent to which the actual respondents from that class reflect the characteristics of the entire class.

One disadvantage of the anonymity which was a necessary outcome of using official Revenue registers as the sample frame was that the names of non-respondents were not known. Thus, non-respondents could not be followed up to see if they differed in essential characteristics from respondents. However, it is believed that this limitation was not important because the relevant economic categories of the non-respondents were known and taken into account in the grossing up, as described in the previous paragraph (e.g. the distribution of non-respondents amongst businesses of different sizes, or individuals of different income groups).

It is sometimes suggested that responses to compliance cost questionnaires will give an upward bias to the findings, because the dissatisfied feel more strongly and have most to gain from any improvement that might result and are therefore more likely to reply. Such evidence as exists does not support this hypothesis. Firstly, the most dissatisfied tend to be those who abhor form-filling; but they will also be the ones most averse to filling in questionnaire forms. Secondly, external evidence suggests that the most dissatisfied with the compliance costs of taxes falling on businesses (VAT, PAYE, corporation tax and even Schedule D income tax) are the proprietors/directors of the smaller businesses; but it is amongst the smaller businesses that response is generally lowest. The conclusion would be that if there is any bias of this kind, it is in the direction of under-stating compliance costs.

(2)   In considering the appropriateness of the questions it will be recalled that all the draft questionnaires were extensively discussed with Customs and Excise and/or Inland Revenue and other knowledgeable people, and the first three were piloted. These measures should have helped to ensure that the right questions were included and minimised ambiguity in the questions. The subsequent interviews with respondents and tax advisers should have removed ambiguities in the answers. In three of the four surveys respondents were asked if they were willing to answer further questions and invited to identify themselves so that they could be contacted if the researchers had any queries. About half the respondents indicated a willingness to answer further questions.

(3)   As well as misunderstanding of the question, responses may be inaccurate as a result of deliberate misrepresentation or inadequate recall or estimation. The latter is more likely where the respondent is being asked questions on what happened over an earlier twelve-month period. The extreme form of deliberate misrepresentation is highly unusual but not difficult to spot and the response can be discarded. It is elements of slight exaggeration or inadvertent error that are more difficult to identify and deal with.

    With some questions, such as the fee paid to a tax adviser, there is a documentary record which should keep the respondent from error; but even here there may be an element of judgement about how a fee should be divided when the adviser has not apportioned it amongst several tasks.
    In fact a number of measures were taken to cross-check accuracy, especially in respect of the first survey, VAT 1. Thus, examples of the fees said by respondents to be paid advisers for VAT work were checked with accountants; the value attributed to the time of employees was checked against the rates of the appropriate type of labour in national statistics published annually in the Department of Employment's *New Earnings Survey*. Although more difficult to validate, the value a proprietor or director puts on his own time was cross-checked with the rates of corresponding occupations in the *New Earnings Survey*.
    Small firms, where the proprietor does much of the work himself, contribute a large proportion of the compliance costs of VAT and are

amongst the most difficult items to check. The VAT 1 study revealed two businesses with very similar charges, which specialised in high quality VAT work for small firms. They received from their clients all the quarterly invoices, processing them, doing the VAT return and providing the client with a management print-out. As an overall check on the general accuracy of the responses from small firms it was assumed that all firms below £100,000 taxable turnover (in 1977-78) employed one of these specialist firms. The compliance costs were calculated on this assumption, which could be considered as the opportunity cost of VAT compliance work for small firms. The outcome was a figure a little lower, but not much lower, than that derived from the questionnaire responses.*

The result of all these cross-checks was to substantiate the general validity of the findings. (Details can be found in Sandford *et al*, 1981). The degree of cross-checking with external data was less in the later surveys; but there seems no reason to believe that people would be inaccurate in them any more than in the earliest survey. Even so, the interviews and recalls are a method by which the accuracy of doubtful statements has been tested.

Data on Other Taxes

Personal income tax (including capital gains tax), national insurance contributions and VAT together comprised 70 per cent of central government revenue in 1986-87. After these taxes the next largest revenue contribution to central government revenue came from corporation tax (11 per cent), followed by the main excises, hydrocarbon oils (6 per cent), tobacco products (4 per cent), alcoholic drinks (3 per cent). Of the remainder of the central government taxes included in the study, none, not even petroleum revenue tax (PRT) in 1986-87, raised more than one per cent of revenue (to the nearest whole number).

The relatively small revenue contribution of these other taxes did not justify surveys as extensive and rigorous as those of the three main revenue yielders. As indicated above, some specific questions on corporation tax were included with VAT 2, but the sample frame was not fully representative. With PRT and two of the main excises, small surveys were undertaken (described in the relevant chapters). The main object with the taxes of small revenue yield was to establish the nature and broad

---

* Responses to the questionnaire resulted in a figure of £392m.; the total using the charges of the specialist firms were £343m. for one firm and £327m. for the other.

order of magnitude of the compliance costs, primarily from documentary material and from interviews. The figures arrived at for these taxes have a much lower degree of reliability than for the main revenue yielders; but even if they are very substantially out, the broad picture would be little affected.

Local authority rates in 1986-87 were the fourth largest revenue yielder — after income tax, national insurance contributions and VAT. They are unique amongst the large revenue yielders in that, by common observation, compliance costs are very low and much less than administrative costs. Some fairly rough and ready methods have therefore been adopted to assess the compliance costs.

Exclusions from the Study

The intention of the study was to provide as comprehensive a coverage as possible of the United Kingdom taxes so that a reliable estimate could be made of the cost of operating the United Kingdom tax system. This we believe we have achieved. All Inland Revenue duties have been included in the study and almost all Customs and Excise duties as well as national insurance contributions and local rates, but certain taxes or near taxes have been excluded on grounds of principle or practicality.

The exclusions are as follows:

(1)   *The excise on matches and mechanical lighters.* This excise has the insignificant yield of £18m.

(2)   *Customs duties.* These duties present a series of problems. The administration of customs duties (and compliance with them) is associated with a variety of regulatory functions which constitute, in the words of senior customs officials, a 'seamless robe'. The object of customs duties is often protection rather than revenue-raising; customs officials have to check where licences are needed for import and export; they have to collect information about trade for national statistics and check for smuggling and drug trafficking. Moreover, the revenue accruing from customs duties does not directly benefit the United Kingdom Exchequer but counts as 'own resources' of the European Community. In all these circumstances, and bearing in mind that customs duties constitute

only a little more than one per cent of tax revenues, it seemed less misleading to omit them from the study than to include them.

(3)   *Motor vehicle licence duties.* These duties are not collected by either revenue department. Whilst the compliance costs are clearly very small (a once or twice per annum payment at the post office or by mail) the administrative costs, rather like customs duties, are inflated by regulatory functions. We were informed that there was no realistic way of distinguishing the tax collecting cost from the regulatory cost. Moreover, it is not unlikely that, but for the regulatory purposes, the duty would not exist but would be subsumed in the excise on hydrocarbon oils. The yield is well under one per cent of tax revenue and these duties have been excluded.

(4)   *Radio and television licences.* This duty is not administered by either of the revenue departments. Its yield goes directly to the BBC and can be considered very much as an indirect payment for services rather than a tax. The yield is under one per cent of total revenue.

(5)   *Oil and gas royalties.* It is arguable whether or not these should be treated as a tax. Some data was collected about their compliance costs in the survey on petroleum revenue tax; but the royalties are not collected by either revenue department and no figures of administrative cost are available.

Pattern of Part II

In the remainder of Part II we consider each tax included in the study. We briefly outline the tax itself, including particular reference to features relevant to its administration. We then seek to answer three main questions. (1) What were the total administrative and compliance costs at the time of our study? (2) What were the characteristics of these costs, what was the composition of compliance costs and, in particular, what features resulted in high compliance costs? (3) What benefits were there, if any, acting as offsets to the compliance costs?

At the end of each chapter or section there is a summary of the main conclusions and of the estimated costs. Also at the end of each chapter or section, whenever relevant, reference is made to studies elsewhere which may be compared to the findings on the United Kingdom taxes.

Where the initial studies relate to an earlier period the figures are updated to 1986-87, taking account of changes in the legislation, the relevant population and appropriate indices.

The next three chapters deal with income tax, capital gains tax on individuals and national insurance contributions. These taxes are too interconnected to enable us to separate out completely the administrative and compliance costs of each. The income tax and capital gains tax (CGT) are dealt with on the same tax return. Employers operating the Pay-As-You-Earn (PAYE) system cannot distinguish the costs of collecting national insurance contributions from those of collecting income tax from their employees. Some of the administrative costs of collecting national insurance contributions fall on the Inland Revenue whilst others fall on the Department of Social Security.

The procedure followed in respect of these taxes is that Chapter 5 outlines income tax and CGT and then examines the findings on the compliance costs of personal income tax and CGT from the PIT survey 1983-84. Chapter 6 introduces the contributory aspects of the national insurance scheme and gives more detail on the employers' collection of PAYE income tax and national insurance contributions and examines the cost to employers of collecting these taxes from their employees for 1981-82, the time of the PAYE survey. Then Chapter 7 estimates the aggregate costs of all three taxes in 1986-87. It introduces the administrative costs for that year; up-dates to 1986-87 the findings of the PIT and PAYE surveys; and completes the picture on the compliance costs of these taxes by adding in some very approximate estimates of the compliance costs of the national insurance contributions of the self-employed, the special compliance costs imposed on financial institutions and the income tax and CGT compliance costs in respect of trusts.

In Chapter 8, on VAT, because we are in the unique position of having two main surveys a decade apart, the approach adopted is to compare the findings and seek to explain the differences. Chapter 9 deals with corporation tax and petroleum revenue tax, Chapter 10 with excise duties, whilst the final chapter in Part II deals with the minor taxes together with the local rate. The findings from the analyses of the various taxes in Part II are brought together at the beginning of Chapter 12 in Part III where we examine the incidence and burden of compliance costs and consider the policy implications of the study.

CHAPTER 5

INCOME TAX — I: PERSONAL INCOME TAX AND CAPITAL GAINS TAX

Introduction

In this chapter we outline the United Kingdom personal income tax and CGT. We then examine the findings of the PIT survey on the compliance costs of these two taxes in 1983-84.

Outline of Taxes

Personal Income Tax

Income tax is administered by the Department of Inland Revenue. Although first introduced by Pitt, and operational 1799-1802, it was the re-introduction of income tax by Addington in 1803 which established two principles which have remained fundamental to its administration: deduction at source wherever possible and the schedular system. Income is divided into a number of categories, or *schedules*, of which currently the most important are Schedule E, which includes employment income, and Schedule D, which includes earnings from self-employment. Taxpayers are categorised as Schedule D or Schedule E according to the main source of their income. Over 99 per cent of Schedule E income tax is collected by the *Pay-As-You-Earn* (PAYE) system.

Employers are usually responsible for collecting Schedule E tax and paying it over to the Inland Revenue. The United Kingdom PAYE is unusual in that the tax is assessed cumulatively throughout the year; thus, taken in conjunction with deduction of tax at source on interest and dividends and other measures such as the payment of mortgage interest net of tax, most taxpayers end the year having paid exactly the correct amount of tax (provided they have notified the Inland Revenue of casual earnings and of any change in circumstances affecting their allowances). As most of the work required to calculate liability is carried out by the Inland Revenue and the employer, the majority of employees with simple tax affairs only receive a tax return about every five years.

A much wider range of expenses can be deducted under Schedule D than under Schedule E: under Schedule D, the broad criterion is that the expenditure is allowable if wholly and exclusively incurred for the purpose of earning the income: more stringent conditions ('wholly, exclusively and necessarily') are applied under Schedule E.

Schedule A, which includes rent income, also retains some significance.

Every taxpayer is entitled to a *personal allowance*, a fixed amount of income which can be received free of tax. Income in the next band above the allowance is taxed at the *basic* rate of tax, a very wide band taxed at a fixed percentage. When taxable income exceeds the basic rate, a higher marginal rate or rates are applied.

The Finance Act of 1977 provided for the annual up-rating of the main personal allowances and the higher rate threshold and bands in line with the increase in the retail price index. A single taxpayer or a working wife generally receives the ordinary personal allowance (referred to in the case of a working wife as the 'wife's earned income allowance', and in the case of a single taxpayer as 'single person's allowance'). A husband, however, receives a higher personal allowance, which in very special circumstances may be transferred to the wife (e.g. a non-working husband could transfer the higher allowance to his working wife). Married couples are treated as one *tax unit*, with the husband responsible for the joint tax return; they may elect, however, for separate assessment, in which case the same tax liability is distributed between them; or they may opt for the 'wife's earnings election' in which each spouse is separately taxed on their earned income, but as this involves foregoing the husband's higher personal allowance, it is only advantageous for couples well into the higher rate tax bands. There are also a number of other allowances, of which the most significant are relief for mortgage interest paid and for pension contributions. Other special allowances include one for blind taxpayers and one for single-parent families.

In 1983-84, the year of the PIT survey, there was an investment income surcharge — an additional 15 per cent rate of tax on investment income above a threshold (£7,100 in 1983-84); but this surcharge was abolished in the Finance Act, 1984. The rates of income tax prevailing at the time of the PIT survey and in 1986-87 are set out in Table 5.1.

Table 5.1 Rates of Income Tax and Thresholds
1983-84 and 1986-87

	1983-84	*1986-87*
Basic rate	30%	29%
Higher rates (with thresholds of taxable income)	40% (£14,601) 45% (£17,201) 50% (£21,801) 55% (£28,901) 60% (£36,001)	40% (£17,201) 45% (£20,201) 50% (£25,401) 55% (£33,301) 60% (£41,200)
Single person's allowance	£1,785	£2,335
Married person's allowance	£2,795	£3,655
Investment income surcharge	15% (£7,100)	Not applicable

Capital Gains Tax

Capital gains tax (CGT) was introduced in 1965, though it has been subject to many changes since. It superseded a short-term capital gains tax which applied from 1962 to 1965. Gains on normal trading activities are classed as income.

In 1983-84 CGT was levied on realised gains with gifts but not death being treated as a realisation (though since 1980 the parties have been able to elect to defer the tax). Losses can be offset against gains. The net gains and net losses of each spouse are computed separately, but are included in a single assessment. The tax also applies to gains on assets held by trustees, but with a threshold which is generally half that of individuals.

A wide range of assets is exempt from capital gains tax, including life insurance and superannuation benefits, a principal private residence, chattels under £3,000 and government and government-guaranteed securities. (Up to 2 July 1986, to benefit from the exemption these securities had to be held for more than twelve months; but this restriction was abolished from that date). There is also a substantial retirement relief (subject to conditions).

As from March 1982 capital gains and losses were adjusted for inflation by up-rating acquisition (and any enhancement) value by increases in the retail price index since that date. The threshold is similarly increased.

Both at 1983-84 and at 1986-87 the rate of tax was a single 30 per cent. The threshold for individuals in 1983-84 was £5,300 and in 1986-87, £6,300.

Main Findings of 1983-84 PIT Study

Excluding psychic costs, the compliance costs for personal income tax and CGT are predominantly of two kinds: hours spent on tax work and fees paid to professional advisers. In addition there are minor miscellaneous costs, such as time and money spent visiting a tax adviser or Inland Revenue officer, the purchase of literature to help in completing tax returns, and the like.

Time Spent on Income Tax and CGT Compliance

On the basis of the PIT survey it was estimated that 40 per cent of taxpayers and 83 per cent of taxpayers' wives spent no time at all on income tax and capital gains tax affairs in 1983-84. This figure reflects the infrequency with which many taxpayers on PAYE, with simple tax affairs, receive a tax form. This feature of the United Kingdom tax system is unique or almost unique (Ireland also has a cumulative PAYE system). At the other extreme 2.3 per cent of taxpayers (over half a million) spent 20 hours or more per annum on their personal tax affairs and 0.2 per cent (some 50,000 taxpayers) spent 100 hours or more. On average between three and a half and three and three-quarter hours was spent on income tax and CGT per taxpaying unit.

It was estimated that the total number of hours spent by taxpayers on income and capital gains tax in 1983-84 was about 90 million, the equivalent of over 11.5 million (eight-hour) man days or some 65,000 man years.

Valuation of Time in PIT Survey

The total value of the time spent on income tax affairs by the taxpayers themselves, on their own valuation, was estimated at £532 million. The PIT survey was unique among the surveys of compliance cost in that we had official figures on the income of respondents from the Survey of Personal Income (SPI). Thus, we were able to make comparisons between the value set on time by respondents to the survey, and a value estimated from the earned income of the individual respondent contained in the SPI for those respondents in full-time employment. (It was not possible to do the same analysis for part-time employees or the self- employed, because of lack of data on hours worked).

National data on hours worked and the amount of paid holiday from the *New Earnings Survey* showed that, on average, those in full-time work worked around 38.5 hours per week for 46 weeks of the year (including overtime) — giving a total of 1772 hours worked per year. Earned income of the respondent, excluding the income of the spouse, was then divided by 1772 to give an estimated hourly value of time which could be compared to the valuation given in the survey. Table 5.2 summarises the results. The comparison bears out the general validity of respondents' own valuation of their time. For basic rate taxpayers the estimates based on income data are slightly higher than taxpayers' own valuations. For higher rate taxpayers the reverse is true but the excess is not huge; and it is not unreasonable to suppose that higher rate taxpayers put a particularly high valuation on leisure.

Table 5.2 Comparison of Valuation of Own Time with Estimated Value from Income Data, 1983-84

	Ratio *Own Valuation* *Estimated Valuation*
Basic Rate Taxpayers, under £9,500	0.99
Basic Rate Taxpayers, £9,500 and over	0.93
Higher Rate Taxpayers	1.27

Employment of Tax Advisers

It was estimated that 2.6 million taxpayers, or 10.5 per cent of the tax-paying population, employed paid tax advisers in 1983-84. This estimate accords well with that of 8.5 per cent in 1970, by Sandford who considered that, for statistical sampling reasons, his estimate was probably on the low side (Sandford, 1973, pp.162-165). Moreover there has been a very considerable increase in the numbers (and in the proportion of the population) self-employed since 1970 and the self-employed particularly use paid tax advisers (see below). Accountants interviewed in relation to the PIT study also considered that personal tax work had increased since 1970. Of those taxpayers seeking paid tax advice the overwhelming majority employed an accountant as their sole adviser (nearly 95 per cent), a further 2.5 per cent sought additional advice from valuers, banks and members of the legal profession. A small number of taxpayers sought advice only from a bank or a solicitor. Of those seeking tax advice solely from a bank, three-quarters were either retired or were widows not seeking employment.

The reasons given by respondents for employing a tax adviser are set out in Table 5.3.

Table 5.3 Reasons Given for Employing a Paid Tax Adviser

	Percentage agreement, unweighted		
	Overall	*Sch.D*	*Sch.E*
	(N=896)[1]	*(N=527)*	*(N=344)*
I want to be sure of getting all the allowances I am entitled to	69.5	69.3	70.3
I feel happier knowing my returns are accurate	67.5	69.4	65.7
I wish to take every opportunity the law allows to cut my tax bill	59.8	58.6	63.7
I can't find/afford the time to deal with tax myself	38.8	39.5	38.7
My income comes from too many sources for me to cope easily	34.3	26.8	45.6
The tax forms are too complicated to understand	33.0	36.2	27.3
Discussions with my tax adviser help me with other financial matters	32.3	32.1	33.4
My adviser saves me more than I pay him	30.1	30.0	29.9
Changes in my circumstances have made me seek advice	15.8	10.4	23.5
I have been wrongly charged in the past	12.4	9.9	16.9
Inland Revenue suggested I use professional advisers	5.3	6.6	3.8
Other reasons (written in)	14.9	11.8	19.2

[1]Also includes 25 responses from taxpayers making repayment claims (see Appendix A).

As there is some difference of emphasis between Schedule D taxpayers (predominantly the self-employed) and Schedule E taxpayers (predominantly employees) they have been distinguished in the table.

Many taxpayers gave more than one reason for employing a tax adviser. Of the 898 members of the sample survey who responded to this question over 500 cited each of 'accuracy', 'making sure of claiming all allowances' and 'taking every legal opportunity to cut the tax bill'. These three reasons topped the list for both Schedule D and Schedule E taxpayers; but a much larger proportion of Schedule E taxpayers cited numerous income sources as a reason for employing an adviser. Of the written-in reasons, 48 respondents indicated that their personal tax work was integrated with their business accounts; this situation is likely to be true of other taxpayers, particularly those on Schedule D.

The main reason given by both Schedule D and Schedule E taxpayers for *not* employing a tax adviser was that 'My affairs are simple'. 'I am capable of handling my own affairs' was the next most usual reason for Schedule E taxpayers and 'I am qualified to handle tax affairs' came second for Schedule D taxpayers.

Total fees paid to tax advisers were estimated at £593 million in 1983-84, consisting of £565.5 million in 'normal fees', i.e. those incurred on a regular basis, and £27.5 million in special fees, arising from particular problems. It seems likely that these fees understate the resource costs of the use of tax advisers for personal tax work. There was a consensus amongst accountants interviewed that fees to personal clients were something of a 'loss leader'; they were often under-priced because accountants didn't like to turn down work of a personal nature for a finance director or even a small businessman (who might provide other work) or a person recommended by a bank or solicitor who might later recommend some bigger clients.

Estimated Total Compliance Costs

Table 5.4 brings together the time costs and the costs of fees to professional advisers, together with miscellaneous costs, to give the estimated total of compliance costs of income tax and CGT to the personal taxpayer, 1983-84, of £1149m. or 3.6 per cent of the revenue from income tax and CGT.

Table 5.4 Estimated Compliance Costs to Personal Taxpayer of Income Tax and CGT, 1983-84

	£m.	*Per cent of total costs*
Fees to tax advisers	593	51.6
Time costs (90m. hours)	532	46.3
Miscellaneous costs	24	2.1
Total	1149	100.0

Characteristics and Distribution of Compliance Costs

Employment Category and Income. The survey demonstrates very clearly that the two most crucial factors in determining the level of compliance costs are employment category (self-employed or employee) and income level.

Table 5.5 analyses compliance costs by reference to tax schedule, sub-divided into higher rate and basic rate taxpayers, whilst Table 5.6 compares Schedule D and Schedule E taxpayers in respect of hours spent on tax compliance and fees paid to advisers analysed by income band. The main differences between taxpayers in the two schedules are as follows:

(1)   A much higher percentage of Schedule D taxpayers employ advisers, especially amongst the basic rate taxpayers: of Schedule D taxpayers 80 per cent of higher rate payers employ advisers and 75 per cent of basic rate payers compared with, respectively, 35 per cent and only 2 per cent of Schedule E payers. Allowing for those Schedule D taxpayers who are not self-employed (see below), the proportion of self-employed taxpayers employing advisers is, overall, around 85 per cent.

(2)   On average Schedule D taxpayers spend more hours on tax work than Schedule E taxpayers at almost all income levels, but with no discernible upward or downward trend. Hours spent by Schedule E taxpayers tend to rise with incomes.

Table 5.5   Compliance Costs 1983-84 Analysed by Income Tax Schedule and Bands

| Schedule and Bands | Population 000 | Time | | | | Advisers | | | Misc. £m. | Total Compliance Costs £m. |
| | | Hours | | Costs | | % employing advisers | Cost | | | |
		mean	total m.	mean £	total £m		mean fee £	total £m.		
Schedule D										
Higher rate	280	16	4	227.9	64	80	500	112	1.3	177
Basic rate or less	2,280	19.9	45	110.6	252	75	213	364	12.5	629
Schedule E										
Higher rate	719	7.5	5	122.5	88	33	308	73	2.1	163
Basic rate or less	18,002	1.8	32	6.1	110	2	96	34	7.7	152
Other	3,434	0.8	3	5.2	18	3	87	9	0.2	27
Overall	**24,715**	**3.6**	**90**	**21.5**	**532**	**10.5**	**225**	**593**	**23.8**	**1149**

(3)   Under both Schedules, fees to advisers tend to rise with income; but fees paid by Schedule D taxpayers tend to be higher.

These differences are broadly in line with expectations. Schedule D taxpayers, who are predominantly self-employed, with the exception of about 10 per cent, mainly in the construction industry, receive their income gross, unlike most Schedule E taxpayers, whose income has had tax deducted at source. There is thus greater possibility of non-disclosure of and under-reporting of income by Schedule D taxpayers. Moreover their taxable income is arrived at by subtracting from this gross income substantial expenditures which are tax deductible. Because of the bigger possibilities of tax evasion the Inland Revenue are more likely to scrutinise carefully the returns of Schedule D taxpayers and both for this reason and because some of the tax deductible items may be complicated and require some element of negotiation it is usual for a self-employed Schedule D taxpayer to employ an adviser. Indeed, many businesses would employ an accountant anyway for audit and general financial advice.

Table 5.6 Comparison of Average Time and Fees in respect of Tax Compliance Work for Schedule D and Schedule E Taxpayers. Analysed by Income Group, 1983-84

Income band £	Mean Number of Hours		Mean Fees to Advisers £	
	Sch D	*Sch E*	*Sch D*	*Sch E*
up to 7,499	20.8	3.4	193	60
7,500-14,999	17.9	4.6	248	247
15,000-29,999	20.4	7.0	500	270
30,000-49,999	9.1	11.7	444	505
50,000 and over	16.8	10.7	1654	554

Perhaps the more interesting question is not why such a high percentage of Schedule D taxpayers employ advisers, but why does the figure fall short of 100 per cent. Partly the answer is to be found in the inclusion within the Schedule D category of taxpayers from the finance and banking sector, fully qualified to do their own accounts — particularly relevant to the top income brackets. At the lower end of the scale, taxpayers who do not employ an adviser are often retired or widowed, separated or divorced. A remarkably high proportion of female respondents to the survey fell into this category.

Table 5.7 compares the total compliance costs of Schedule D and Schedule E taxpayers analysed by income band. The table shows that up to £30,000 income level Schedule D respondents report consistently higher compliance costs than Schedule E. Above that level, however, the figures are more comparable. It should be recalled that the designation of Schedule relates to the main source of income and at the top income ranges, taxpayers in both Schedules became more akin to each other, each with considerable subsidiary income sources.

Table 5.7 Comparison of Average Compliance Costs of Schedule D and Schedule E Taxpayers, 1983-84

Income band £	Schedule D		Schedule E	
	Mean Compliance Cost £	*As % of Income*	*Mean Compliance Cost £*	*As % of Income*
up to 7,499	274	6.79	1	0.13
7,500-14,999	411	3.87	122	1.06
15,000-29,999	618	2.93	182	0.85
30,000-49,999	513	1.49	606	1.51
50,000 and over	1397	1.65	607	0.83

The overall pattern is for costs to rise with income. However, when costs are examined as a percentage of income, differences are apparent: percentage costs under Schedule D tend to fall as income rises — they are 'regressive', being proportionately greater for low income respondents. Under Schedule E, by contrast, the trend is for percentage costs to rise with income, at any rate up to the £50,000 income level. The U.K. income tax system is designed so that Schedule E taxpayers below the higher rate threshold, who form the great bulk of all taxpayers, incur low costs.

Table 5.8 Comparison of Compliance Costs of Taxpayers Employing an Adviser with the Other Taxpayers, 1983-84

	Taxpayers Employing Adviser *£m.*	*Taxpayers Not Employing Adviser* *£m.*
Time costs	340	178
Miscellaneous costs	15	9
Fees to adviser	<u>593</u>	<u>-</u>
Totals[1]	<u>948</u>	<u>187</u>

[1] The combined total (£1,135m.) is slightly less than the total in Tables 5.4 and 5.5 because grossing up the two groups (with and without advisers) separately yields slightly different mean costs from grossing up the overall sample means.

Table 5.8 reinforces the point that, under the United Kingdom system, a large proportion of taxpayers have few, if any, compliance costs, whilst a small proportion incur substantial costs. The 10.5 per cent of taxpayers employing tax advisers incur over 80 per cent of total compliance costs; not only do they face advisers' fees, but their total time costs are also almost twice as high. Employing an adviser cannot remove all the chores from tax compliance.

Besides the predominating influence of employment category and income on compliance costs, regression analysis (see Appendix B) revealed the level of capital allowances and the presence of capital gains as the next most important features affecting the level of compliance costs of Schedule D taxpayers. For Schedule E taxpayers the significant variables after income were the presence of business profits and directors' fees, i.e. non- Schedule E type income.

Capital Gains. Both capital allowances and capital gains tax may give rise to complex calculations and difficult business decisions. Capital gains tax, in particular, deserves some further consideration.

Some questions on CGT were included in the PIT survey. The responses indicated that only 3 per cent of all income tax payers reported capital gains in 1983-84 and three-quarters of these (including their wives) spent less than an hour on CGT; at the other extreme 2.8 per cent spent over 20 hours and 1.2 per cent spent over 50 hours. Capital gains tax emerges as a tax on which Schedule D taxpayers spend much more time than Schedule E payers; all the taxpayers spending over 50 hours on CGT compliance were Schedule D tax payers.

Unfortunately we do not have a reliable breakdown of tax advisers' fees between income tax and CGT work; but CGT is clearly a tax which normally requires the skills of the professionally qualified. Besides the evidence from the PIT survey there are many other indications of the high compliance costs of CGT. The tax is essentially 'backward-looking' and may require much delving for past records or enquiries to make good missing information. Sandford (1973) identified CGT as peculiarly a tax with high compliance costs. Interviews with professional accountants following the PIT study stressed the same point and in particular indicated the indexation provisions as generating high compliance costs. A recent report from a group of tax specialists set up by the Institute for Fiscal Studies in September 1987 stated: 'It would hardly be an exaggeration to say that the complexities of indexation and the rules for matching share transactions are such that they maximise rather than minimise compliance costs. It would be difficult to think up a more complex tax structure' (IFS, 1988).

Benefits of Compliance

For a few taxpayers there may be some benefits from tax compliance in so far as the work they are obliged to do to complete their tax returns helps to increase their grasp on their own financial affairs. This may be especially true of Schedule D taxpayers. Without the tax requirement, some self-employed taxpayers might not employ an accountant; in the event the accountant may offer them useful advice on other matters concerned with the finance and management of the business.

The cash flow advantages to employers we discuss in the next chapter; there are no cash flow benefits to employees. However, the self-employed do receive a cash flow benefit. They are required to make their payments of tax in two instalments on 1 January and 1 July each year based on profits earned for the accounting period which ended in the tax year to the previous 5 April. However, when a trade or profession commences, the profits of one accounting period may serve as the basis for two or three years. (For details see Appendix B). If incomes are unchanged from year to year the deferment they enjoy is approximately six months, or less in so far as Schedule D profits are calculated on an accruals basis and receipts tend to lag. However, if incomes are rising (even if it is only an inflationary rise) the value of the deferment is increased. In 1983-84 the revenue collected from the self-employed was of the order of £2,600m. If we assume an average deferment of six months, at the average Bank Rate of 9.35 per cent during that year, the value of the cash flow benefit works out at £122m.; thus, the net compliance cost for Schedule D taxpayers was of the order of £680m. The cash flow benefit thus represents a substantial offset to the compliance costs of the self-employed, who tend to have the heaviest compliance costs.

International Comparisons

There have been recent studies of the compliance costs of personal income tax in the U.S.A. and Canada.

United States

Slemrod and Sorum (1984) despatched a mail questionnaire to a random sample of 2,000 Minnesota residents in April 1983 relating to the 1982 tax year. They obtained a response rate of 33 per cent. After eliminating non-taxpayers and incomplete responses they were left with 600 usable replies.

The basic measure used for valuing time was the estimated hourly rate of the respondents net of tax. The researchers weighted the Minnesota sample to make it more representative of the United States taxpaying population as a whole and, after making various adjustments, concluded that the aggregate time spent on compliance in 1982 was between 1.4 and 2.1 billion hours and that the total resource cost of compliance was between 17 and 27 billion dollars. This represented between 5 and 7 per cent of the revenue levied by the federal and state income tax systems combined. No attempt was made in the study to value the costs of employers and of the federal and state collection agencies.

The fact that the sample was drawn from only one geographical region and was a tiny fraction of the total United States taxpaying population, together with the use of (necessarily) somewhat arbitrary procedures in grossing up the sample to include the federal income tax for the whole country, reduces the reliability of the results.

The Arthur D. Little Corporation also undertook a study for the U.S. Treasury (Arthur D. Little, 1988) with the particular goal of developing a methodology for estimating the 'paperwork burden' imposed on taxpayers by the federal income tax, measuring this burden in hours for 1983.

The part of the study concerned with individuals was based on two national surveys, a diary study in which 750 individuals were asked to keep a daily record of the time taken to perform tax paperwork-related activities and a mail survey covering similar ground, which resulted in 4,038 responses from a sample population of 6,200 (a 65 per cent response rate). Unlike the Slemrod and Sorum study, the Arthur D. Little study excluded time spent on the state and local taxes and out-of-pocket financial expenses and sought to convert paid preparers' fees into equivalent hours had the respondents completed the tax work themselves. After a reconciliation between the diary study and the recall study, the burden for individuals, on average, was estimated at 26.4 hours aggregating to 1.59 billion hours.

In comparing U.S.A. studies with the United Kingdom it must be remembered that the lower level of United States taxation tends to raise the compliance cost:revenue ratio. Furthermore, the United States self-assessment system means that more work is left to the taxpayer; the corollary is that the administrative costs of the federal government have always been a substantially lower proportion of revenue than the United Kingdom costs; for example, federal costs were 0.48 per cent of revenue in 1984 (Internal Revenue Service, 1985) against the U.K. costs of 1.49 per cent. (Inland Revenue Annual Reports).

Canada

Vaillancourt's study (Vaillancourt, 1988) was based on face to face interviews, with questions bought in from a national commercial polling organisation. A modified probability sample of 2,040 residents, aged eighteen or over, was interviewed. The interviews were spread across the ten Canadian provinces and took place in May-June 1986. Of the 2,040, 1,673 had returned a 1985 income tax return and constituted a representative sample of the 16 million Canadian taxpayers. A series of very detailed questions on tax compliance costs was asked.

In valuing time Vaillancourt took the gross wage rate as representing the approximate value to society of the output that could have been produced in the time period. (Vaillancourt's valuations thus accord closely with those of the PIT survey where taxpayers' own valuations were used, but a cross-check on full-time employees showed a close correspondence with their estimated wage rates).

Vaillancourt concludes that the average compliance cost per Canadian taxpayer in 1985 was $122.50 with a total cost to individuals of $1.95bn. or 2.5 per cent of taxes collected.

Vaillancourt's study, unlike that of Slemrod and Sorum or the Arthur D. Little study, does extend to the other compliance costs of income tax and to the administrative costs and we consider his overall conclusions in Chapter 7.

Summary of Main Conclusions

In 1983-84 United Kingdom taxpayers spent an estimated 90 million hours in aggregate on income tax and CGT affairs, or about 3.6 hours per taxpaying unit. Some 10.5 per cent of taxpayers employed paid advisers. The total compliance costs were estimated at £1149m. or 3.6 per cent of revenue from income tax and CGT. The most important factors determining the level of compliance cost were size of income and category of employment. CGT was also an important source of high compliance costs but affected relatively few taxpayers. For Schedule D taxpayers, largely the self-employed, compliance costs showed a regressive pattern, being proportionately heavier on the lower income groups. Because of the timing of the tax payments the self-employed received a significant offset in the form of cash flow benefits.

CHAPTER 6

INCOME TAX — II: COST TO EMPLOYERS OF COLLECTING PAYE INCOME TAX AND NATIONAL INSURANCE CONTRIBUTIONS

Outline of Taxes

PAYE Income Tax

The main features of the United Kingdom withholding system of income tax, known as PAYE, were outlined in the previous chapter. Employers have the responsibility to deduct income tax from the wages and salaries of their employees and pay it over to the Inland Revenue by the 19th of the following month. All employees are allocated a tax code by Inland Revenue determined by their allowances and the employer receives a set of tables enabling him to convert tax codes to the appropriate tax deductions for different weekly, fortnightly or monthly wage and salary payments so that he can deduct the right amount of tax. The system is cumulative; in principle, taxpayers on basic rate, with no complicating tax circumstances, who have correctly reported their circumstances, have the correct amount of tax deducted by the year end. Besides deducting tax the employer has to make a return of payments in kind made to employees and, at the year end or when the employee changes jobs, has to supply, to the Inland Revenue and to the employee, a statement of tax and national insurance payments made.

National Insurance Contributions

National insurance (NI) contributions are levies on employers, employees and the self-employed. Over time they have increasingly ceased to have the characteristics for insurance of pre-determined benefits from flat rate contributions; they are in the main compulsory; the rate of contribution and of disbursements from the fund are wholly determined by government policy; contributions vary with income within certain limits although the basic benefits are identical; and, until very recently, part of the income to the fund has come from a General Exchequer contribution. It is appropriate to treat them as a tax, following the practice of OECD revenue statistics.

The employers' and employees' NI contributions (known as Class 1 contributions) are collected from employers at the same time as PAYE income tax but then paid over by Inland Revenue to the Department of Social Security. In 1981-82 at the time of the PAYE survey, both the employers' and employees' contributions were fixed percentages of earnings between a lower threshold and a ceiling, neither of which was related to income tax thresholds. In 1981-82 there was also a surcharge on the employers' contribution solely for revenue-raising purposes. By 1986-87 a number of changes had taken place: the surcharge had gone (1984); the ceiling on employers' but not on employees' NI contributions had been abolished and two lower rates had been introduced for low paid workers applying to the contributions of both employers and employees (1985). (Note that the rates of national insurance contributions were average or 'slab' rates, not marginal or 'slice'; so that the benefit from the lower rates accrued only in respect of the lower paid). It is possible to contract out of the state earnings related pension scheme (SERPS) and pay a lower rate.

The Class 1 contributions provide the overwhelming bulk of the revenue (e.g. in 1986-87, when there was no surcharge to bias the figures, £24,935m. out of a total of £25,663m. or over 97 per cent of revenue, came from Class 1 contributions).

Class 2 and Class 4 contributions are paid by the self-employed; Class 2 is paid at a fixed rate and Class 4 also at a fixed rate in excess of a lower profits limit and less than an upper profits limit. Class 2 contributions may be paid to the Department of Social Security by banker's order or by stamped card and Class 4 contributions are collected by Inland Revenue along with income tax on the self-employed.

Class 3 relates to voluntary payments to improve a contributions record; the receipts are minimal and for our purposes Class 3 can be ignored.

The rates of Class 1 for 1981-82 (the year of the PAYE survey) are set out in Table 6.1 along with the rates for Class 1, 2 and 4 for 1986-87.

Table 6.1 Main Rates of National Insurance Contributions, Employers and Employees, 1981-1982 and 1986-87

Employers and Employees (Class 1)

Not Contracted Out

	1981 - 82			1986-87	
Weekly Earnings (£)	Employer %	Employee %	Weekly Earnings (£)	Employer %	Employee %
27.00-200.00	13.7[1]	7.75	38.00 - 59.99	5	5
			60.00 - 94.99	7	7
			95.00 - 139.99	9	9
			140.00 - 284.99	10.45	9
			285.00 or more	10.45	no additional liability

Contracted Out

	1981 - 82					1986-87			
Weekly Earnings (£)	Employer on first £27 %	on rest %	Employee on first £27 %	on rest %	Weekly Earnings (£)	Employer on first £38 %	on rest %	Employee on first £38 %	on rest %
27.00-200.00	13.7	9.2	7.75	5.25	38.00 - 59.99	5	0.9	5	2.85
					60.00 - 94.99	7	2.9	7	4.85
					95.00 - 139.99	9	4.9	9	6.85
					140.00 - 284.99	10.45	6.35	9	6.85
					285.00 or more	10.45	10.45[2]	no additional liability	

[1] Includes employers' surcharge.
[2] 6.35% to £285; excess over £285, 10.45%.

Self-Employed

Class 2, 1986-87: £3.75 per week; no liability if earning below £2,075 per year.
Class 4, 1986-87: 6.3 per cent on profits in *excess* of Lower Profits Limit (£4,450) and less than Upper Profits Limit (£14,820).

Main Findings 1981-82 PAYE Study

Size and Composition of Compliance Costs

It had been hoped to measure compliance costs separately for PAYE income tax, employees' NI contributions, and employers' NI contributions. However, it was found from the pilot study that, because of shared costs, few employers were able to separate out these elements. Consequently, overall costs were estimated for the three elements combined, including the employers' NI surcharge which existed in 1981-82.

Compliance costs were measured as the sum of:

(1)   Total value of time spent by directors, partners or proprietors on PAYE and NI work.

(2)   Total value of time spent by employees other than computer staff on PAYE and NI work.

(3)   Total value of time spent by computer staff on PAYE and NI work.

(4)   Fees paid to accountants and specialist agencies.

(5)   Any other costs.

Table 6.2 gives the estimated total compliance costs to employers of collecting PAYE and NI contributions arrived at by grossing up the average compliance costs recorded by respondents for each of the size categories supplied by Inland Revenue (see Appendix C). The table indicates that staff time contributed over 80 per cent of the cost and that the overall compliance cost in 1981-82 was of the order of £450 million. This figure represented about 1.8 per cent of the yield of PAYE income tax and just over 1 per cent of the yield of PAYE income tax and NI contributions combined. Administrative costs to the Inland Revenue were just under 1 per cent of the yield of income tax and NI contributions.

Table 6.2 Estimated Compliance Costs to Employers of Collecting PAYE and NI Contributions 1981-82

Regular Costs	*£m*	*Per cent of Total Costs*
Value of time spent by:		
Directors, partners, proprietors	147	33
Computer staff	16	4
Other staff	211	47
Other costs within the firm	18	4
Payments to advisers	54	12
Non-regular Costs		
Costs of special problems	3	1
	449	100

The *composition* of compliance costs varied with business size: for small- and medium-sized firms, the value of time spent by directors, partners and proprietors, together with fees to advisers, predominated. For large firms, these items were negligible: employee costs predominated and the costs of computer staff rose steadily with the size of firm.

Characteristics and Distribution of Compliance Costs

(1) Size of Firm. The survey reveals size of firm as the predominating influence on the level of compliance costs. The most relevant measures of size obtained from the survey data were number of employees and the amount of PAYE and NI payments (hereafter referred to as 'tax payments'). Tax payments were particularly convenient both because they

were the basis of the Inland Revenue classification of employers from which the sample was drawn and because they provided the basis for a cost/revenue comparison — a form of input/output ratio. Both measures (and, indeed, a less useful turnover measure) revealed a marked regressiveness in compliance costs.

Compliance costs are analysed by tax payments in Table 6.3. Whilst in absolute terms costs rise with payments, they fall in proportionate terms: the lower the payment, the higher the compliance cost as a proportion of that payment, and *vice versa*. In 1981-82, the compliance cost:yield ratio ranged from 33 per cent for the smallest PAYE and NI payers to under 1 per cent for the largest.

Table 6.3 Analysis of Compliance Costs of Businesses as Percentage of PAYE and NI Payments 1981-82

Total PAYE and NI in year	*Number of Respondent Businesses in each Category*	*Mean Compliance Cost (£)*	*Compliance Cost/Yield Ratio (mean %)[1]*
£1- £1,000	71	89	32.8
£1,001- £2,500	106	145	8.7
£2,501- £5,000	94	306	8.7
£5,001- £10,000	98	380	5.2
£10,001- £15,000	64	439	3.6
£15,001- £25,000	48	567	2.8
£25,001- £50,000	61	657	2.0
£50,001- £100,000	28	822	1.2
100,001- £250,000	31	1,864	1.3
Over £250,000	18	7,818	0.7
	619		

[1] For each case, compliance cost is expressed as a percentage of annual PAYE and NI payments. These percentages are then averaged within each group.

Table 6.4 analyses compliance costs by number of employees. Average annual compliance cost per employee ranged from £58 for businesses with 1-5 employees to £11 for businesses with over 500 employees.

Table 6.4 Analysis of Compliance Costs per Employee in Businesses Classified by Number of Employees 1981-82

Number of Employees	Mean Compliance Cost per Employee (£)	Compliance Cost/Yield (%)
1- 5	58	14.2
6- 10	39	6.0
11- 20	38	4.6
21- 50	29	3.8
51- 100	17	1.7
101- 500	18	1.3
Over 500	11	0.8
Number of Respondents	687	619

Note: Some respondents gave information on employment and compliance costs but not tax payments, hence the smaller number of respondents in the cost/yield column.

(2) Other Influences. Although size of firm was clearly the major determinant of compliance costs, businesses of similar size often reported widely different costs. Other influences which were found to be important were mechanisation, staff training, and type of documentation used. Of these factors, the most significant was the type of documentation used. Firms using standard Inland Revenue documents reported higher cost:yield ratios than firms using 'substitute' documentation approved by Inland Revenue. In firms using their own documentation, PAYE and NI procedures were fully incorporated into an integrated accounting system. Table 6.5 demonstrates this difference clearly.

Table 6.5 Comparison of Compliance Costs as a Percentage of PAYE and NI payments, for Users of Standard and Substitute Documents 1981-82

Compliance cost/yield ratios (mean %)[1]

Employment	Businesses Using Standard Documents		Businesses Using Substitute Documents	
1- 5	14.5	(234)	5.6	(5)
6- 10	6.3	(141)	3.4	(14)
11- 20	5.3	(79)	2.2	(22)
21- 50	4.4	(42)	2.1	(12)
51- 100	3.2	(13)	0.7	(19)
Over 100	1.6	(7)	1.0	(16)

Numbers of respondents in brackets

[1] Compliance costs are calculated as a percentage of annual PAYE and NI payments for each respondent. These percentages are then averaged within each group.

There was some indication that computerised firms had lower compliance costs than similar firms without computers, but the number of firms where matched comparisons could be made was small.

The follow-up interviews revealed that experienced book-keepers were considerably faster at PAYE and NI work than other people. A 'learning curve' effect was also reported in cases where staff were unused to PAYE work: as they gained experience, costs diminished markedly over time.

Analysis by business sector revealed no clear pattern of differences. There was some indication that the professional and other services and primary sectors had higher cost:yield ratios than average. It was anticipated that labour turnover would be important; this did not appear to be so, but labour turnover was highly correlated with number of employees, making the effects of firm size and of labour turnover difficult to distinguish. There were also some indications that frequency of payment affected compliance costs — firms with predominantly monthly-paid workers having lower costs than those with predominantly weekly-paid workers.

(3) End Year Costs. Another aspect of the composition of compliance costs deserves note. At the end of the year, employers are required to prepare an annual statement, declaration and certificate (form P35) and to make a return for each employee (forms P14 and P60). Respondents were asked to distinguish between such year-end costs and all other PAYE and NI costs, including the issue of P45 forms (statement of tax paid when employees leave an employment). Although this factor did not influence the overall level of costs in any consistent way, it provided an insight into differences in firms' accounting practices.

Many respondents were unable to distinguish end-year from other costs, but the analysis of those who did is set out in Table 6.6. While the trend is not uniform, end-year costs tend to represent a higher proportion of the costs of smaller firms, especially in the case of businesses employing outside advisers to do some or all of their PAYE work. End-year costs were invariably less than half of total costs, and were less than one-third of total costs for all but the smallest firms. The evidence suggests that there was a tendency for small firms to put off doing a large proportion of their PAYE and NI work until the end of the year, while larger firms dealt with it more systematically.

**Table 6.6 Percentage of Total PAYE & NI Compliance Costs
Attributable to End-year Work 1981-82**

Numbers of respondents in brackets

Number of Employees	All Respondents (%)		Businesses Doing all PAYE Work In-house (%)		Businesses Using Outside Advisers (%)	
1- 5	39	(194)	34	(109)	49	(85)
6- 10	23	(125)	23	(87)	25	(35)
11- 20	21	(87)	24	(61)	14	(26)
21- 50	17	(45)	15	(36)	25	(9)
51- 100	31	(24)	29	(19)	..	(5)
Over 100	20	(30)	21	(27)	..	(3)

.. means too few responses (5 or less) for useful comparison.

Benefits of Compliance

While an employer incurs costs in complying with PAYE and NI regulations, he also gains a cash flow benefit. The size of this benefit depends, amongst other things, on what assumptions are made about the effective incidence of the tax, i.e. who really pays it. There would probably be little dispute with the view that the effective incidence of PAYE income tax is wholly or largely on the employee — in other words, that if income tax were abolished, employers would be paying the same gross wage or salary to employees without deduction of tax. A similar argument can be presented in respect of the employees' NI contributions. More open to dispute is the incidence of employers' NI contributions. But to the employer this payment is part of his total labour costs and there are respectable precedents (Meade, 1978) for treating employers' contributions in the same way as employees' contributions and PAYE income tax. In other words, for assuming that if all these payments were withdrawn, in the long run wage and salary rates would rise to absorb them. That is the simplifying assumption made in the following calculations; in so far as it is not true, the cash flow benefit is over-stated; and, it must be admitted that it is particularly suspect in relation to the temporary employers' surcharge existing in 1981-82.

Thus, in effect, the employer is treated as paying out part of the wage/salary bill to the employee on one date and another part to the Inland Revenue at a later date. The Exchequer is therefore lending cash to the employer for the period between the two dates.

The extent of the cash flow benefit depends on the length of time elapsing between the payment of wages and the payment of PAYE and NI. Thus, the benefit differs between monthly and weekly paid employees. In the case of monthly paid employees, tax payments are due on the 19th of the month following the payment of the wage. Thus, if employers pay on the last legitimate date, the benefit consists of the tax held from the pay-day up to the 19th of the following month.

In the case of weekly paid employees, the benefit is composed of two elements: (1) the grace period between the *end* of the tax month and the date on which tax is due, and (2) the collection period in which the tax accrues week by week *during* the tax month — thus, tax withheld from the first week's pay is retained by the employer for seven days longer than tax withheld from the second week's pay, and so on. As with monthly paid employees, tax is due on the 19th of the month following the payment of the wages.

Clearly, in so far as employers pay the collected tax to Inland Revenue before the due date, they reduce their cash flow benefit; if they pay after without incurring cash penalties, they increase their benefit. The assumption in the calculations is that all payments are made on the final due date, but some smaller employers, in particular, tend to pay late.

On these bases, an estimate was made of the cash flow benefit of PAYE and NI contributions to employers. (For technical details of the calculations see Appendix C). The overall results are set out in Table 6.7. For each size group of businesses, estimates are made of (gross) compliance costs, cash flow benefits and their value at current bank base rate (13.3 per cent) and of net compliance costs (gross costs minus the value of cash flow benefit). In aggregate the value of this benefit was estimated at £878m.

On this estimate, in 1981-82, overall, the compliance costs of collecting PAYE and NI contributions were more than wiped out by the cash flow benefits. But whereas the largest firms had negative net compliance costs, i.e. the cash flow benefit exceeded the compliance costs, the medium and small firms had positive net costs which, proportionately, were heavier for the smaller firm.

In considering these findings the main assumptions on which they rest must be stressed: (1) that the effective incidence of employees' income tax and of both employers' and employees' NI contributions rests wholly on the employee; (2) that all businesses made all due payments to Inland Revenue on the last official day for payment; and (3) that the value of the extra cash can be taken as the average clearing bank base rate, April 1981 to March 1982. During this period bank base rates were exceptionally high, averaging 13.3 per cent. These assumptions are additional to the more general ones of the representativeness of the sample and the validity of the grossing up procedure.

Indeed, a particular problem arises in connection with these general assumptions. The figures of cash flow benefit are probably biased in an upward direction by the existence in the sample of one giant company with an enormous cash flow benefit. Unfortunately it has not been found possible to estimate the extent of this bias. To omit the firm altogether would create a bias in the opposite direction.*(See bottom of next page).

The reservations about the assumptions, particularly with respect to the incidence of the employers' NI contribution and the surcharge, together with the sample bias, mean that these figures must be treated with considerable caution and that a qualitative rather than a quantitative conclusion should be drawn. There is no doubt that the value of the cash flow benefit is a significant offset to the compliance costs to businesses of administering PAYE and NI contributions. For the larger firms, but only for the larger firms, it is likely to exceed the gross compliance costs.

It should further be recalled (Chapter 3) that the cash flow benefit is not a resource saving, but simply a transfer payment within the economy.

International Comparisons

Ireland

A study very similar in approach to that of the United Kingdom PAYE study, but on a much smaller scale, was undertaken in Ireland (Leonard, 1986) to assess the administrative and compliance costs to employers of the Irish PAYE and PRSI (Pay Related Social Insurance) contributions. Leonard drew a representative sample of the members of the Federated Union of Employers (FEU) whose membership comprised 2,526 firms, approximately 3.3 per cent of total firms. This FEU population was not, itself, fully representative of the total population. The sample size was 300 and a response rate of nearly 40 per cent was obtained, giving a usable response of 119 (representing about 0.16 per cent of the total number of Irish businesses) to a mailed questionnaire which had first been piloted. Comparison with the PAYE study is particularly relevant both because the Irish PAYE system is cumulative, like that of the United Kingdom, and the finance of the social security system rests primarily on contributions from employers and employees; and because the questions in the questionnaire and definitions of cost were almost identical to those used in the United Kingdom study. Leonard's study related to 1983.

---

* The effect of excluding this giant firm is to reduce the overall cash flow benefits by a staggering £442m. Firms in the top size bands continue to have negative net compliance costs but overall the cash flow benefit just about equals the compliance costs.
As an alternative to omitting this large firm, the grossing up of the figures for the largest size band could be amended by noting that the giant firm is in the UK Top 100. Thus we could regard this one firm as representative of the top 100 employers, and the other respondents in the band as representative of the remaining 22,310 employers. Such a procedure reduces the total gross compliance costs for the size range by £7m (to £118.3m), and the total value of the cash flow for the size range by £231m (to £533.1m). The total value of the cash flow benefit for all firms is then reduced from £878m to £647m, and the estimated net compliance cost becomes -£205m (ie there is an aggregate net benefit of £205m).

Table 6.7   Estimated Cash Flow Benefits and Net Compliance Costs of PAYE and National Insurance Contributions 1981-82

Annual amount of PAYE and NI paid £	(1) Number of employers	(2) Average gross compliance cost per employer (£)	(3) Total gross compliance cost (1) x (2) (£m.)	(4) Average cash flow benefit per employer (£)	(5) Average value of cash flow benefit (4) x 13.3% (£)	(6) Total value of cash flow benefit (5) x (1) (£m.)	(7) Average net compliance cost (2) - (5) (£)	(8) Total net compliance cost (1) x (7) or (3) - (6) (£m.)
Under 1,200	265,395	91	24.2	38	5	1.3	86	22.8
1,200 - 5,999	448,558	232	104.1	238	31	13.9	201	90.2
6,000 - 41,999	237,139	496	117.6	1,336	177	42.0	319	75.6
42,000 - 179,999	61,231	1,272	77.9	6,971	920	56.3	352	21.6
180,000 or more	22,410	5,594	125.4	256,407	34,102	764.2	-28,508	-638.9
Overall	1,034,733	434	449	6,382	849	878	-415	-428.7

Leonard's findings closely match those of the United Kingdom PAYE study. He finds that whilst total compliance costs rise with size of firm (whether measured by employment, size of tax payments or turnover) average compliance costs (per employee) fall with size. Leonard also calculated cash flow benefits on assumptions broadly similar to those of the U.K. PAYE study and found that, for the larger firms, (but only the larger firms) the cash flow benefit exceeded the compliance cost. Overall, however, net compliance costs remained positive.

Administrative costs were officially estimated at 1.1 per cent of total receipts from PAYE and PRSI whilst the estimate for the total costs of employers in the sample (without allowing for the offset of cash flow benefits) was 2.7 per cent. For the various reasons given in Chapter 1, the absolute levels of such ratios may be misleading, especially in international comparisons; but the higher ratio of compliance to administrative costs in Ireland than in the United Kingdom is interesting. It has been suggested that the Irish have a more complicated structure of social insurance contributions than the United Kingdom. It is also probable that Ireland has more small firms and that giant firms represent a smaller proportion of its economy; if that is so, it might also help to account for the relatively smaller estimate of cash flow benefit.

Table 6.8 Mean Compliance Costs as Percentage of Tax for Employers of Different Sizes - Ireland and United Kingdom Compared

Size of Business measured by No. of Employees:	0-25	26-50	51-100	101-200	201-400	401+
Ireland Mean Compliance Cost:	4.0	2.5	1.2	1.1	0.5	0.9
United Kingdom Mean Compliance Cost:	9.6	3.4	1.7	1.5	0.4[1]	0.8

[1] This unexpectedly low figure is based on only 6 cases.

One of the most significant conclusions from the United Kingdom PAYE study was the regressiveness of compliance costs — their tendency to fall much more heavily on the small firm than the large. On this point, Leonard's findings fully support those of the United Kingdom PAYE study. Table 6.8 compares the findings, using number employed as the measure of size. The United Kingdom data have been re-grouped to match the size bands of the Irish study. There are differences especially in the smallest bands (where the mix of firms within the size band has a considerable effect on the average compliance cost); but overall the similarity of pattern is striking.

Canada

We have already discussed the compliance costs of personal income tax in Canada (Vaillancourt, 1988). Professor Vaillancourt also sought to measure the costs to employers, in 1986, of withholding income tax. He conducted a mail survey of a sample of employers, achieving a 9.8 per cent response rate on a sample of over 4,000, yielding 385 responses, of which 309 (7.4 per cent) were usable. The coverage of his questionnaire was rather different from that of the United Kingdom and Irish studies; with detailed cost questions including the costs of completing particular tax returns required under the Canadian system he grossed up his results on the basis of the average time taken to complete them. The differences of system and approach mean that detailed comparison with Vaillancourt's study is neither possible nor fruitful; but his general conclusions are relevant and interesting. He estimates that 'the compliance costs of employers having to retain and remit personal income taxes are of the order of 1/10th of 1 per cent of their gross business income'. Further, that these 'compliance costs decrease as a percentage of size with an increase in size. This relationship is a robust one, which holds when other factors are taken into account.' More specifically he estimates that the cost ratio for all employers falls from 3.36 per cent of gross business income for small employers to 0.064 per cent for large employers. The total cost to employers was calculated at $2.75bn. or 3.5 per cent of tax collected. Vaillancourt accepts that this estimate is high in comparison with other estimates in the literature and attributes the difference in part to the high costs associated with the Canadian unemployment insurance system.

Summary of Main Conclusions

In 1981-82, for the United Kingdom, the aggregate compliance costs of collecting PAYE income tax and NI contributions was estimated to be £449m., about 1.8 per cent of the yield of PAYE income tax and just over 1 per cent of the yield of PAYE income tax and NI contributions combined. There was a marked tendency for the average compliance cost to fall with size of firm, i.e. the impact of compliance costs was regressive.

Of a number of factors influencing compliance costs other than size, the most important appeared to be the use of approved substitute documents instead of official documents.

A cash flow benefit was a substantial offset to compliance costs and probably exceeded these costs for the largest firms.

The regressiveness on employers of the compliance costs of collecting PAYE income tax and social security contributions is well attested by international comparisons, in particular recent studies in Ireland and Canada.

CHAPTER 7

INCOME TAX — III: AGGREGATE COMPLIANCE AND ADMINISTRATIVE COSTS OF INCOME TAX, CGT AND NI CONTRIBUTIONS, 1986-87

Introduction

In this chapter we seek to update the PIT and PAYE surveys to arrive at estimates of compliance costs to personal taxpayers and employers in 1986-87; to take account of other income tax compliance costs and national insurance compliance costs; and to compare compliance and administrative costs.

Legislative and Administrative Changes

Personal Income Tax and CGT

Between 1983-84 and 1986-87 a number of legislative changes were made to income tax and CGT. Those most likely to have an effect on compliance and administrative costs are the following:

(1)   Over the period as a whole the basic personal allowances were increased by some 12 percentage points more than required to keep pace with the Retail Price Index (RPI).
(2)   In 1984 the investment income surcharge was abolished.
(3)   The basic rate of income tax was reduced from 30 to 29 per cent in 1986.
(4)   As from 1985-86 a new scheme was introduced by which a composite rate tax was applied to interest paid by banks and other

deposit takers which simplified the position for deposit holders and was expected to generate Inland Revenue staff savings.

(5)   Life assurance relief was withdrawn for premiums paid under insurances made after 13 March 1984.

(6)   In 1984 stock relief was abolished and it was provided that 100 per cent first year capital allowances and 75 per cent initial allowances would be phased out. They were replaced by 25 per cent reducing balance depreciation allowances for plant and machinery and 4 per cent straight line allowances for industrial buildings.

(7)   In 1985 a number of changes were made to the CGT indexation allowance.

(8)   The 1986 Finance Act introduced personal equity plans which gave relief from CGT and income tax subject to conditions.

(9)   In 1986 changes were made in respect of employee share schemes and the Business Expansion Scheme.

(10)   Computerisation of the records of PAYE taxpayers was extended (see next section).

Although the responses to the PIT survey relate to 1983-84, the sample was necessarily drawn from a somewhat earlier register for which the total taxpaying population was 24,700,000. For 1986-87 Inland Revenue Statistics record a figure of 24,100,000 individual taxpayers. Thus there was a fall of 600,000 (or 2.4 per cent) between the population from which the sample was drawn and 1986-87. However, there was an increase from 860,000 to 1,060,000 (a rise of 18.7 per cent) in the numbers of higher rate taxpayers and also a significant increase in the numbers of the self-employed.

On balance it is extremely difficult to judge whether the effect of all these changes has been to increase or reduce compliance costs. Accountants interviewed after the PIT survey pointed to ways in which compliance costs had been reduced for individuals, e.g. the composite interest scheme with banks and the abolition of stock relief. On the other hand they held that the Business Expansion and stock option schemes, while they had brought benefits to taxpayers in lower taxes, had complicated compliance; that there was increasing work in respect of payments in kind (P11Ds) because the limits had remained unchanged; and they complained that compliance costs were increasing because of harsher Inland Revenue attitudes in relation to back duty cases and PAYE investigations. They attributed the change in attitudes to the adoption of performance indicators and targeting of Inland Revenue investigations which pre-dated but has been further developed under the Financial Management Initiative. (See Chapter 1).

Similarly the reduction in the total of the taxpaying population can be expected to have reduced compliance costs, but the increase in the proportion of higher rate taxpayers to have increased them.

All in all, it does not seem possible to make any realistic assessment of the net effect of these legislative and administrative changes in arriving at a figure of compliance costs for 1986-87. We have simply up-rated the 1983-84 figures to allow for the changes in the appropriate price and wage levels.

PAYE and NI Contributions

Between 1981-82 and 1986-87 a number of changes were made in the PAYE and NI systems with some implications for compliance costs. The legislative changes to the rates and structure were outlined in the opening section of Chapter 6. Of these, the introduction, in 1985, of the two lower rates of NI contribution is likely to have made the biggest impact. It has meant that employers have not only had to distinguish between contracted in and contracted out employees, but also between staff in three earning bands. This additional complication must have increased compliance costs.

The period 1981-82 to 1986-87 has also seen dramatic changes in tax administration practices with the increasing computerisation of Inland Revenue activities. The PAYE computer came on line at 14 offices in 1983, and was expected to extend its coverage to the whole country by 1987-88. As more work became computerised, 121 local collection offices and 164 local tax offices were scheduled for closure. To the extent that managerial and technical improvements at Inland Revenue have resulted in a better service to taxpayers, compliance costs may have fallen. But the closure of local tax offices may well have made compliance more irksome and time-consuming for the small employer.

Other changes which must have had some effect on compliance costs have been changes in the number of employers and a fall in the number of taxpayers by some 300,000 (or 1.4 per cent). It is not possible to make any reasonable calculations as to the net effect of these changes on compliance costs, but we would not expect them to be large.

The VAT 2 survey contained questions directed to employers about the compliance costs of PAYE and NI contributions; but of 318 employers identified in the survey only 147 supplied full information compared with some 600 in the original (1981-82) survey. Moreover the sample in the later survey, unlike the earlier, was not structured in relation to the size of PAYE and NI payments. Thus reliance has been placed on uprating the original survey rather than on grossed up results from the new survey. One point of interesting contrast arose between the two surveys however — in the original survey fees to external advisers accounted for 12 per cent of total compliance costs; for the sample in the new survey they were double, at 24 per cent; this trend towards greater use of external advisers was also strongly evident for VAT (see Chapter 8).

Up-Dating the Earlier Estimates to 1986-87

The same principles have been employed in up-dating the PIT and PAYE estimates. The *New Earnings Survey* (NES) has been drawn on for the most appropriate data for wage and salary increases. The NES publishes data relating only to April each year and where up-rating relates to the time costs of staff, the April figures for the beginning of each financial year have been used to obtain the percentage increase. As a proxy for fees to professional advisers accountants' earnings have been used, but here the April ending the financial year has been taken as the relevant date because accountants' charges would generally be submitted some time after the period to which the tax work related. With miscellaneous charges the Retail Price Index (RPI) has been used and the September month (a mid-year figure) used. Table 7.1 gives the up-rate for the personal taxpayers' costs and Table 7.2 the up-rate for the costs to employers.

Table 7.1 Personal Taxpayers' Compliance Costs for Income Tax and CGT, 1983-84 and 1986-87

Costs	*1983-84 £m.*	*Index for Up-rating*	*Per cent Increase*	*1986-87 £m.*
Fees to tax advisers	592	NES Accountant	27	753
Time costs	532	NES full-time adult males	24	659
Miscellaneous costs	24	RPI	14	27
	1,149			1,439

Table 7.2 Employers' PAYE and NI Costs 1981-82 and 1986-87

	1981-82 £m.		Index for Up-Rating	Per cent increase	1986-87 £m.
Regular Costs					
Value of time spent by:					
Directors, partners, proprietors	147	NES office managers		54	226.3
Computer staff	16	NES computer programmers		43	22.9
Other staff	211	NES costing & account clerks		44	303.0
Other costs within the firm	18	RPI		29	23.2
Payments to advisers	54	NES accountants		53	82.7
Non-Regular Costs					
Costs of special problems	3	NES accountants		53	4.6
	449			47	662.7

The cash flow benefits to Schedule D taxpayers and to employers are also changed for the later year. With Schedule D income tax revenue at around £3,600m. in 1986-87 and average bank base rate at 10.5 per cent the cash flow benefit for the self-employed was of the order of £189m.

On the basis of the 1981-82 survey some broad assessment can be made of the cash flow benefit to employers in 1986-87. In 1981-82 the combined gross PAYE and NI collection amounted to £44,000m. and the cash flow benefit to £6,500m. or approximately 15 per cent of the tax payments. In 1986-87 the gross tax payments were £60,000m. Assuming the same ratio of cash flow benefit to tax payment (which implies no changes in the average frequency with which employees are paid) the cash flow benefit in 1986-87 would be £9,000m. At the 1986-87 average clearing bank base rate of 10.5 per cent this would give a figure of £945m for the aggregate value of the benefit. This estimate would indicate that, in 1986-87 as in 1981-82, the cash flow benefit overall exceeded the compliance costs but by a considerably smaller amount both in absolute and percentage terms. In 1981-82 the overall net benefit was 96 per cent of the gross compliance cost; in 1986-87 it was 43 per cent. The main reasons for the reduction are the abolition of the NI surcharge and the fall in interest rates. The removal of the surcharge makes more reasonable the assumption (detailed above) that the incidence of the employers' NI contribution is wholly on the employee. But, in other respects the conclusions for 1986-87 must be treated with even more caution than those of 1981-82 because they involve both the original assumptions and additional ones.

Other Compliance Costs of Income Tax and NI Contributions, 1986-87

Besides the major costs covered in the two main surveys, a number of other, lesser costs arise from compliance with the requirements for payment of income tax and NI contributions. Banks and building societies are required to undertake certain actions on behalf of the revenue authorities; compliance costs are incurred in respect of trusts, as well as by individuals; and businesses incur costs in deducting income tax on interest payments of debenture interest. The self-employed also incur costs in complying with the requirements to pay NI contributions.

In this section we describe those costs involved and attempt to make some rough estimates of their size.

Banks

In addition to the compliance costs which they incur in common with other businesses, i.e. those associated with corporation tax, deduction of PAYE income tax and NI contributions from their employees and deduction of tax from the interest due to their debenture-holders, banks face a series of other compliance costs arising from their borrowing and lending activities. To some extent these costs arise from the application, in income tax administration, of the principle of deducting tax at source wherever possible to minimise evasion. Further, even when deduction of tax is not at issue, it is often cheaper and easier for the Inland Revenue to deal with a fairly small number of banks than with millions of depositors and borrowers. The use of the banking system in this way is an example of the transfer of costs from the public to the private sector.

The responsibilities of the banks in respect of the income tax of their customers fall into three main categories.

(1)   *Application of Composite Rate Tax (CRT) to interest due to depositors in settlement of basic rate liability and payment thereof to the Inland Revenue.*

The banks were brought into the CRT system in 1985. Previously CRT had applied only to building societies and banks had paid interest gross, with the individual depositor responsible for recording his receipt of interest in his tax return and paying tax directly. Since 1985 CRT has applied in respect of individuals ordinarily resident in the United Kingdom for all deposits up to £50,000 and some in excess thereof. Banks pay interest net of basic rate tax to these depositors and pay over to Inland Revenue, once per quarter, CRT at a rate below the basic rate of income tax, determined on the basis of the proportion of interest paid to taxpayers and non-taxpayers (although non-taxpayers cannot recover tax).

The composite rate is fixed before 31st December each year for the following fiscal year. The CRT is paid over to the Inland Revenue fourteen days after the end of a quarter.

When the system was first introduced there were heavy commencement costs; regular costs are incurred in monitoring the process, trying to ensure that nothing goes wrong and, when it does, correcting the errors. The largest banks have a small central section concerned with CRT and it affects the day-to-day working of the branches.

One large cost associated with the CRT is the provision of a large sample of depositors, one year in four, which is required by Inland Revenue for the formula which determines the CRT.

Another continuing cost is that the banks have to make an annual return of the interest payments made to depositors including those under the CRT scheme where these payments exceed a certain sum which was £400 in 1986-87. This requires a major computer printout exercise of names, addresses and amount of interest received.

(2)   *Mortgage Interest Relief at Source (MIRAS)*

As indicated in the outline of income tax in Chapter 5, taxpayers benefit from income tax relief on the interest on the first £30,000 of a loan in respect of a principal private residence; for some years most taxpayers have received that relief under the MIRAS scheme by which the borrower pays interest net of income tax to the lender, who recovers the balance from the Inland Revenue. MIRAS has involved more complications for the banks than payment of interest gross. Where mortgages are over £30,000 part of the payment is net of tax and part gross. The largest banks have a section of staff at Head Office dedicated to MIRAS but staff in the branches who are not so dedicated have to apply it. The MIRAS form requires explanation to customers and the system is open to abuse; bank staff are expected to look out for indications that the borrower may not be eligible and inform the Inland Revenue. As with CRT, regular monitoring is required and there is a higher error rate. Moreover, the Inland Revenue requires certificates from taxpayers of interest paid and they in turn have a right to demand these certificates from the banks.

(3)   *Certificates of Interest Paid*
Apart from house purchase, customers borrow from banks for a wide range of purposes. Under the United Kingdom law income tax is not relieved on loans for consumption purposes, but it is relieved on loans for business purposes (as a cost of generating a business income) and, in 1986-87, it was also relieved on loans for home improvements. In order to obtain the benefit of income tax relief on eligible loans outside MIRAS, customers require a certificate from the bank of interest paid which they can forward to Inland Revenue. The banks are therefore in the business of providing many thousands of bits of paper certifying interest paid for tax purposes.

There is another compliance cost which falls on the bigger banks in that, because they have a maintenance department using sub-contractors, they come into the special scheme for deducting income tax at source in respect of payments to builders. But this is not a cost unique to banks.

Through the good offices of the British Bankers' Association, an attempt has been made to estimate the compliance costs of the U.K. banks for the year 1986-87 under the first three items listed. The items have been costed out in respect of one bank and then grossed up to arrive at a figure for the banking system as a whole. Clearly such a procedure has obvious limitations; for example, it is not easy to give accurate costs of procedures which are diffused throughout the banking system and closely inter-connected with normal banking functions; and the bank concerned may not be of average efficiency. But at least the estimate does provide some rough indication of the orders of magnitude. A more extensive survey would have been difficult to justify in the context of a study of the total administrative and compliance costs of the U.K. tax system.

On the basis of this sample study the British Bankers' Association estimated that, for 1986-87, the total costs of the special tax compliance requirements laid on the U.K. retail banks amounted to approximately £50m. Although such costs are only a small part of the total picture and cannot affect our general conclusions, they are nonetheless at a significant level for the banks themselves.

Building Societies

The building societies also have to apply the composite rate system (CRT) and have been doing so much longer than the banks, and operate mortgage interest relief at source (MIRAS), with the attendant costs. They are not, however, concerned with the wide variety of loans for business and other purposes which characterise the operations of the retail banks. Moreover, in respect of CRT and MIRAS they are in a more favourable position than the banks. The requirements imposed on them to provide annual returns (name, address and interest received) of depositors is more limited than that of the banks; in 1986-87 it was restricted to depositors receiving over £2,000, as against £400 for the banks, although it is understood that the limits are to be brought into line over time. Secondly, in respect of MIRAS, building societies make a return of all mortgage interest paid — comprising, for each borrower, name, account number, tax deducted, net interest and balance. This return can be made on magnetic tape and, unlike the banks, the building societies do not have to issue certificates of interest paid to each borrower on a mortgage.

These differences, together with the much smaller number of building societies than banks (around 120 as compared with 500) mean considerably lower compliance costs for building societies. Some limited enquiries, undertaken for this study by the Building Societies Association, suggest that the total cost arising from the special tax compliance requirements imposed on the building societies might be contained within a figure of £18m.

The picture for banks and building societies is not all black. The MIRAS scheme means that, at current tax rates, one quarter of the interest on mortgages eligible for tax relief is paid by the government; this component of interest is guaranteed to arrive regularly even if the borrower gets into arrears.

Trusts

The total number of trusts is not known as there is no requirement to register a trust or trustees in the United Kingdom. However, trustees must notify the Inland Revenue of any taxable income, gains or transfers and, at that time, provide a copy of the trust deed or other governing instrument; it is clearly only trusts subject to tax that are of interest for the purposes of this study.

A recent publication of the Inland Revenue (Robson and Timmins, 1988) casts some light on this rather obscure area. The Inland Revenue study gives the following numbers of trusts known to the Inland Revenue in respect of the financial year 1985-86.

	Approx. No.
Discretionary (and accumulation and maintenance):	55,000
'Special arrangement' trusts:	91,000
Trusts dealt with by Claims Branch, Foreign Division:	7,000
Trusts with interests in possession:	112,000

'Special arrangement' trusts are those for which composite returns are made (e.g. where the clearing banks are the trustees); they are mostly small and non-discretionary. The Inland Revenue study is essentially concerned with the 55,000 discretionary trusts, but some limited information is given about the special arrangement trusts.

Even of those discretionary trusts notified to the Department a very large number have no or very small amounts of income, because they are dormant with negligible assets, or holding only assets yielding no taxable income (such as National Savings Certificates or life insurance policies).

Of the 55,000 discretionary trusts, 42 per cent were apparently in this category in 1985-86. The size of discretionary trusts varied considerably; 1,394 (3 per cent of the total) were identified as having income above £25,000, but this 3 per cent generated almost a half of the total income from the discretionary trusts.

In the Inland Revenue study, on the basis of a sample survey, it is estimated that the trustees' expenses against income for all the 55,000 discretionary trusts taken together, amounted to £22m. in 1985-86. Discussion with practising accountants suggested that about one quarter of these expenses would be a reasonable estimate of the compliance costs of income tax in 1985-86, i.e. £5.5m. The compliance costs of CGT would not be included in the £22m. of trustees' expenses against income, as they would be a charge against capital. CGT compliance costs would be irregular in their incidence but could be very heavy in particular cases. If we allow a somewhat arbitrary £2m. the compliance costs in respect of discretionary trusts comes out at an estimated £7.5m. in 1985-86.

Any estimate of the compliance costs in respect of the other 210,000 trusts must be still more speculative. Trusts with income in possession are essentially taxed as income in the hands of the beneficiaries, so that the trustees have little to do in respect of income tax, though more when there are capital gains tax liabilities. Accountants' experience suggests that a conservative figure might be an average cost of £50 per trust for tax work, giving a total of £4.5m. With special arrangement trusts and trusts with an overseas component a reasonable figure would be an average of £75 which would give an estimated total for these trusts of £8.9m. The combined total compliance costs of income tax and CGT in respect of all trusts would then come out at £20.9m. As the figures for trustees' expenses of discretionary trusts related to 1985-86, this sum could be rounded up to £21m. to give a somewhat conservative estimate for 1986-87.

We make no pretension that this estimate is anything other than a reasonable guess, but, even should it be very wide of the mark, none of the conclusions of the study are affected. As a minimum we have set down a marker recognising the existence of compliance costs in respect of trusts.

Deduction of Income Tax at Source from Debenture Stock

Certain questions addressed to corporations in the VAT 2 survey enable us to make a rough estimate of the cost to companies of deducting income tax at source from debenture stock, i.e. £2.25m.

NI Contributions of the Self-Employed

The self-employed are required to pay Class 2 contributions (unless they are already paying Class 1 by virtue of being also employees) and, in certain circumstances, Class 4 national insurance contributions. In principle, when operating smoothly, the compliance costs of these payments should be minimal. Class 2 contributions can be paid either by direct debit or by stamped cards for which stocks can be purchased in advance from the post office. In 1986-87 rather more than half chose the stamped card method. Class 4 contributions, based on the level of profit, are normally collected along with income tax by Inland Revenue and any normal compliance costs are likely to have been included with income tax. Difficulties, and hence compliance costs, arise, as it were, at the edges of the system — over the definition of self-employment, over movement into and out of self-employment, over taxpayers' changing methods of payment or paying in arrears, over disputes on the level of taxable profits and claims for exemption or deferment. Without a very detailed survey, which would certainly not be justified in the context of this study, a reliable estimate would be impossible to arrive at.

The official (provisional) estimate of the numbers of self-employed paying Class 2 contributions in 1986-87 was 1.933 million, with a similar number (not always the same people) paying Class 4. If we arbitrarily assume that their compliance costs average £10 per annum per head, for Class 2 and Class 4 combined, we have a figure of £19.3m. £10 per annum for each self-employed person will be more than the compliance costs where the system is working smoothly, but is likely to be an understatement where there are hiccoughs, which may be fairly frequently. There is no pretence that this is other than a reasonable guess, but the figures we are dealing with are relatively small. In 1986-87 Class 2 and Class 4 contributions together raised only £697m. in contributions as against £24,935 from Class 1. A compliance cost of £19m. would represent 2.7 per cent of revenue collected.

Administrative Costs

Administrative costs relate to both Inland Revenue and (in respect of NI contributions) to the Department of Social Security. The Inland Revenue figures are taken from the annual report and include the costs incurred in collecting NI contributions (both Class 1 and Class 4) on behalf of the Department of Social Security. These costs are extremely low because they represent a marginal addition to the costs of collecting income tax.

The costs of the Department of Social Security are less precise. Our concern is with the costs associated with collecting contributions and not with costs on the benefit side. Whilst, as we have seen, the bulk of the contributions are collected initially by Inland Revenue, the costs of enforcing payment of contributions due and dealing with difficult problems falls to the Department of Social Security. Figures provided by the Department give an estimate of the salary costs of this work as £37.8m., but it is stressed that the estimate represents only a broad order of magnitude as the distribution of staff at local offices is at the discretion of local managers. If we up-rate the salary figure in line with the general pattern of costs within the civil service, we reach a figure of around £50m.

Summary of Administrative and Compliance Costs

Table 7.3 summarises the yield of these three taxes — income tax, CGT and NI contributions — and sets down the findings on administrative and compliance costs.

Overall, administrative costs amount to 1.5 per cent of the revenue from the three taxes and compliance costs to 3.4, giving a combined operating cost of 4.9 per cent. The administrative costs of income tax and CGT amount to 2.3 per cent of the revenue of these two taxes and their compliance costs to individuals alone, represents 3.6 per cent.

International Comparisons

The one study which has hitherto attempted to cover all the compliance and administrative costs of income tax is that of Vaillancourt (1988) for Canada. He concludes that in 1986 the total operating costs of the Canadian income tax system were 7.1 per cent of revenue. The findings of the two studies are compared in Table 7.4.

Given the Canadian self-assessment system it is not surprising to find the costs to individuals somewhat higher and the costs to government somewhat less. The surprisingly large difference is in the costs to employers. The difference could be accounted for by higher levels of PAYE income tax and NI contributions in the United Kingdom, and (as suggested by Vaillancourt) the high costs associated with the Canadian unemployment insurance system.

Table 7.3 Summary of Revenue Yield, Administrative and Compliance Costs of Income Tax, Capital Gains Tax and National Insurance Contributions 1986-87

Revenue Yield	*£m.*
Income tax	38,499
CGT	1,064
NI contributions	25,663
	65,126

Administrative Cost	
Income tax	883
CGT	18
NI contributions collected by IR	46
NI contributions collected by DSS (including enforcement costs)	50
	997

Compliance Costs	
Income tax and CGT — individuals	1,439
Collecting PAYE and NI contributions — employers	663
Income tax — banks and building societies	68
Income tax and CGT — trusts	21
Deducting interest at source — companies	2
NI contributions — self-employed	19
	2,212

Table 7.4 Comparison of Operating Costs of Income Tax and Social Security Payments, U.K. and Canada (Percentages of Revenue)

	U.K. 1986-87	*Canada 1986*
Costs to individuals	2.21	2.53
Costs to employers	1.02	3.57
Other private costs	0.17	0.03
Costs to government	<u>1.53</u>	<u>1.0</u>
Total operating costs	<u>4.93</u>	<u>7.13</u>

CHAPTER 8

VALUE ADDED TAX

Introduction

Unlike any of the other taxes considered in this book, for value added tax (VAT) we have two surveys, VAT 1 and VAT 2, a decade apart. Each consists of a large or fairly large sample of registered businesses drawn from the ideal source — the VAT register — and checked for representativeness by size of business (as measured by taxable turnover) and economic category. VAT 1 has been written up fully elsewhere (Sandford *et al*, 1981); VAT 2 has not been previously published and is the less detailed and comprehensive survey. Despite the limitations of VAT 2, rather than following the pattern of the previous two chapters of detailing the findings of an earlier survey and then seeking to update them to 1986-87, it seemed more interesting and useful to present the findings of the two VAT surveys side by side. We then concentrate on describing and trying to explain the broad differences revealed, taking into account the interviews with respondents and especially professional advisers. Indeed, it was because there were reasons for believing that significant changes in VAT compliance costs might have taken place that the second survey was undertaken.

Thus, after an initial section briefly outlining the tax as it operated in the United Kingdom at the time of the surveys, we then compare both administrative and compliance costs as at 1977-78 (VAT 1) and 1986-87 (VAT 2) and suggest reasons for the differences. We conclude with reference to the limited material available for international comparisons on VAT.

Outline of VAT

VAT was introduced into the United Kingdom in 1973. It is administered by Customs and Excise. In principle VAT is a single tax on domestic consumption, but the tax is collected multi-stage. Under the invoicing or credit system which applies in the United Kingdom,

111

throughout the European Community and practically everywhere where VAT has been introduced, the actual value added by each business is never calculated. Instead every registered business pays VAT on its purchases of goods and services (inputs), charges VAT on its sales (outputs) and hands over the difference between output tax and input tax to Customs and Excise for each accounting period. If input tax should exceed output tax, the business receives a refund.

Traders (using the term for producers of all kinds, not just retailers and wholesalers) whose taxable turnover is below a specified level are exempt, but may register voluntarily. Certain outputs are also exempt. A good or service may be zero-rated in which case no VAT is charged on its sale, but (unlike exemption) VAT paid on inputs is recoverable. All exports are zero-rated at present and all imports pay VAT on entry; but these provisions may change in respect of European Community countries in 1992 (see Chapter 13). Outputs other than exports may be zero-rated and the United Kingdom is unusual in the wide range of goods and services which are subject to a zero rate.

Traders who regularly make net payments of VAT are required to make quarterly VAT returns and to pay over the net VAT collected not later than one calendar month after the end of the quarter. Regular repayment traders may make monthly returns and receive monthly refunds.

A series of special schemes for retailers has been designed to make compliance less irksome and costly.

At the time of VAT 1 in 1977-78 there were two positive rates of VAT, a standard rate of 8 per cent and a higher rate of 12.5 per cent applying to petrol, most domestic electrical goods, photographic equipment, furs, jewellery, boats, aircraft and most caravans. At the beginning of 1977 the minimum annual turnover for compulsory registration was £5,000 but this was raised to £7,500 in October 1977. Exempt activities included the renting of land and buildings, insurance, postal services (where provided by the Post Office), betting and gaming, financial services, education, medical services, burials and cremations. As well as exports, zero-rated products included most foodstuffs (but not when served in a restaurant), children's clothing and footwear, books and newspapers, fuel, new building and public transport.

At the time of the VAT 2 study, 1986-87, there was a single positive rate of VAT of 15 per cent. (The additional rate had been abolished in 1979 and all the goods assimilated to the new 15 per cent standard rate). The VAT annual registration threshold stood at £20,500. Certain outputs, previously zero-rated, had become standard-rated: lubricating oils, building extensions and alterations, hot take-away food, newspaper advertisements. Transactions between credit card companies and their outlets had been exempted in 1985. Additionally a large number of changes (to which we refer later) had taken place in administrative practice.

VAT Administrative and Compliance Costs 1977-78 and 1986-87

Administrative Costs

Table 8.1 summarises the basic administrative data on VAT for the years 1977-78 and 1986-87.

Table 8.1 Administrative Data on VAT: 1977-78 and 1986-87 Compared

	1977-78	*1986-87*
No. of VAT registered businesses	1,274,178	1,505,500[1]
VAT revenue	£4,235m.	£21,423m.
Administrative costs	£85.5m.	£219.9m.
Administrative costs as per cent of VAT revenue:	2.02	1.03
No. of staff (including administrative services):	12,246	12,813

[1] Note that the number of businesses recorded here is slightly less than that from which the sample was drawn (1,526,162); the sample was drawn in Autumn 1987, but the questions in the questionnaire referred to compliance costs 1986-87.

Source: Customs and Excise Annual Report, 1987, Cm. 234.

An interesting feature is the 18 per cent increase in registered businesses, which compares with a 4.6 per cent increase in VAT administrative staff. Perhaps the most important feature is the increase in VAT revenue, reflecting, in probable order of importance, the change in VAT rates, the rise in retail prices, the growth of real incomes, the extension of standard rating and the success of Customs and Excise control policy. There has been a steady reduction of tax arrears, doubtless helped in 1986-87 by the imminence of a new penalty structure, and inspection visits have concentrated on those areas where tax has been most at risk. As a result of these various influences the ratio of administrative costs to VAT revenue has halved over the decade.

Total and Composition of Compliance Costs

Table 8.2 Compliance Costs of VAT Analysed by Components, 1977-78 and 1986-87 Compared

Nature of compliance cost	1977-78 £m.	%	1986-87 £m.	%
Value of time spent in compliance by:				
Directors, partners, proprietors	224	57.1	444	56.2
Qualified accounting staff	38	9.7	82	10.4
Other staff	108	27.6	91	11.5
Fees to professional advisers	20	5.1	136	17.2
Other costs	2	0.5	38	4.8
Total	392	100.0	791	100.0

Table 8.2 gives the estimated total and components of compliance costs in 1977-78 and 1986-87. The grossing up procedure is described in detail in Appendix D; it should be noted that, because of the smaller

sample size and the lower response rate for VAT 2, the estimates do not have the same robustness as those of VAT 1 and must be regarded as indicators of magnitude rather than impeccable data. Despite this caveat, the overall figures tell a reliable story. Overall VAT compliance costs have approximately doubled between 1977-78 and 1986-87, from an estimated £392m. to £791m. During this period the Retail Price Index increased by 109 per cent (September 1977 to September 1986) and average weekly earnings by some 162 per cent. Thus, whichever of these broad measures is used as a deflator, VAT compliance costs have fallen in real terms. When allowance is made for the increase in number of traders, average compliance costs are seen to have fallen still more.

Interesting changes have taken place in the components of compliance costs. The value of the time of directors, partners and proprietors (taken together) has remained much the same as a proportion of total compliance costs, as has that of qualified accounting staff. But the proportion of 'other staff' in costs has plummeted, whilst the fees to professional advisers in 1986-87 were almost three-and-a-half their proportion in 1977-78. The rise in 'other costs' is also interesting: they include computer and legal costs which are more prevalent in the 1986-87 survey than in VAT 1. (We comment more fully on these features, below, in seeking to explain the changes which have taken place).

Distribution of Compliance Costs

The most important finding of the 1977-78 survey was the extremely regressive pattern of compliance costs; thus, on average, the cost for every £1,000 of goods sold by a business in the taxable turnover band of £10,000-£20,000 (1977-78 prices) was £12.30; for a business with taxable turnover over £1 million the corresponding cost was 40p; with higher taxable turnovers the cost dropped still further, to as low as 0.5p per £1,000 sales for firms in the 1977-78 sample with taxable turnover greater than £50m. The 1986-87 survey amply supports this finding. Table 8.3 records compliance costs as a proportion of taxable turnover 1977-78 and 1986-87.

Benefits of Compliance

The VAT 1 study recorded two offsets to the costs of compliance — a substantial cash flow benefit and managerial benefits accruing primarily to smaller businesses.

Table 8.3 Compliance Costs as a Percentage of Taxable Turnover, 1977-78 and 1986-87 (Current prices)

1977-78		*1986-87*	
Taxable Turnover (£000s p.a.)	*Compliance Costs as per cent of Taxable Turnover (mean percentage)[1]*	*Taxable Turnover (£000s p.a.)*	*Compliance Costs as per cent of Taxable Turnover (mean percentage)[1]*
0- 9.9	1.64	0- 20.5	1.94
10- 19.9	1.23	20.5- 49.9	0.78
20- 49.9	0.74	50- 99.9	0.52
50- 99.9	0.54	100- 499.9	0.42
100- 999.9	0.24	500- 999.9	0.26
1,000 and over	0.04	1,000- 9,999.9	0.04
		10,000 and over	0.003
Overall weighted mean	0.92	Overall weighted mean	0.69

[1] For each case, compliance cost is expressed as a percentage of taxable turnover. These percentages are then averaged within each size band.

A VAT trader who is not a repayment trader collects VAT over a three-month period on the difference between output and input tax (the collection period) and can legally hold it for another month (the grace period) before handing it over to Customs and Excise. Assuming a smooth cash flow over the quarter, constant stocks and payment on the last due date, a trader on average throughout the year is holding 5/24 of his total VAT payments: 1.5 month's VAT as a result of the collection period and three months' VAT for one month every three months (the equivalent of one month throughout the year) as a result of the grace period.

A repayment trader, on the other hand, is entitled to make monthly returns although not all of them do so. Customs and Excise reckon to pay over 95 per cent of claims (by value) within ten days of receipt. If we assume that VAT refunds are received, on average, one month after the end of a monthly return period, the repayment trader is, in effect, making a loan to Customs and Excise. Assuming an even flow of payments, this loan is composed of 1/24 of the VAT due for repayment (the average paid out during the month) plus 1/12 (the average waiting time for repayment after the end of the return period) which together total 1/8 of the repayments due.

Using Customs and Excise published data on payments and repayments the net cash flow benefit (the benefit to payment traders less the detriment to repayment traders) can be calculated. In both survey years the VAT liability of all traders related to the invoice date rather than the date of payment. Thus, the *distribution* of the cash flow benefit or detriment was determined largely by commercial credit conditions. A retailer selling for cash and buying on long credit terms did particularly well; and even a repayment trader could get a cash flow benefit by buying his inputs late in the month and not paying for them until after he had received his VAT refund. Thus, in practice the cash flow benefits tend to merge into the general commercial pattern of credit and competition. Nonetheless, the private sector as a whole receives the net cash flow benefit; and the estimation of the amount of that benefit does not rest (as with NI payments) on somewhat dubious assumptions about incidence.

Table 8.4 compares the net cash flow benefit in 1977-78 and 1986-87 at current prices. In real terms the value of the net cash flow benefit was very much higher in 1986-87 both because VAT revenue has increased much more than the general price level and because of higher interest rates.

Table 8.4 Comparison of Net Cash Flow Benefit, 1977-78 and 1986- 87

Year	Net Cash Flow Benefit £m.	Interest Rate (MLR or bank base rate)	Value of Cash Flow Benefit
1977-78	1,049	7	73
1986-87	5,519	10.5	580

The other main benefit from compliance was a managerial benefit. In 1977 the Consultative Committee of Accountancy Bodies (1977) recorded: 'The demand for quarterly figures for VAT purposes has improved the quality of records maintained by many small businesses.' This was borne out by the VAT 1 study. Of respondents to the 1977-78 survey, overall 32 per cent agreed with the statement, 'My purchase records are better kept since VAT came in' and 26 per cent agreed, 'My sales records are better kept since VAT came in'. The benefit was most applicable to smaller firms. Of firms with a turnover of under £100,000 in 1977-78, the respective figures were 42 per cent and over 30 per cent.

Some businesses turned the improved records to financial advantage, by saving on accountants' fees because they did more of their own accounts (25 per cent of the sample); by improved stock control (8 per cent); by claiming discounts more frequently (6 per cent); by reduction in losses from bad debts (5 per cent) and in other miscellaneous ways (4 per cent).

In the 1986-87 survey it was not possible to reproduce precisely the format of VAT 1. The passage of time since the introduction of VAT (1973) had rendered meaningless a question such as 'My purchase records are better kept since VAT came in'. The question employed in VAT 2 was much briefer and more general: 'Does record-keeping for VAT give you any benefits, e.g. saving money by doing more of your own accounts and giving less work to outside advisers?' To that question 204 respondents, 30 per cent of the sample, responded positively; most, as requested, gave examples, of which the main one was that the respondents saved money by doing more of their own accounts.

Thus, it is clear that there are continuing and not inconsiderable managerial benefits from the better record-keeping which is necessary to comply with VAT requirements. It is not possible to put a realistic value on these benefits, but they are an important offset to the compliance costs of some of the smaller businesses.

Costs in Relation to Tax Revenue

Table 8.5 summarises the VAT operating costs in 1977-78 and 1986-87 and expresses them as a proportion of tax revenue. They indicate that the costs of operating VAT (administrative plus compliance costs) fell from over 11 per cent of VAT revenue to under 5 per cent; and whilst most of this reduction reflects the changes in VAT rates and revenue, some results from a substantial fall in compliance costs in real terms. When allowance is made for the value of the cash flow benefit, net compliance costs had fallen to 1 per cent of tax revenue in 1986-87; however, that figure is very dependent on the rate of interest which, in 1986-87, was still high historically; if bank base rates fell to half their 1986-87 level (i.e. to 5.25 per cent) the net compliance cost would rise from just under 1 per cent to 2.34 per cent. It must also be remembered that whilst the improved cash flow is a benefit to the trader it does not result in resource savings to the economy.

Table 8.5
Estimated Costs of Operating VAT, 1977-78 and 1986-87

	(1) *Reve-* *nue* *from* *VAT*	*(2)* *Admin* *Costs*	*(3)* *Compliance* *Costs*	*(4)* *Value of* *Cash* *Benefit[1]*	*(5)* *Net* *Comp-* *liance* *Costs[2]* *(3)-(4)*	*(6)* *Admin* *Costs*	*(7)* *Compliance* *Costs*	*(8)* *Net* *Comp-* *liance* *Costs*
							as percentage of revenue	
	£bn.	*£m.*	*£m.*	*£m.*	*£m.*			
1977-78	4.2	85	392	73	319	2.02	9.25	7.53
1986-87	21.4	220	791	580	211	1.03	3.69	0.983

[1] At average Minimum Lending Rate or bank base rate.
[2] Excluding managerial benefits.

Significance of the Compliance Cost Changes

Two features in the comparison of the VAT 1 and the VAT 2 studies particularly call for explanation: the fall in compliance costs in real terms; and the big increase in the proportion of compliance costs in the form of accountants' fees.

Extent of Reduction in Compliance Costs

Between 1977-78 and 1986-87 compliance costs are estimated to have increased from £392m. to £791m. — i.e. by 102 per cent over a period when the index of retail prices had increased by 109 per cent and other general price and wage indices by considerably more. To show the extent of the reduction in compliance costs in real terms, Table 8.6 up-rates the 1977-78 figures on the same basis as PIT and PAYE survey data were up-rated to 1986-87 (Chapter 7). Thus, if compliance costs had remained the same in real terms, we should have expected them to have been £1,086m. in 1986-87, not £791m. Thus, they are 27 per cent lower than might have been expected.

Table 8.6 Up-rating 1977-78 Compliance Costs to 1986-87

Nature of compliance cost	1977-78 £m.	Percentage increase in proxy	Estimate 1986-87 £m.
Value of time spent on compliance by:			
Directors, partners, proprietors	224	192	654
Qualified accounting staff	38	159	98
Other staff	108	155	275
Fees to professional advisers	20	176	55
Other costs	2	109	4
Total	392		1,086

A note of caution should be sounded about the accuracy of the up-rating. The proxy for the time of directors, proprietors and partners has been taken as the wages of office managers, which, over this period, increased considerably more than average wage rates (192 compared with 162 per cent). For much of this period unemployment was growing and small proprietors, in particular, may well have accepted a reduction in their hourly remuneration; if so the estimate would be an overstatement. As this is the largest component in the compliance costs of VAT (57 per cent) any over-statement in this figure would lead to an appreciable over-estimation of the total.*

However, if the up-rating may have erred in over-estimation, no allowance has been made for the increase in the number of businesses between the two dates.

Table 8.7 shows the numbers of traders in size bands which can be matched very roughly by reference to the increase in retail prices. This table shows that there has not only been a growth in the total number of registered businesses, but also a general growth in their size. The number of registered businesses with the smallest turnovers has declined and

---

* If all the time and fee components were up-rated by the average increase in weekly wages, the estimate of compliance cost in 1986-87 would come out at £1,026m.; if by the RPI the 1986-87 figure would be £819m. These compare with the estimated costs of £791m.

the number in the three largest turnover bands has each grown by a surprisingly similar amount. Customs and Excise believe that the number of voluntarily registered businesses has remained fairly constant at a little over 200,000.

Table 8.7 Size Distribution of Firms: Matched Bands
1977-78 and 1986-87

Comparative Bands 1977-78 1986-87 £m.	No. of Traders 1977-78	1986-87	Percentage of Traders 1977-78	1986-87	Per cent change in no. of traders
0- 9.9} 0- 20.5}	270,000	192,000	21.1	12.6	-28.9
10- 49.9} 20.5- 99.9}	611,000	831,000	48.0	54.5	36.0
50-499.9} 100-999.9}	339,000	432,000	26.6	28.3	27.4
500 and over} 1m. and over}	54,000	70,000	4.2	4.6	29.6
Total	1,274,000	1,526,000	100.0	100.0	19.8

The process of matching bands does generate an upward bias in 1986-87. (It assumes, for most bands, a 100 per cent increase in RPI as against an actual 109 per cent increase). Even so, the extent of the increase in the number of larger firms, which have the highest absolute compliance costs, means that we should have expected a growth in compliance costs more or less in line with the growth in number of businesses. Taken with the reduction we have already identified it would appear that the average reduction in real costs has been a third or more.

Attitudes to VAT

The VAT 1 study had shown that, as one might expect, the average compliance costs of pro-VAT traders were well below those of anti-VAT traders (Sandford *et al*, 1981, p.112). If compliance costs had fallen in real terms as the VAT 2 survey indicated, we should expect to find some change in attitudes towards VAT.

The VAT 1 study included a comprehensive set of measures to test attitudes. The briefer VAT 2 questionnaire did not repeat the full panoply of VAT 1 measures, but did include two central attitude questions which had been included in the earlier survey. The responses, for the two years, are set out below:

Percentage Response to Statement
'I do not mind doing VAT work'

Year	Agree strongly	Agree	Disagree	Disagree strongly
1977-78	2.0	36.9	31.6	29.5
1986-87	2.3	47.1	26.1	24.4

Percentage Response to Statement
'As it stands, VAT is unreasonably complicated'

Year	Agree strongly	Agree	Disagree	Disagree strongly
1977-78	17.6	37.2	40.7	4.5
1986-87	17.5	36.2	40.8	5.5

The different responses to these questions between the two dates do, in fact, suggest some change in attitudes, especially because the 1977-78 sample, from which the responses are drawn, included a disproportionate weighting of large firms which generally had a more pro-VAT attitude than the smaller firms. The responses to the statement that 'VAT is unreasonably complicated' have changed only a little and to an extent which is not statistically significant; but the change in attitude to doing VAT work is very marked.

Reasons for Compliance Cost Reduction

Abolition of higher rate tax. One factor which has indisputably reduced overall compliance costs has been the abolition of higher rate tax, in 1979. In the VAT 1 survey an attempt was made to estimate the effect of the higher rate on compliance costs. Two samples of businesses were compared, matched as closely as possible save that the businesses in one sample were all subject to higher rate. It was concluded that, if the higher rate were abolished and the higher rated outputs taxed at standard rate, compliance costs in 1977-78 would have been £32m. less (out of £392m.). When the 1977-78 figure is reduced by this sum and then up-rated in proportion, the up-rated figure is appreciably lower at £994m. but is still much above the 1986-87 figures derived from the VAT 2 survey.

Rating Changes in the Construction Industry. It was the view of accountants interviewed as part of the VAT 2 study that the rating changes introduced in 1984 for the construction industry, by which new building work in the form of improvements, alterations or extensions became standard-rated (like repairs and maintenance), removed a difficult borderline; and whilst it left a borderline which continues to create some problems, the effect was to reduce compliance costs. The size of the 1986-87 sample makes detailed analysis by firm and size sector unreliable. Nonetheless, analysis of the average compliance costs in the construction industry supported the view of a particularly large fall in real costs of compliance in that sector. Whereas in the VAT 1 survey the construction sector consistently showed high percentages of compliance cost to taxable turnover in each size band, in the VAT 2 survey, the ratios were in line with the average for the size band.

Customs and Excise Simplification Measures. A series of policy measures by Customs and Excise have been aimed at simplifying VAT, especially for small traders. A new simplified single sheet VAT return was introduced shortly after the period to which the main VAT 1 survey related, 1977-78, and was the subject of a special telephone survey; 73 per cent of the interviewees said they found the new form easier to complete than the old one. The new form required figures to be inserted in a maximum of 12 boxes instead of 26.

The new simplified form was one of several changes which followed a review of the tax undertaken by Customs and Excise in 1977-78 (Cmnd. 7415, 1978). The rules concerning partial exemption were modified, so that the number of traders who had to apply restrictions to their deduction of input tax was reduced from about 20,000 to

3,000; (although the remaining 3,000 partly exempt traders had more complicated compliance duties than before, they were generally large businesses with adequate accounting systems). Certain businesses with turnover under £50,000 were allowed to align their VAT year with their financial year, which had previously not been permitted. Small businesses were also encouraged to adapt their cash book record to serve also as the VAT record of purchases. The maximum value of a supply by a retailer for which a less detailed invoice might be issued was raised from £10 to £25.

Table 8.8 Reduction in Compliance Costs, 1977-78 and 1986-87 Comparison of Small and Larger Firms

Matched Turnover Bands	*(1) Average Compliance cost 1977-78 £*	*(2) Average Compliance cost (survey) 1986-87 £*	*(3) Average Compliance cost (update) 1986-87 £*	*(4) Ratio (2) as % of (3)*
Small firms				
1977-78: £10,000-£50,000	226		624	51
1986-87: £20,000-£100,000		321		
Larger firms				
1977-78: £50,000 and over	572		1579	62
1986-87: £100,000 and over		982		
All firms	308	518	850	61

Later simplifications have included permission to use electronically submitted invoice information (1980-81); the revision of the VAT Guide, with information on liability broken down into a series of separate trade booklets; and a new 'Visits by VAT Officers' booklet issued (from 1984). A departmental Deregulation Unit was set up in 1985, but its proposals for changes in VAT relate mainly to the period after the VAT 2 survey.

Given the limitations of the data it is hardly possible to make any quantitative estimate of the effect of Customs and Excise measures to simplify VAT but it is interesting that the measures were aimed particularly at the smaller firms and Table 8.8 suggests that, whilst average compliance costs have fallen across the board, it is the smaller registered traders who have enjoyed the biggest reduction — i.e. where the 1986-87 survey costs represent the lowest proportion of the expected (up-dated) costs.

No allowance has been made in Table 8.8 for the effect of the abolition of higher rate tax. Column 4 shows, for two matched size bands of small and larger firms, the estimated decline in average VAT compliance costs in real terms. It is clearly much more pronounced for the smaller band of compulsorily registered traders than the rest.

We should have liked to test out the effect of the change in partial exemption rules. There were few instances of partly exempt traders in the sample; but in any case, the purpose and effect of the simplification was to reduce the numbers in the partly exempt category, so unless we had asked a specific question on whether a trader had ceased to be partly exempt as a result of the 1978 changes, no analysis would have been useful.

Customs and Excise Policy on Inspection Visits. There is one other aspect of Customs and Excise policy which may have some influence on the level of compliance costs and more particularly on the decline in the costs of small firms. Control visits to small firms have been reduced as part of the policy of concentrating control activity where most revenue is at risk. The reduction in visits and perhaps in the strictness of control over the smaller firms may have reduced their compliance costs somewhat. On the other hand, Customs and Excise have reduced 'educational' visits and now only aim to visit a trader for this purpose once in fifteen to eighteen months after registration — and this may have increased compliance costs and led traders to seek the advice of accountants more frequently.

Other Factors. Several other hypotheses were tested as possible reasons for compliance cost reductions between the two dates, but yielded negative results. In particular the average costs of computer users and non-computer users were compared. In 1986-87 there were substantially more computers used for VAT compliance than in 1977-78; but, even in the later year, only 12 per cent of the sample (80 businesses) used either their own computer or a computer bureau. Of these, 19 were in professional services and 11 in retailing. Twenty-four of the 80 did not supply full information so the analysis was restricted to 56 cases, which ruled out a size by sector comparison. A size only comparison yielded inconclusive results and certainly did not suggest that computer use was a significant factor in the cost reduction. If anything the figures suggested the opposite, but, given the limitations of the data, no hard conclusions can be drawn.

Learning Curve and General Productivity Improvements. Finally it can be observed that, at the time of the 1977-78 survey, VAT had been in operation for under five years. Even though we would expect the learning curve to be flattening out, we could still expect some learning effects after 1978. The longer VAT had been in operation, the more used to it traders would have become and the more likely to have come across and resolved difficulties at some earlier stage. That observation, however, depends on the system not being subjected to radical change. It should be noted that traders registered in the twelve months prior to the survey were excluded from the sample because they could not answer questions relating to the survey period; thus, no newly registered traders (who might have had particular difficulties) appeared in the sample. Further, general factors raising productivity (e.g. improved office equipment, such as word processors instead of typewriters) would affect compliance costs as well as other business activities.

Increased Use of Accountants

In Table 8.2 we showed the big proportionate increase between 1977-78 and 1986-87 in fees to accountants for VAT work, almost three-and-a-half times in the later year what they had been in the earlier. Other evidence in the survey also indicated the increased use of accountants for VAT purposes.

In 1977-78 only 13 per cent of respondents paid accountants for VAT work, although 46 per cent had used an accountant at one time or another. A typical situation appeared to be that some traders had used an accountant for early VAT work, which they then (often with the encouragement of the accountant) took over themselves. Further, the accountant who did the firm's auditing and accounting for other purposes might be consulted on an *ad hoc* basis if a particular VAT problem arose.

In 1986-87 56 per cent of the sample claimed to employ a VAT adviser (though he often would not do all the VAT work) and 60 per cent said they used a VAT adviser on occasion. Table 8.9 compares the main sources of tax advice used by respondents, and their assessment of the helpfulness of these sources, in 1977-78 and 1986-87. The table shows some interesting changes in the use made of the main sources of information. In 1986-87 much less use is being made of all the official sources of information — presumably because many traders have become much more accustomed to the working of the tax than in 1977-78. However, the table does indicate the increased use being made of accountants, who from fourth position in 1977-78 move up to top position in 1986-87 as the prime source of advice (a fraction of a per cent above the visiting VAT officer). There is virtually no change between the two periods in the degree of satisfaction the users derived from each source.

Table 8.9 Main Sources of Advice and their Helpfulness,
1977-78 and 1986-87

Main Sources	*Users (% of sample)*		*Finding Helpful (% of users)*	
	1977-78	*1986-87*	*1977-78*	*1986-87*
Official VAT booklets	76	55	64	63
Visiting VAT officer	71	60	82	82
Local VAT office	48	41	80	78
Accountant	46	60	86	88

In fact, casual observation of the market, let alone the interviews with accountants and other VAT specialists as part of the VAT 2 study, have made very clear the increased interest of accountants in VAT. The last few years have seen a pattern by which the large accountancy firms have established a VAT department first in London, then in the main provincial cities. Moreover, they have staffed these departments to a large extent from former Customs and Excise officials. The other side to that medal is the acute staffing difficulties experienced by Customs and Excise as they have lost many of their best senior executive officers (SEOs), higher executive officers (HEOs) and staff from the solicitor's office to the private sector (see Customs and Excise Annual Reports).

Why More Accountants are dealing with VAT

The interviews with accountants and VAT specialists mainly took place in the early part of 1988, following the VAT 2 survey distributed in the Autumn of 1987. The message from a series of interviews, mainly with VAT specialists in large accountancy firms, was consistent. Accountants were expanding VAT work and marketing it fairly hard. They held that VAT was becoming more complicated, or that it had always been a complicated tax but the complications had not hitherto been widely appreciated, either by accountants or Customs and Excise; now that had changed for both. Accountants had woken up to the fact there was money to be saved for their clients and money to be made for themselves. The increase in the standard rate to 15 per cent meant that there was more at stake. (Moreover, the relative importance of VAT payments had increased with the reduction in income tax and corporation tax). The penalty system increased the need for clients' returns to be accurate and on time. The European Community decisions and proposals complicated the picture and made it more necessary for clients to be kept aware of possibilities. Accountants wanted to offer a full range of services to clients and if some large firms established VAT departments others felt bound to follow suit to prevent loss of clients. Moreover one accountant suggested that the full range of services, including a thorough knowledge of VAT, was needed for purposes of indemnity.

At the same time interviewees held that changes in Customs and Excise policy were pushing traders towards accountants. Visits of an educational nature by VAT inspectors had been cut back. (Specific educational visits were discontinued in the mid 1970s, but were replaced by registration visits, which were made shortly after the business was registered and had much the same effect; this practice continued until the early 1980s, when it was replaced by a first visit which took place only after the business had bedded down — about 15 months after registration.) When inspectors visited, because of their tight schedules, they were not prepared to spend as much time as before helping traders. As part of improved Customs and Excise control there was a large increase in assessments for under-declarations (up from 144,985 in 1976-77 to 206,618 in 1986-87); if the books were unclear, some accountants maintained, inspectors were more inclined to make an assessment and let the trader sort things out. The FMI put inspectors under pressure to increase their number of visits and discover more revenue-yielding mistakes.

At the same time, the quality of Customs and Excise staff had fallen, not least because so many had been creamed off to the private sector; but, even apart from this cause of reduction in quality, accountants took the view that Customs and Excise staff were less good than Inland

Revenue staff; that the visiting inspectors often lacked understanding of the business situation and of accounts; and that they did not know the Finance Acts but were guided by the VAT notices, so that they were unable to go back to basics to deal with an unusual problem.

The Paradox

We are faced with a paradox. On the one hand our VAT 2 mail survey suggests that, even after allowing for the compliance cost reductions resulting from the abolition of higher rate tax, compliance costs fell in real terms between 1977-78 and 1986-87, especially for the smaller firms. At the same time the survey itself and much general evidence points to the increasing use of accountants for VAT advice. For this reason alone one might have expected to see compliance costs rising. Indeed, as Table 8.10 indicates, the costs of those traders employing accountants were significantly higher than of those who did not.

Table 8.10 Comparison of Average Compliance Costs of Those Employing and Those Not Employing an Outside Adviser, 1986- 87

Taxable Turnover		Mean Compliance Costs	
£000 p.a.	All Traders	With Adviser	No Adviser
	£	£	£
0- 20.5	199	416	135
20.5- 50	273	483	195
50- 100	387	424	376
100- 500	960	1,441	614
500- 1m.	1,950	4,036	281
1m.- 10m.	1,268	3,012	809
10m. and over	1,453	—	1,453
	(N=371)	(N=115)	(N=256)

Note: N = number in analysis. The table includes only those respondents who provided full information. The biggest reason for incomplete information was a failure of those specifying that they employed a VAT adviser to indicate what proportion of their total fee for tax advice related to VAT.

Moreover, it was the clearly stated view of VAT specialists interviewed that VAT was in practice becoming more complicated and Customs and Excise inspectors were becoming less helpful. With the increased employment of accountants and the complications to which they referred, we should have expected compliance costs to have risen.

The resolution of the paradox may, perhaps, be sought in two directions (apart from the possibility, discussed above, that the statistical proxies used overstate the fall in compliance costs in real terms).

(1)   For the large majority of traders, compliance costs fell in real terms between 1977-78 and 1986-87; these were traders with relatively straightforward VAT situations. They did not employ an accountant, or, if they did, only on a fairly informal basis on particular issues. Their compliance costs were primarily their own time or that of a book-keeper. Even in 1986-87 the proportion of total compliance costs taken up in fees to external advisers was only 17 per cent. However, by 1986-87, some traders were beginning to make more use of accountants perhaps because they were running into problems or because the accountants were pointing them towards methods of tax saving, or because they were concerned at the forthcoming implementation of proposals for automatic penalties for default or serious misdeclaration. Accountants were primarily dealing with this minority of traders. Whether costs are seen as having fallen or risen is partly a matter of perception; and the perception of accountants is coloured by the cases with which they deal.

(2)   There is a significant timing difference between the period to which the mail survey related, 1986-87, and the time of the interviews, the first half of 1988. A large proportion of the examples given by accountants at interview related to changes introduced in 1987 or which were becoming more significant post 1987. Most important of these were the changes in partial exemption, effective from April 1987, which brought more traders into the partly exempt category (though only affecting about 15,000); the rules for apportionment of petrol between private and business use; the gradual implementation of the penalty system which may have frightened traders into taking greater care; and the growing significance of European Community law. It would also appear that

much of the expansion of VAT work by the big accountancy firms, especially in the provinces, took place after the beginning of 1987.

Thus, a scenario which fits the facts is that, following the VAT 1 survey, relating to 1977-78, the abolition of higher rate tax led to an abrupt drop in compliance costs. Thereafter they continued to fall gradually for most of the next decade, particularly because traders became more accustomed to the tax and Customs and Excise introduced a series of measures to simplify it and particularly reduce the burden for small firms. From perhaps the middle 1980s the situation changed. Although costs continued to fall or remain stable in real terms for the majority of traders, there was a growing interest of accountants in VAT work and an appreciation of tax savings that could be made. At the same time Customs and Excise attitudes, under the influence of FMI, were changing and tending to push traders with problems towards accountants. Compliance costs for some traders and overall had started to rise by 1986 but this rise accelerated from 1987 for a variety of reasons, not least the changes in partial exemption rules and the threat of the new penalty system.

Two small pieces of evidence would tend to support this hypothesis. The number of appeals to the VAT tribunal, after several years of stability, began an upward rise from 1982-83 which has continued ever since. Also, although precise information is lacking, it would appear that the number of SEOs, officers leaving Customs and Excise for the private sector has been increasing; certainly the 1987-88 combined figure of resignations from the grades of senior executive officer (SEO), higher executive officer (HEO) and executive officer (EO) was 70 or 80 per cent above that of the year before.

If this scenario is true, then the compliance costs of VAT are currently increasing; whether this increase will be only temporary, settling down when traders have adjusted to the changes, especially the penalty system, or whether the level of compliance costs will continue to grow with an increasing component of accountancy services is unclear. There are also influences in the opposite direction, i.e. a series of measures, introduced in 1987, with the objective of reducing the costs for small firms (see Chapter 13).

International Comparisons

Some comparative figures have recently been published on the administrative costs of VAT in a number of OECD countries (*Taxing*

Consumption, OECD, 1988) and these are reproduced in Table 8.11, below, with the original footnotes. As the OECD publication rightly stresses: 'It remains impossible to make any judgments on the relative efficiency of the administration of value added taxation amongst Member countries only on the basis of the information available. By way of illustration, a relatively high level of administrative cost per registered trader may indicate either a relatively inefficient administration or one of relatively higher quality (manifesting itself in less evasion and avoidance, better taxpayer services, faster return and payment processing, etc.). Further, relatively high administrative costs may simply be the result of a tax authority having to cope with a tax that is by its nature complex, and conversely, relative low administrative costs may be due to the tax in question being simple to control.' (op.cit. p.203)

The limitations of measuring administrative costs as a percentage of tax revenue were stressed in Chapter 1 (above); it is also important to emphasise again that administrative and compliance costs need to be considered together, as one may fall at the expense of the other.

On compliance costs the evidence is much thinner than on administrative costs. The one study in English of the compliance costs of VAT in other countries is that of Graham Bannock and Partners in conjunction with Professor Horst Albach under the auspices of the Anglo-German Foundation (Bannock, 1987). The study sought to compare the compliance costs of and attitudes towards VAT for smaller firms in Britain and Germany. It was based on mailed surveys carried out early in 1987 and related to 1985, supplemented by telephone interviews. The samples in both countries were derived from private sources: a response rate of 44 per cent in the U.K. and 25 per cent in Germany yielded 262 and 197 usable responses respectively in the two countries.

There are considerable methodological difficulties in respect of the study. Because of their source the surveys are less representative than any based on an official register; the German firms in the sample tended to be older and larger than the U.K. firms; and there are particular problems about the basis of comparison across countries. Nonetheless, whilst the detail may be suspect, the general findings are of considerable interest.

In each country the familiar regressive pattern of compliance costs is evident. The novelty of the study, however, lies in the differences between the two countries. In the United Kingdom small firms spent more time on VAT work and were less inclined to use accountants than in Germany. Taking time and money costs together, whilst the differences were not large, there was a tendency for compliance costs as a proportion

Table 8.11   Administrative Costs of Value-Added Tax[1]

	Administrative Costs[2]		Administrative Costs Per Registered Trader		Administrative Costs Per Staff Member		Admin. Costs as a percentage of Revenue[2]
	Domestic Currency	US Dollar Equivalent[3]	Domestic Currency	US Dollar Equivalent	Domestic Currency	US Dollar Equivalent	%
Belgium	BFr 4,109M[10]	$101.7M	BFr 7,103	$175	BFr 1,038M	$25,686	1.09
Denmark	DKr 420M	$57.2M	DKr 1,135	$155	DKr 221,053	$30,106	0.69
Finland	FMk 102M	$21.3M	FMk 1,128	$235	FMk 209,016	$43,599	0.41
France	FFr 1,576M[4]	$224.2M	n.a.	n.a.	FFr 150,741	$23,353	0.4
Ireland	IR£ 15M	$21M	IR£ 140	$196	IR£ 20,520	$28,718	1.08
Italy	L 200B	$147.3M	L 142,653	$105	L 33.3M	$24,544	0.49
Luxembourg	n.a.	n.a.	n.a.	n.a.	n.a.	n.a.	0.99
New Zealand	NZ$ 20M[5]	$ 10.5M	NZ$ 87	$ 46	NZ$ 20,000	$10,490	0.49[6]
Norway	NKr 140M	$ 18.9M	NKr 495	$ 67	NKr 233,333	$31,531	0.32
Portugal	Esc 2,350M[7]	$ 16.1M	Esc 7,119	$ 48	Esc 2.6M[8]	$17,870[8]	1.07
Sweden	SKr 212M[9]	$31.1M	SKr 466	$ 68	SKr 258,537	$37,914	0.35
U. Kingdom	£200.4M[10]	$294M	£136	$200	£20,569	$30,175	0.95[11]

[1] Refer to text for reservations regarding the comparability of the data in this table.
[2] 1985 unless otherwise indicated.
[3] At end of 31 December 1986 (Source: 'IMF Survey').
[4] Does not include costs of Customs Authorities.
[5] 1987
[6] Revenue is 1987-88 estimate taken from '1987 Budget' (NZ Govt. Printer, Wellington), administrative costs are for 1987.
[7] 1986; does not include costs of Customs Authorities.
[8] Does not include staff in local tax offices or in tax control services.
[9] 1988; does not include costs of Customs Authorities (est. SKr 132M, 1982), costs of collecting the tax (est. SKr 29M, 1982) or costs of courts (Est. SKr 5M, 1982).
[10] 1986
[11] Revenue is for 1985, administrative costs are for 1986.

Source: OECD 1988

of turnover to be higher in the United Kingdom than in Germany for all size bands except the smallest.

The differences in attitudes to VAT between the two countries were very marked. In the United Kingdom VAT was clearly regarded as more costly and troublesome than other taxes to a greater extent than in Germany. Further, whilst 80 per cent of German respondents agreed 'VAT is a simple method of collecting tax', only 48 per cent of United Kingdom respondents took the same view. Similarly, 48 per cent of United Kingdom respondents held that 'As it stands, VAT is unreasonably complicated', as against 18 per cent of German respondents. Although the larger proportion of younger, smaller firms in the United Kingdom sample can be expected to have biased the responses so as to exaggerate the differences, they are far too large to be explicable solely in such statistical terms. Bannock suggests two main reasons for the differences in costs and attitudes, and hints at other possibilities.

There is a much longer tradition and experience of broadly based indirect taxation administered by business in Germany than in Britain. In Germany VAT superseded an unpopular turnover tax affecting the majority of businesses. In the United Kingdom VAT replaced purchase tax, levied only at the wholesale level and collected by some 70,000 businesses, and selective employment tax, which though more widespread and unpopular was administratively simple, collected with the national insurance payments.

Secondly, Bannock states that German traders dealing with VAT tend to be more highly trained than their United Kingdom counterparts. In many trades in Germany a pre-qualification is required as a condition of registering a new enterprise with the local chamber of trade which helps to ensure that business proprietors have some knowledge of tax procedures.

His more tentative suggestions were that there was some (very limited) evidence to suggest that German businesses might make more use of computers than their United Kingdom counterparts. Further, the Germans operate a compensation scheme for the smaller firms with a deduction which tapers to zero as size increases, thus preventing an abrupt change between those just in and those just out of the system; however, the German threshold is much lower than that in the United Kingdom and the scheme only applies at levels below the U.K. threshold. (For details of the working of the German scheme and a similar one in the Netherlands, see Godwin and Sandford, 1983). Thirdly, it may help to reduce compliance costs that in Germany, unlike the United Kingdom, one tax office is responsible for all business taxes.

Another possibility which emerges from a study of the history of VAT in the two countries is the greater stability of the German VAT. Despite its longer existence, it has been subject to less changes than the United Kingdom tax.

Summary of Main Conclusions

In 1986-87 the official cost of collecting VAT was £220m. (1.03 per cent of VAT revenue); the estimated (gross) compliance cost was £791m. (3.69 per cent of VAT revenue). The compliance costs were very regressive in their impact, falling with disproportionate severity on the smaller firms.

There were important offsets to the compliance costs of VAT in the form of cash flow benefits, from which the largest firms probably benefited more than proportionately; and managerial benefits, mainly accruing to the smaller firms.

Compliance costs in real terms appear to have fallen significantly between 1977-78 and 1986-87 mainly as a result of the abolition of higher rate tax, the learning effect and a series of simplification measures by Customs and Excise particularly affecting small firms. However, there was some evidence that compliance costs might be beginning to rise. A marked trend in recent years was an increasing role being taken by accountants in VAT compliance work.

A study by Bannock of the compliance costs and attitude to VAT of smaller firms in the United Kingdom and in Germany suggested that compliance costs tended to be higher in the United Kingdom. Certainly U.K. traders were more anti-VAT than their German counterparts.

CHAPTER 9

CORPORATION TAX AND PETROLEUM REVENUE TAX

Outline of Corporation Tax

Corporation tax is administered by Inland Revenue and is chargeable on the profits of United Kingdom resident companies, non-resident companies trading through a branch or agency in the United Kingdom and on unincorporated associations. Corporation tax was first introduced in 1965 in the form of the so-called 'classical' system, by which a company's profits, distributed and undistributed, were taxed at the same rate and then dividends were also taxed to income tax. In 1973 a switch was made to the imputation system, by which a tax credit, equivalent to the basic rate of income tax, is 'imputed' to a dividend in respect of payment of corporation tax. This credit is set off against the income tax liability of the shareholder receiving the dividend and amounts to the deduction of income tax at source. Whenever a dividend is paid, a payment of advance corporation tax (ACT) has to be made.

Assessments of corporation tax are made for accounting periods rather than tax years. The rate of corporation tax is fixed for each financial year, which for corporation tax purposes ends on 31 March. If an accounting period straddles two financial years, the profits may have to be apportioned and charged partly at one corporation tax rate and partly at another.

Payment of corporation tax (except for certain companies trading before April 1, 1965, which are currently being brought into line) is due on whichever is the later of (a) nine months after the end of the accounting period or (b) 30 days after the making of the assessment.

The main rate of corporation tax was 35 per cent for the financial year beginning 1 April 1986. There is a reduced rate for corporations with profits below a certain level, which in 1986-87 was 29 per cent, in line with the basic rate of income tax.

As outlined in Chapter 7, in 1984 stock relief was abolished and major changes took place in respect of capital allowances. At the same time provision was made for reducing the rate of corporation tax from 52 per cent to the 1986 rate of 35 per cent.

Basis of Study

The study was based on a series of semi-structured interviews with tax consultants and tax managers together with responses to a small number of questions included in the VAT 2 survey for those respondents amongst VAT registered traders who were incorporated. (See Appendix D). There is no complete list of companies classified by size available in the United Kingdom. The VAT register is the nearest to such a list but it is not fully comprehensive; it omits companies which are exempt from VAT either because their turnover is below the VAT threshold or because they produce wholly exempt supplies. However, the number of large companies excluded from the register must necessarily be very small.

Table 9.1 Incorporated Respondents to VAT 2 Survey, Analysed by Size

Range of Taxable Turnover *£000 p.a.*	*Proportions of Respondents* *Incorporated* *per cent*
0 up to 20.5	3
20.5 - 49.9	7
50 - 99.9	13
100 - 499.9	30
500 - 999.9	50
1,000 - 9,999.0	76
10,000 and over	100

The VAT 2 survey was much smaller than that of VAT 1, being designed primarily to test for major changes in the compliance costs of VAT since 1978. As most VAT traders are not incorporated, the number of companies responding to the survey was small, 139, of which 36 were members of a group. In fact, it became apparent that the response rate amongst companies was markedly lower than that amongst unincorporated businesses. The number of companies on the VAT register at April 1988, as given by Customs and Excise, was 541,253 (counting the members of group registrations individually). This was around a third of the VAT registered traders (when allowance is made for groups) whereas the proportion of the sample respondents who were incorporated was only just over one fifth. Inland Revenue data indicates that the number of companies has been growing by on average 5 per cent per annum across the size ranges. Thus the estimated number of companies at the time of our survey is approximately 487,000.

The sample response from incorporated traders, as a proportion of total response, analysed by size, is given in Table 9.1.

Unfortunately, Customs and Excise are unable to give a size breakdown of companies from which it would be possible to gross up the compliance costs by size groups. Nor, because of the disproportionately low response rate, can it be assumed that the response rate from companies in each size bracket is the same as the total response rate (for this would only give us a total of 285,000 companies). It is therefore necessary to make a series of assumptions about the distribution of companies over the size bands. It is clear from the data on responses that the degree of under-representation of companies is much higher in the lower size bands. Thus, the total number of companies in each size band was estimated on the following assumptions:

(1)   That the number of companies at the time of the survey in 1986-87 was 487,000 approximately;

(2)   that all registered traders with a taxable turnover over £10m. were incorporated;

(3)   that 90 per cent of traders with a taxable turnover between £1m. and £10m. were incorporated;

(4)   that 75 per cent of traders with taxable turnover between £0.5m. and £1m. were incorporated;

(5)   that the remaining companies were distributed proportionately amongst the other turnover bands.

Whereas there is clearly an element of arbitrariness in these assumptions, they do not conflict with the known facts and are not unreasonable in themselves. Moreover the scope for error lies primarily at the bottom of the size distribution, so that it least affects the estimation of total compliance costs. Nonetheless, given the small size of the sample, the incomplete sampling frame and the assumptions which have had to be made, it must be stressed that the estimates of compliance costs of corporation tax are considerably less reliable than those of income tax and VAT. The distribution of companies given by the assumptions is set out in Table 9.2.

Table 9.2 Assumed Distribution of Companies by Size Bands

Range of Taxable Turnover *£000 p.a.*	*Assumed Proportion* *of Traders* *per cent*	*Estimated Number* *of Companies*
0 up to 20.5	27	51,989
20.5 - 49.9	27	138,833
50 - 99.9	27	86,484
100 - 499.9	27	100,959
500 - 999.9	75	44,911
1,000 9,999.9	90	55,487
10,000 and over	100	8,819
Overall	32	487,482

Table 9.3 Composition of Compliance Costs of Corporation Tax,
1986-87

Type of Cost	*£m.*	*Per cent of Total*
Time costs of:		
Directors	28.6	9.5
Accounting staff	47.6	15.9
Other staff	13.1	4.4
External adviser	141.1	47.0
Group tax administration fees	24.5	8.2
Other costs	45.2	15.1
	300.0	100.0

Main Findings on Corporation Tax

Size and Nature of Compliance Costs

Grossing up the sample of corporation tax respondents on the basis of a distribution of companies by size bands, as set out in Table 9.2, yields an aggregate figure for the compliance costs of corporation tax in 1986-87 of £300m. or 2.2 per cent of revenue collected. The composition of those costs is set out in Table 9.3. As with the other studies the costs of in-house staff are derived from time costs at the respondents' valuation.

Of the total costs of compliance, approximately half were fees to external advisers. As Table 9.4 shows, the costs of the smallest firms are predominantly those for external advisers (84 per cent in the turnover range up to £100,000). The costs of external advisers as a proportion of total costs decline as the size of firm increases, although the cost of these advisers remained over 50 per cent of total costs for all sizes of firm except the largest (with a turnover of £10m. and over). In the largest companies it is in-house accountants together with 'other costs', about half of which were group tax administration fees, which constitute the largest categories. (It should be noted that the proportional distribution of compliance costs within size bands is not affected by the assumptions used to calculate aggregate compliance costs; it can therefore be regarded as having a greater reliability.)

Table 9.4 Composition of Compliance Costs Analysed by Size of Company, 1986-87

Turnover Range	External Adviser		In-house Staff Costs Directors		Accounts		Other		Other Costs		Total
£000 p.a.	£m.	%	£m.	%	£m.	%	£m.	%	£m.	%	£m.
0- 99.9	49.5	84	3.5	6	2.3	4	3.6	6	0	0	58.9
100- 499.9	31.8	69	6.6	14	1.8	4	1.2	3	5.0	11	46.4
500- 999.9	11.5	74	4.1	26	0	0	0	0	0	0	15.6
1,000- 9,999.9	44.7	54	5.0	6	6.8	8	0.8	1	24.9	30	82.3
10,000 and over	3.5	4	9.4	10	36.7	38	7.5	8	39.6	41	96.8
Overall	141.1	47	28.6	10	47.6	16	13.1	4	69.5	23	300

The final column of Table 9.4 gives a distribution of aggregate compliance costs by size. A fuller distribution is given in Table 9.5, together with mean costs for each size (which are also unaffected by the grossing up assumptions).

Table 9.5 Compliance Costs of Corporation Tax by Size of Company, 1986-87

Taxable Turnover *£000 p.a.*	*Mean Compliance Cost* *£*	*Total* *£m.*
0 up to 20.5	100	5.2
20.5 - 49.9	293	40.6
50 - 99.9	151	13.0
100 - 499.9	460	46.4
500 - 999.9	347	15.6
1,000 - 9,999.9	1,484	82.3
10,000 and over	10,980	96.8
Overall	616	300

Taxable turnover is used as the measure of size because this is the form in which the VAT register is compiled which was the basis of the survey. We should like to have analysed compliance costs in relation to either profits (before tax) or corporation tax payments, but the response to these questions was poor (no doubt because, at the time of the survey, many companies would not yet have that information available for 1986-87). However the VAT 2 questionnaire, in the PAYE section (Appendix D) did include questions on employment. Analysis is restricted to 66 companies (many small companies did not have employees) but is of considerable interest. We thus have two measures for showing the variation of compliance costs with size — costs as a percentage of taxable turnover for each turnover band and costs as a percentage of taxable turnover in relation to number of employees. These measures are set out in Tables 9.6 and 9.7. Both tables reveal the familiar regressive pattern of compliance costs in respect of business taxes.

Table 9.6 Compliance Costs of Corporation Tax as a Percentage of Taxable Turnover, 1986-87

Taxable Turnover £000 p.a.	*Compliance Costs as Per cent of Taxable Turnover*	*No. of Cases*
0 up to 49.9	0.77	11
50 - 99.9	0.20	6
100 - 499.9	0.17	31
500 - 999.9	0.07	9
1,000 - 9,999.9	0.03	15
10,000 and over	0.01	3

Table 9.7 Compliance Costs of Corporation Tax as a Percentage of Taxable Turnover, Analysed by Size of Employment, 1986-87

Size of Company by No. of Employees	*Compliance Cost as Per cent of Taxable Turnover*	*No. of Cases*
1- 5	0.48	18
6 - 10	0.19	14
11 - 25	0.09	13
26 - 50	0.05	8
51 - 100	0.07	7
100 - 500	0.02	4
Over 500	0.01	2

In the VAT 2 questionnaire, respondents were also asked to indicate, of the time spent by in-house staff on corporation tax, what proportion was on planning work and what on 'administration (e.g. maintaining additional ACT records)'. The answers are recorded in Table 9.8.

Table 9.8
Proportion of Time Spent on Corporation Tax
Compliance Devoted to Planning

Percentage

Company directors	28.3
Qualified in-house accountants	18.8
Other office staff	16.2

The general picture of compliance with corporation tax which emerges from the survey data was confirmed by the interviews. Most of the data needed to calculate corporation tax liabilities are required anyway in order to fulfil the requirements laid on companies by the company legislation. The questions in the mail survey were phrased so as to stress that we were concerned strictly with the *additional* costs of corporation tax. In order to arrive at corporation tax liability profits have to be recalculated in accordance with the definitions for tax purposes, e.g. adding back certain items which are non-tax deductible, calculating depreciation according to the tax rules and the like. Our interviewees stressed that for most small and medium-sized firms this is usually a very straightforward exercise. Many small firms leave corporation tax entirely to their accountants, but the average compliance cost for the smallest size group of companies was only £100 (Table 9.5). It is also noticeable from the VAT 2 responses that there were hardly any adverse comments on corporation tax in the 'suggestions' section at the end of the questionnaire, though this may partly reflect the fact that, because they tend to leave corporation tax to their advisers, small businessmen are not qualified to comment.

Whilst the costs of complying with corporation tax tend to diminish with size, some very substantial costs may be incurred by the biggest firms, especially multi-nationals concerned with buying or selling subsidiaries or transferring companies to this country. Then the ramifications may be considerable, such as double taxation complications and the interconnections between taxes. Even the largest firms in such cases call on specialist legal and accounting advice to make sure that the changes are being effected in the least tax-costly way and that there is no danger of falling into a tax trap.

A word of warning: because of the close relationship between audit activities and corporation tax activities, the division of accountants' bills may not be precise. Furthermore, as we noted under personal taxation, there is some tendency for personal tax work to be undertaken by accountants at below cost, as a 'loss leader' for other work. It is therefore possible that, on the one hand, compliance costs of corporation tax may be understated because they are hidden in audit work; on the other hand they may be overstated because they include an element of cost (e.g. for a director's personal tax account) which in strict economic terms belongs to personal taxation.

Benefits of Compliance

As companies have to produce accounts for other purposes than taxation, there is little likelihood of a managerial benefit resulting from corporation tax. But there is a very substantial cash flow benefit.

The principle we have adopted (Chapter 3) in relation to cash flow benefits or detriments is that they relate to the date at which the economic transaction giving rise to the liability takes place. Thus, even though the shareholders cannot get their hands on the money until much later, the cash flow benefit dates from when the profit is actually earned.

Corporation tax is payable nine months after the end of the accounting period, or one month after the issuing of an assessment (whichever is the later). Certain companies which were trading in 1965 are given more than nine months to pay their tax but that benefit is in the process of being withdrawn.

The payment of a dividend accelerates the payment of corporation tax. A liability for advanced corporation tax (ACT) is incurred when the dividend payment is made. The ACT has to be paid to the Inland Revenue within 14 days after the quarterly period in which the dividend was paid. The ACT is then available for set off against the company's corporation tax (CT) liability for the accounting period in which the dividend was paid. The amount of CT the company eventually pays, after setting off ACT, is known as mainstream CT.

Corporation Tax: Estimation of Value of the Cash-Flow benefit

In 1986-87 the total amount of CT collected was £13,495m of which £4,456m was ACT. Thus the amount of mainstream CT collected was £9,039m.

An estimate of the cash flow benefit can be made by assuming:

(1)   that all profits and hence CT liability arise evenly throughout the accounting period;   and (2) that payment is made at the last possible legal date — i.e. nine months after the accounting period for mainstream CT;   and 14 days after the end of the quarter in which distribution of dividends is made for ACT. This assumption seems reasonable as interest is chargeable on late payments.

Then, for mainstream CT, the cash flow benefit can be estimated as:

0.5T held throughout the year on average (where T is mainstream CT)

plus

T held for 0.75 years (a further nine months after the end of accounting period)

Tax received as ACT in tax year 1986-87 could arise from

(1)   dividends paid after the end of the accounting period 1985- 86, or

(2)   interim dividends paid during accounting period 1986-87

However, ACT on dividends paid within a particular accounting period is available for offset against the CT on the profits *for that period.* Thus *any* dividend paid during accounting period 1986-87 is offset against the CT due to be paid nine months *after the end of accounting period 1986-87.* Thus it does not matter whether we are talking about interim or final dividends — they both give rise to prepayment of the 1987-88 CT liability, and thus of a loss of cash flow benefit. The extent of the loss of cash flow benefit clearly depends on when the dividend is paid — the earlier the payment, the greater the loss of benefit.

To illustrate the above point, suppose firstly that *all* CT receipts accruing during 1986-87 had been *mainstream* CT, and *none* ACT. Then

the cash flow benefit enjoyed by companies would have been
£(1.25 x 13,495)m
and the *value* of the benefit, using the average bank base rate for 1986-87 of 10.5 per cent, would have been

£(1.25 x 13,495 x 0.105)m
= £1,771m

However, £4,456m receipts comprised ACT, and were thus a prepayment of 1987-88 CT. If *all* the ACT arose from a dividend paid half-way through the accounting period — e.g. September 30 for a company whose accounting period starts April 1 — then ACT would have been payable six months and two weeks into the accounting period (October 14 for a company whose accounting period starts April 1) — some 14.5 months (63 weeks) *earlier* than if no dividend had been paid. The *reduction* in the value of the cash flow benefit as a result of paying ACT would then be

£(63/52 x 4,456 x 0.105)m
= £567m

reducing the value of the overall cash flow benefit to £1,204m.

Similarly, if all dividends had been paid at the end of the first quarter — 30 June for a company with accounting period starting April 1 — then the value of the cash flow benefit would have been reduced by a *further* £117m.

Clearly the exact loss of cash flow benefit cannot be estimated without accurate knowledge of the pattern of dividend payments. But it is clear that in comparison with the estimated compliance cost of £300m the operation of the corporation tax system confers considerable cash flow benefits on the corporate sector.

A further qualification is that some companies are affected by a general restriction in set-off of ACT. Broadly the set-off cannot exceed a figure calculated by applying the basic rate of income tax to the profits chargeable to CT. However, restrictions of this sort have become very much less significant as a result of:

(1)   the abolition of stock relief;
(2)   the phasing out of high initial and first year capital allowances;
(3)   the extension of a company's right to carry back ACT from two years to six.

Administrative and Compliance Costs of Corporation Tax, 1986-87

Table 9.9 sets out the administrative and compliance costs of corporation tax in relation to tax revenue.

Table 9.9 Administrative and Compliance Costs of Corporation Tax 1986-87 in Relation to Tax Revenue

Corporation Tax Revenue £m.	Administrative Costs £m.	%	Compliance Costs £m.	%	Operating Costs £m.	%
13,495	70.3	0.52	300	2.22	370	2.74

It is notable that the administrative costs at 0.52 per cent of revenue are very low compared with other Inland Revenue taxes. They have fallen substantially in recent years with the rise in corporation tax revenue; in 1984-85 the administrative costs were 0.72 per cent; but this was still comparatively low. Compliance costs are also low compared with income tax and VAT, but are more than four times the administrative cost.

Summary of Main Conclusions

In 1986-87 the compliance costs of corporation tax were estimated to be £300m., though for reasons of sample size and structure, this finding is less robust than the findings on income tax and VAT. Administrative costs were £70.3m.

About half of the total compliance costs were fees to external advisers and these fees dominated the compliance costs of the smaller companies.

As with VAT and PAYE, the compliance costs of corporation tax were disproportionately heavy on small firms; however, corporation tax in 1986-87 appeared to be relatively simple for most small and medium-sized firms, though it could raise substantial problems for big multi-nationals.

The value of the cash flow benefits from corporation tax much exceeded compliance costs in aggregate.

There are no known international studies of recent origin of the compliance costs of corporation tax with which the findings can be compared; however, a study is under way in Australia under the auspices of the Australian Tax Research Foundation. Also recorded, in Appendix A, is a study (Arthur D. Little Corporation 1988) of the time taken by businesses (partnerships and corporations) to complete the U.S. federal income tax returns.

Outline of Petroleum Revenue Tax

The taxation associated with the extraction of oil and gas is highly complex and has been subject to frequent change since 1979. Our purpose is not to analyse and explain the technical intricacies except in so far as some understanding is required to appreciate their significance for the level of administrative and compliance costs in 1986-87 and the influences on these costs. A convenient account of the history and summary of the current position is to be found in Stephen Bond *et al*(1987), on which this study has drawn.

In 1986-87 the income from North Sea oil and gas was subject to three levies: licence royalties, corporation tax and petroleum revenue tax (PRT). (1) Royalties (where due) are paid six-monthly at the rate of 12.5 per cent on the proceeds of sale, less some costs for transport and treatment of oil; since April 1982 royalty payments apply only to fields licensed before that date. (2) Corporation tax is levied on the same basis as for on-shore companies except that it is 'ring fenced', i.e. profits from the North Sea have to be calculated separately from the on-shore activities of the company, to ensure that profits earned in the North Sea cannot be used to offset losses from other trading activities (although trading losses in respect of ring fence activities may be offset against profits from non-ring fence activities according to normal corporation tax rules). Corporation tax is calculated after deducting royalties (if any) and PRT. (3) PRT is a special regime introduced in 1975.

In this study on administrative and compliance costs, as indicated in Chapter 4, we have omitted licence royalties, which are arguably not a tax, are not collected by the revenue departments but by the Department of Energy, for which no figures of administrative costs are available and which, in any case, have been abolished for new fields. Corporation tax has already been considered in the earlier part of this chapter. In this part we examine the administrative and compliance costs of PRT together with any additional costs arising from the ring fencing of corporation tax.

When PRT came into operation in 1975, it was set at a rate of 45 per cent. It applied to profits in each field treated separately. It contained a series of special provisions to try to ensure that the state obtained the full benefit from the 'economic rent' associated with a scarce national resource, whilst at the same time encouraging production in small marginal fields and promoting new exploration. A desire for short-term revenue has also influenced Government policy.

The principal special provisions were:

(1)   An oil allowance: for every field, 1 million tonnes of oil per annum was exempted from PRT, up to a cumulative limit of 10 million tonnes. (The allowance is divided amongst the producers exploiting the field in proportion to their output.)

(2)   An uplift: in computing allowable cost, capital expenditure was entitled to an uplift originally set at 75 per cent. Thus, at the time of introduction, a business could offset 175 per cent of capital expenditure against taxable profits.

(3)   A 'safeguard' provision which limited the PRT liability in any six month chargeable period to 80 per cent of the amount by which gross profit exceeded 15 per cent of cumulative capital expenditure.

Between 1979 and 1983 the tax regime was made much stiffer. The PRT rate was raised from 45 per cent to 60 per cent (1979), then to 70 per cent (1980) and then to 75 per cent (1982). Also in 1980 a supplementary petroleum duty (SPD) was introduced — charged on a field-by-field basis at 20 per cent of gross oil revenue less an oil allowance of one million tonnes per annum. The 1981 Budget set limits to the safeguard provision and the uplift related to a concept of 'payback'. In 1982 SPD was replaced by advance PRT (APRT), which differed little from SPD except that it could be offset against PRT liabilities and any still outstanding by the end of the field's life was to be refunded. Meanwhile the uplift was reduced to 35 per cent and the oil allowance halved. Another move was to accelerate payments of PRT in 1980 and again in 1982, when they became monthly.

From 1983 the climate changed, in view of fears that taxation was having detrimental effects on new developments. As well as the abolition of licence royalties for new fields, the oil allowance was restored to its original level for new fields (except Southern Basin fields), APRT was phased out and exploration expenditure leading to development of new fields could be offset against PRT on existing fields. This breach in the field-by-field principle was followed by a further breach in the 1987 Budget when a new 'cross field' allowance was introduced by which companies could immediately offset up to 10 per cent of capital expenditure otherwise upliftable on offshore fields outside the Southern Basin against PRT generated on other fields. The 1987 Budget also permitted *general* expenditure on research and development to be offset against PRT after a three year delay period.

The system also had to accommodate to the changes in corporation tax 1984-86, described above, which reduced capital allowances, although some drilling costs still received 100 per cent first year allowances.

Revenue and Administrative Costs

The revenue from PRT has been subject to major changes from one year to the next. In 1986-87 the yield was £1.2 bn. but this figure represented a drastic fall from the previous year (£6.4 bn.); the yield in 1987-88 has increased again, but to nothing like the 1985-86 figure. Table 9.10 records the PRT yield and administrative cost for the years since 1983, when SPD effectively ended.

Table 9.10 PRT Revenue and Administrative Cost

	(1)	(2)	(3)
Year	PRT Revenue £m.	Admin Cost £m.	Cost/Yield Ratio (2) as % of (1)
1983-84	6,016	0.7	0.01
1984-85	7,178	0.9	0.01
1985-86	6,376	1.1	0.02
1986-87	1,189	1.4	0.12

At the time of the 1987 Budget the estimated yield for 1987-88 was

£1,680m.; provisional figures of yield, however, are appreciably higher at £2,330m.

Because of the extreme fluctuations in revenue yield, administrative costs have varied markedly as a percentage of tax revenue; there has also been a tendency for administrative costs to rise somewhat in real terms as the yield has fallen. However, even in 1986-87, at the highest ratio of cost:revenue, PRT remains a very cheap tax to administer, primarily because of the small number of taxpayers, listed in the Inland Revenue Annual Report at 83 for 1986-87.

Compliance Costs

The basis of the study of the compliance costs of PRT in 1986-87 was a survey by mail questionnaire, carried out with the support and co-operation of the United Kingdom Oil Industry Taxation Committee. The survey was distributed to the fourteen leading companies represented on the Committee of whom nine, including the three largest oil producers, responded.

Because the accounting period of the companies does not precisely correspond with the Government's financial year, two of the responses related to 1987 rather than to 1986-87. In consequence the PRT paid by the nine respondents (at £1,324m.) exceeded that received by the Inland Revenue in 1986-87 (£1,189m.) and was the equivalent to approximately 80 per cent of the yield anticipated for 1987-88 at the time of the 1987 Budget.

The recorded compliance costs for 1986-87 from the respondents to the survey amounted to £3.25m. or approximately 0.25 per cent of the tax they paid. Of the nine respondents, three paid no PRT in 1986-87 but did incur compliance costs amounting in total to £200,000 (averaging £60,000-£70,000 each). To obtain the total compliance costs we must allow for the 74 companies recorded by the Inland Revenue as PRT taxpayers. Clearly almost all these businesses pay no tax at all and some may well be moribund. Nonetheless, bearing in mind the compliance costs incurred by respondents who paid no PRT in 1986-87, on a conservative estimate we must allow another £2 million for their compliance costs. On this basis the estimated compliance costs in 1986-87 are £5.25m. or 0.44 per cent of tax revenue in that year. This figure represents a very modest compliance cost for the level of revenue. It is much below the average compliance cost for central government taxes. On the other hand, it is more than three times the level of administrative costs.

Had we estimates of compliance costs for a series of years, as with administrative costs, there is no doubt that, because tax revenue has been so volatile, we should have observed the ratio of cost to revenue varying markedly. Because of the low revenue yield, 1986-87 will have had a relatively high ratio of compliance cost to yield. For this reason less attention should be paid to this ratio than to that of compliance to administrative cost, where both will be similarly affected by changes in revenue yield.

Amongst the nine respondents there was some evidence of compliance costs varying inversely with size as measured by revenue yield, but there was no consistent pattern. This is hardly surprising when three of the nine paid no PRT but yet incurred compliance costs and when PRT liability in any particular year may be wiped out by some of the offsets we have earlier described. As there exists a provision by which costs incurred in abandoning a field will be allowed against PRT in so far as these costs relate to safety and the prevention of pollution, there will be years in which some businesses will be receiving repayments of PRT. It must therefore be expected that at some future date compliance costs as a proportion of revenue could rise very substantially.

All the respondents to the questionnaire did all or almost all the compliance work in-house. Three of the nine firms had used external advice in 1986-87 but in no case did the costs of this advice exceed five per cent of total compliance costs. All the companies had their own tax departments but in most cases some compliance work was undertaken by the accounting department and in five cases some work was also undertaken in the commercial department.

The frequent changes in PRT taxation and the special rules on field-by-field treatment (with exceptions) all tend to add to the level of compliance costs.

As with corporation tax PRT generates a cash flow benefit to the payers in the sense that the income giving rise to the tax liability is received some time before the tax has to be paid. However, Government has imposed conditions of payment which drastically shorten the period between generation of liability and payment of tax. The chargeable period is six months.

Instalments of PRT for a chargeable period are payable from the third month of the period onwards, for six months. Each instalment equals one eighth of the PRT assessments for the previous chargeable period. A balancing payment is then made two months after the end of the chargeable period on the basis of the operator's own assessment followed later by an official assessment.   In relation to the official assessment interest is paid on any under- or over-payment of PRT.

Summary of Main Conclusions

In 1986-87 the revenue from PRT was £1,189m., the administrative cost was £1.4m. (0.12 per cent of revenue) and the compliance cost, on a somewhat conservative basis, is estimated at £5.25m. (0.44 per cent).

The 1986-87 revenue yield was particularly low and the volatility of the tax yield makes the cost:yield ratios particularly unreliable; but, primarily because of the small number of taxpayers, the PRT has so far proved a tax with very low operating costs. Compliance costs are more than three times the administrative costs.

CHAPTER 10

EXCISE DUTIES

Outline of Duties on Oil, Tobacco and Alcoholic Drinks

Excise duties are typically narrow based, high rate taxes imposed at the production or import stage on specific commodities. The principal requirements of a traditional excise duty are large production by a small number of producers; low price elasticity of demand; clearly defined boundaries between dutiable and exempt goods; and non-availability of untaxed substitutes for the dutiable goods. Oil, tobacco and alcoholic drinks duties all meet these criteria well. They are the main excise taxes in the United Kingdom, together raising £16,470m., or 40 per cent of Customs and Excise revenue in 1986-87; revenue is generally buoyant in terms of GNP. Taken together the administrative costs were £4.1m., or 0.25 per cent of revenue.

The rates of duty in 1986-87 are set out in Table 10.1, where the taxes are listed in order of revenue importance. All the duties were unchanged from the previous year.

Basis of Study

The research methods employed were mainly semi-structured interviews together with a mail survey on alcoholic drinks. Much of the initial work took place in 1983, with subsequent update. Representatives of Customs and Excise were interviewed on several occasions. Representatives of the oil industry's taxation committee, and of three major oil companies, were interviewed in 1983 and 1988. Representatives of seven tobacco manufacturers were interviewed during 1983. Representatives of the industry's trade body, the Tobacco Advisory Council, were also interviewed in 1983 and 1988 and representatives of the National Association of Warehouse Keepers were interviewed in 1988.

Questionnaires for the alcoholic drinks survey were mailed to all U.K. members of the seven major trade associations. The questionnaire was piloted to 10 per cent of the sample in November 1983, and the main survey was despatched in February 1984. Response is set out in Table 10.2.

Table 10.1 Duty Rates for the Main Excise Duties, 1986-87

Duty	*Duty Rates*	
Hydrocarbon Oil duty	Light oil:	19.38p per litre
	Road vehicle fuel(DERV):	16.39p per litre
	Fuel oil:	0.77p per litre
	Gas oil:	1.1p per litre
Tobacco duty	Cigarettes:	21 per cent of recommended retail price plus £30.61 per thousand
	Cigars:	£47.05 per kg
	Hand rolling tobacco:	£49.64 per kg
	Other tobacco:	£24.95 per kg
Beer duty	£25.80 per hectolitre (hl) of worts at 1030 degrees original gravity (og), plus 86p per additional degree of og	
Cider duty	£15.80 per hl (for strengths below 8.5 per cent; otherwise charged at the same rate as wine)	
Spirits duty	£15.77 per litre of alcohol	
Wine duty	Strengths up to 15 per cent:	£98 per hl
	Sparkling wines:	£161.80 per hl
	Strengths from 15-18 per cent:	£169 per hl
	Strengths from 18-22 per cent:	£194.90 per hl
	An additional £15.77 was charged for every percentage point or part of one per cent by which strength exceeded 22 per cent.	

Table 10.2 Alcoholic Drinks Survey: Sample and Response

Product	Pilot Sample	Pilot Response	Main Sample	Main Response	Total Sample	Total Response
Spirits	15	3 (20%)	94	14 (15%)	109	17 (16%)
Beer	14	5 (36%)	175	67 (38%)	189	72 (38%)
Other	3	2 (67%)	30	8 (27%)	33	10 (30%)
Total	32	10 (31%)	299	89 (30%)	331	99 (30%)

Table 10.2 excludes 38 members of the original sample who fell outside the real sample frame. Of these, 23 were subsidiary or administrative companies only; others had gone away, or were in liquidation. It could well be that a number of the 92 members of distilling associations from which no reply was received were also out of frame; it is otherwise hard to explain why the virtually identical questionnaires sent to the other types of drink manufacturer received double the response obtained from distillers. However that may be, the respondents to the questionnaire represented a much higher proportion of output than the 16 per cent response might suggest. Amongst distillers, 'ownership, and therefore employment, is concentrated in some 15 major firms' (NEDO,1978). Respondents to the questionnaire on spirits paid 60 per cent of total spirits duty receipts in 1982-83, so response from major distillers was good.

Nature of Administrative and Compliance Costs of Excise Duties

General Pattern and Recent Changes

From the interviews it was clear that Customs and Excise officials and registered traders generally agreed that record-keeping for excise duties did not involve high marginal costs. The main costs imposed on registered firms collecting excise duties were physical costs, such as the installation and reading of checking meters; costs of co-operating with Customs and Excise random examinations; cash flow costs in some industries; and costs of payment guarantees — traders must take out guarantees if they are deferring payment to any extent.

As one interviewee from the Tobacco Advisory Council put it, 'the industry has lived with the government's hand in its pocket for hundreds of years; the costs are an essential part of the way we work'. This is typical of excise duties: it can be argued that, particularly in a period of unchanging duty regulations, the marginal compliance costs of excise duties are minimal. Clearly, however, costs may rise in a period of change.

It is clear that some costs are transferable between the revenue administration and the registered trader. There have been several major changes in excise duty practice since 1976. In particular, a major overhaul of the system for oil, tobacco and alcoholic drinks has taken place. In general terms, Customs and Excise have been moving towards a more accounts-based checking system. More reliance is now placed on the trader's own records and security than in the past (though Customs and Excise have powers to insist on improvement in record-keeping or security standards wherever they are deemed inadequate). There is a trend towards withdrawal of Customs and Excise presence at the factory/terminal: and there has been a transition period during which there has been a move away from Customs and Excise maintaining their own, definitive set of books for each registered trader, to a system which accepts the trader's records as definitive. These moves, whilst relieving traders from certain compliance costs, e.g. providing on-site accommodation for Customs and Excise staff, have to some extent shifted costs which were once part of the administrative burden on to the trader.

Deferred payment arrangements have also been introduced: previously, excise duties were payable as goods left the warehouse. In most cases, accounting periods run from the 15th of one month to the 14th of the next, with payment generally due on the 29th of the month following clearance at importation or removal from warehouse. In the case of tobacco products cleared from U.K. registered stores however, the accounting periods are calendar months, and duty is due on the 15th of the month following the month of clearance. The trader must produce a daily accounting advice at the time of remitting or deferring duty. Deferral of payment is only permitted on presentation of payment guarantees from a bank or insurance company, otherwise Customs and Excise require payment as each consignment of goods leaves the registered premises or bonded warehouse. (Some prospective entrants may experience difficulty in obtaining such guarantees).

The changes to individual duties are set out below.

Oil duty. A warehousing review, carried out by Customs and Excise, was implemented in October 1985. The duty point, beyond which duty becomes payable, was pulled back from the oil terminal (or 'distribution warehousing' stage of production) to the refinery (or 'manufacturing' stage). (Some import and export warehouses and intermediate storage warehouses are still bonded).

Tobacco. In 1976-78, a new system of tobacco duty payment was introduced representing a major change in administration, as a move towards harmonisation within the European Community. Until 1976, duty was paid as the raw tobacco (or 'leaf') came out of bond; thus the duty was payable prior to manufacture. The directives for harmonisation prescribed an end-product duty. The United Kingdom also had strict regulations prohibiting the addition of any non-tobacco substances to the leaf, in order to facilitate Customs and Excise control procedures. Most other European Community countries permitted some additives, and it was ruled that the U.K. regulations constituted a non-tariff barrier.

Spirits. The system of payment for distilled spirits has also been changed. In the control of spirits duty, there has been a move away from warehouses locked by Customs and Excise to a system based on the manufacturer's own security arrangements. The last Crown locks on 'maturation warehouses', in which whisky stocks have to be kept for at least three years, were removed by the end of March 1988.

Beer. The beer duty system remained essentially unchanged from 1894 up to the 1980s. Recently, there have been various moves towards modernisation and simplification. A record of 'brews' is kept at each brewery, and duty is payable according to the quantity and gravity (roughly related to strength) of beer produced. There has been a move from physical to documentary checks, with Customs using the brewer's own records for duty purposes. Responsibility for correct record keeping is now with the brewer. New regulations issued in 1985 allow for flexible arrangements and exceptions to the rule if necessary. From 1986, the use of traders' computerised record has been permitted, and in 1987 the procedures for spoilt beer relief and 'drawback' were simplified (including a special scheme for small brewers). All the brews from one month are included in a single declaration for duty purposes at the month-end. The brewer has 25 days from the date of declaration in which to pay the duty. This allows for the fact that, on average, beer is only ready for sale 10 days after the duty point has been reached. A 6 per cent allowance is made for losses during the production process after the duty point.

Type of Costs

The following categories of compliance cost can be distinguished.

(1)   *Costs associated with the artificially high value of the product.* Many of the costs associated with excise duties arise from the relatively high levels of duty, which mean that manufacturers respond as much to changes in duty regulations as to changes in consumer demand. An example of such 'indirect costs' is considered below.

One direct cost arising from high duty is that although goods are only worth the pre-tax price to the manufacturer, they are worth the post-tax price to the consumer; e.g. the most popular brand of cigarettes was valued by the manufacturers at £12.50 per 1,000 in 1986-87 but the public were prepared to pay the post-duty (and post-VAT) price of £76 per 1,000.

Because the manufacturer is responsible to Customs and Excise for safeguarding the product, and has to pay duty on unexplained losses, insurance and security costs are greater than would be the case if the product were duty-free. One of the largest tobacco manufacturers calculated that these additional costs came to £270,000 in 1983 (of which, strictly speaking, a proportion is attributable to VAT — but the main tax incurred is tobacco products duty — TPD). Thus, the cost of additional insurance at tax-inclusive prices is a major direct compliance cost of excise duties.

(2)   *Clerical costs.*   Most respondents reported that the marginal clerical costs of excise duties were minimal, though there was some evidence that the smaller firms were more conscious of having taken on additional clerical staff solely to deal with tax. This finding is in line with the general observation in compliance cost studies that small firms incur proportionally higher costs than large ones. Export paperwork for TPD is a particularly interesting area, in that manufacturers can opt for either a rebate system, or for a more heavily documented 'suspension' system, under which goods destined for export do not pay tax in the first place. There is thus a

trade-off between an improvement in cash flow and additional clerical work. Unsurprisingly, only the firms with low exports opted for the rebate system.

(3)   Costs of payment guarantees. Most firms (excluding brewers) incurred costs in insurance premiums or bank charges. Although Customs and Excise have the power to insist that duty payments are fully guaranteed, they generally make the concession that monthly guarantees need only cover the first £5m. per month in full, plus 20 per cent of the excess over £5m. As the smaller companies were quick to point out, the structure of this concession imposes disproportionately high costs on the small firm.

(4)   Inward processing/warehousing. There are a number of complications in the warehousing and inward processing, i.e. import regulations, which can cause additional difficulties to the manufacturer, such as the difference between the older bonded warehouses and the newer registered stores. In general, however, Customs and Excise seem to have been very flexible in their interpretation of the rules, and have assisted the manufacturers where possible. After some transitional awkwardness, there is now little distinction in the excise rules applying to bonded warehouses and registered stores.

Measuring the Costs of Compliance

Many of the firms interviewed found it difficult to quantify compliance costs accurately; for example, two large tobacco manufacturers both stated that additional accounting and security costs were 'minimal', and felt unable to make a more precise estimate.

Tobacco Industry. There were no substantial changes to the tobacco duty system between 1983 and 1987. It seems unlikely that any firm incurred total compliance costs of more than £500,000 in the year of the survey, and it is probable that the regular costs of the smaller firms were much less than this — say £100,000 or £150,000. Even on the basis of the incomplete information supplied, the total regular direct costs to the seven manufacturers in the industry were clearly less than £2m. in 1982-83, i.e. about 0.13 per cent of pre-tax turnover. Up-rating these costs in line with the rise in average earnings, 1986-87 compliance costs would have been about £2.7m.

Alcoholic Drinks Industry. Mean costs for distillers as reported in questionnaire responses averaged £124,366, or 0.32 per cent of duty payments, for the 14 respondents providing information. The pattern of costs as a percentage of duty was regressive; but the number of cases was small, and variances were large. Unfortunately, cost:duty ratios are not an ideal yardstick where the industry produces largely for export (and therefore tax-free), selling much of its output to bonded warehousing companies. On the administrative side, Customs and Excise devote substantial resources to the non-revenue activity of ensuring that duty free production does, in fact, go for export. The compliance costs of operating the bonded warehouse system are considered below.

Assuming that the average cost:payment ratio of 0.31 per cent was correct, compliance costs for 1982-83 would have been something over £3m. Up-rating this figure by the rise in earnings between 1982 and 1986 would give compliance costs of £4m. in 1986-87. This latter figure may be something of an over-estimate, bearing in mind that the major changes accompanying the introduction of duty deferment could have caused a temporary increase in costs during the survey year.

Brewers' compliance costs as reported in the survey averaged £20,829 for 46 respondents. A reasonable spread of responses was forthcoming, and the response rate was nearly 40 per cent. However, there were some oddities in the costs when measured as a percentage of duty: for their size groups, costs for two firms were very low, while in one case a very high percentage was reported. There seemed to be no obvious reason for these discontinuities. Other than these three firms, a regressive pattern of costs was apparent.

In percentage terms, brewers' compliance costs were very low: only one-sixth of one per cent of duty payments. Assuming that this average cost:payment ratio was correct, compliance costs would have totalled less than £2.5m. in 1982-83, rising in line with earnings to about £3.4m. in 1986-87.

Since 1983 the transfer to brewers' own records as the basis on which duty is assessed will have increased compliance costs and reduced administrative costs; however, the increased flexibility of recent years may have offset the compliance cost increase.

Only six other drink manufacturers provided adequate information on compliance costs. Mean compliance costs for these six respondents were £12,947, or 0.44 per cent of duty payments. (Again, one case reporting a very high percentage, 15.3 per cent, pushed the average up). Thus, costs would have been around £2.3m. in 1982-83, rising to £3.1m.

in 1986-87; but the small number of cases, and the presence of an outlier, makes this estimate fairly speculative.

Costs of Warehouse Keepers. In addition, the bulk of revenue from wine duty comes from imports, and the mail survey only covered domestic drink manufacture. An interview with the National Association of Warehouse Keepers (NAWK), who represented more than 80 per cent of the warehouse keepers involved with Customs and Excise, suggested that the compliance costs of warehousing excisable goods had increased substantially since the early 1980s. Again, the main reason for the increase in costs is the transfer to the industry of duties formerly carried out by Customs and Excise staff. Costs for 1982-83 were relatively low, averaging £6,000 per warehouse, or £0.3m. altogether. The 1986-87 warehouse keepers' costs would have been about £50,000 per warehouse, or £2.5m. in total (for the 50 NAWK bonded warehouse members). This estimate may be on the low side because of the existence of some warehouse keepers who are not members of the trade association. But the only major importers outside NAWK are supermarkets who use bonded warehouses to keep 'buffer stocks' of their own branded imports. Customs and Excise argue strongly that the compliance costs which the supermarkets choose to incur are actually negative, because they could opt to pay duty on importation (with one month's deferment of duty) but have chosen, for commercial reasons, to incur warehousing costs instead. (Customs and Excise have recently acted to curb this 'short stay' use of bonded warehouses). Neither the Customs and Excise nor the private sector was able to allocate the costs of the warehousing system between the separate duties on alcoholic drinks, although the control of wine was stated, by Customs and Excise, to be more labour intensive than the control of spirits.

Oil Industry. No detailed quantitative data was obtained for the oil industry, but interviews supported the picture given by large tobacco manufacturers and large distillers. There were 74 duty-paying companies, of whom 12 contributed 95 per cent of the revenue. While some definite costs could be identified — such as the costs of separately marking and storing oil qualifying for rebate of duty — the orders of magnitude involved were small relative to tax payments: perhaps no more than one-quarter of one per cent (which is the unweighted average of compliance costs of the duties considered above). Assuming this figure to be approximately correct for 1983, costs would have been around £13.1m.; up-rating this figure by the rise in average earnings would have increased them to £17.6m. in 1986-87.

However, we do know that Customs and Excise saved 110 staff from changes implemented in 1985. Assuming that the functions of the administrative staff saved were in some measure transferred to similar staff in the private sector, it is likely that private sector costs rose despite the reduction in the number of duty points. So some upward adjustment to the 1986-87 private sector compliance cost might be justified.

Indirect Costs of Compliance — the Example of the Tobacco Industry

Before turning to any benefits of compliance and then reviewing administrative and compliance costs together, it is worth examining the way the tobacco industry has been affected over time by its need to comply with duty requirements. The industry provides a remarkable example of how the *form* of a tax, more particularly when that tax is high, can have major economic consequences for an industry (quite apart from the overall effect on the demand for its product); and how there can also be major economic consequences of changes in the manner in which a tax is levied.

Under the reformed system for cigarettes (which constitute the vast bulk of tobacco sales), duty is imposed on the finished product. The duty is of a mixed *ad valorem* and specific type: it is partly a percentage duty on the manufacturer's recommended retail selling price, and partly a specific duty per thousand cigarettes manufactured. This system superseded the very different 'leaf duty' system, under which duty was paid on the raw material rather than the end product.

'The leaf duty system was running the industry, not the other way round' commented one tobacco manufacturer; 'A large number of people were employed sweeping and cleaning wherever possible to reclaim duty on tobacco dust; leaf was dehydrated so as not to pay duty on water whenever possible. Tax was paid with a guaranteed cheque before a consignment of leaf left bond — this necessitated a fixed slab of investment which kept a lot of people out of the industry. We used to gear manufacturing to sales for duty reasons; sales fluctuations led to labour being hired and fired. Now stocks of manufactured goods are duty-free and we can concentrate on training permanent staff to use the new technology'. Adjectives including 'appalling' and 'diabolical' were used by other interviewees to describe the old system.

Although there clearly were direct costs of changing from the leaf duty system to the end product duty, they were not stressed by any interviewee. These costs could all be traced back to the way the tax was administered, because the manufacturing process used expensive, duty-paid material. It also became clear that these costs had virtually disappeared with the new regulations.

The current duty system was relatively popular; Customs and Excise had consulted the Tobacco Advisory Council extensively in designing it. As an 'end product' tax, imposed at point of sale to the retailer, duty is not carried by stocks of raw materials or manufactured goods, so working capital is reduced, and as noted by one interviewee above, costs of entry into the industry are thus cut. The permanent simplifications made possible in the manufacturing process by the switch much outweighed any temporary costs of change.

On the other hand, the indirect effects of the change were substantial. Under the leaf duty regime, manufacturers were given a massive incentive to economise in the use of (duty-paid) tobacco. Consequently, small cigarettes gained a considerable price advantage over large ('king size') cigarettes. Competition took the form of coupon and premium offers, rather than pricing policy. Imperial Tobacco had invested especially heavily in the technology for producing small cigarettes in very large numbers; relatively few king size cigarettes were bought.

United Kingdom cigarette consumption was just over 100 billion cigarettes per annum in both 1982 and 1983, falling to 95 billion in 1986. Consumption has declined substantially from a peak of over 137 billion in 1973. This decline is largely attributable to the continuing fall in the proportion of adults who smoke, which has been influenced by duty increases and government anti-smoking measures.

When the duty was reformed, the form of the large specific element in the new system (i.e. a charge per 1,000 cigarettes regardless of size) reduced the price differential between small and king size cigarettes, and the latter became the biggest selling brands. (Thus, the decline in tobacco consumption is less than the decline in cigarettes smoked, as demand has switched to larger cigarettes). In the mid 1970s, king size cigarettes constituted 12.5 per cent of the market: a decade later they held 85 per cent. Gallagher, who manufacture the leading king size brand, had become market leader by 1988 with about 40 per cent of the cigarette market, whilst the share of Imperial, who had become 'locked in' to the declining small cigarette sector, had fallen from 65.5 to around 35 per cent.

Some direct duty-associated costs peculiar to the tobacco industry remain. An interesting cost is that, since the reform, in accordance with European Community directives, the *ad valorem* element of TPD has been charged on the manufacturers' *recommended* retail price, not the *actual* retail price. If actual retail prices are lower than recommended prices (as is often the case in supermarkets), it can be argued that duty is being overpaid. Given prevailing patterns of discount, the extra duty amounts to about one per cent of the total cigarette duty yield.

One small manufacturer had reduced recommended retail prices in order to cut duty payments, but emphasised that this was only possible because the bulk of their output was sold through cut-price outlets: a firm selling largely at higher prices through traditional outlets would prefer overpaying duty to cutting prices across the board. It is not unlikely that more low-priced brands aimed specifically at the multiple store outlets will be launched, especially if the European Commission proposals, which would increase the *ad valorem* component, are adopted. (See Chapter 13).

During the 1970s the rise of cut-price sales through supermarket chains and cash-and-carry wholesalers partly replaced traditional confectionery, tobacco and newsagent (CTN) retailers. In conjunction with the EEC-inspired competitive improvements, and the overall decline of the industry, this change led to keen price competition from the late 1970s onwards. Two smaller firms, spotting the gaps in the market created by changing conditions, entered the industry, selling largely through supermarkets and other non-traditional outlets and competing mainly on price. It is questionable whether this would have happened under the leaf duty system, under which the large slab of fixed investment in duty-paid raw material served as a barrier to entry.

The 'own-label' market has become of increasing importance since 1983. Given the reluctance of the U.K. major tobacco companies to enter this market, it has come to be serviced largely by importers from Western Europe. Imported cigarettes had around 13 per cent of the total United Kingdom cigarette market in 1986-87.

Thus, the change in the duty structure altered relative prices in the industry and changed patterns of demand radically. Investment in capital equipment, marketing and advertising expenditure specific to the declining small cigarette sector became outdated. Competitive conditions alone did not determine the way in which the industry behaved: the manner in which the duty was imposed also made a major contribution to success and failure in the market.

Benefits of Compliance

Whether there is a cash flow benefit or indeed a detriment arising from payment of the various main excise duties is very difficult to determine with excise duties. As described in Chapter 3, the existence of a benefit (or detriment) to the private sector depends on whether or not the economic transaction giving rise to the tax liability on the part of the final consumer (the intended taxpayer) is before or after the date that the manufacturer is required to pay. If, on average, the final consumer receives the goods for consumption before that date, then there is a benefit; the distribution of that benefit is then a matter of the conditions of commercial credit which are a part of the total competitive situation within an industry. Our study enables us to say something about the cash flow position of the manufacturers, but very little about whether there is a cash flow benefit to the private sector as a whole, which is the more important issue for tax policy.

For all manufacturers of dutiable products the period during which duty is collected is one month. Hence, assuming an even flow of payments, the average tax held by manufacturers each month is one-half of this sum, i.e. $T/24$, where T is the annual duty payment. For all manufacturers (except brewers) the duty is not actually paid over until 15 days after the end of the accounting period; so the *whole* month's duty is retained in the private sector for a further 15 days (i.e. half of one month). Hence the total additional cash available is $T/24 + T/24 = T/12$. This process occurs every month, so the average additional cash held throughout the year since the introduction of duty deferment will be $T/12$, equivalent to one average month's duty payment.

In the case of breweries, the grace period is nominally 25 days, but it begins at the *start* of fermentation, which takes 10 days on average, rather than at the completion of manufacture. Hence the 'net' grace period is again 15 days.

Thus, the existence of a benefit to the private sector as a whole depends on whether the final consumer actually receives the goods within a month of them leaving bond. If they are bought by the final consumer one day in advance of the duty payment date (on average), then the overall benefit to the private sector is $1/365$ T x the going rate of interest; if they are bought one day after the duty payment date, there is an overall detriment to the private sector of the same amount. If the final consumer buys the goods before the duty payment date, but does not pay for them until afterwards, there is still a cash flow benefit to the private sector — but it has all accrued to the final consumer and there has been a net cash flow detriment to producers taken together; however, this is all part of the competitive process, in which credit has been allowed to the final customer as part of the package which makes the product more attractive.

(It will normally be associated with a higher price or some offsetting disadvantage).

Tobacco. Without a detailed examination of the retailing process it is not possible to say whether there is an overall cash flow benefit to the private sector and how much. The time taken for the product to reach the final consumer from the manufacturer depends very much on the nature of the retail outlet. The turnover of goods is very much higher in a supermarket (hence the throughput time is much lower) than with the traditional outlets. From our study we can make a few remarks about the position of the manufacturers, but that does not give us the answer to the more important question of the cash benefit to the private sector as a whole.

It seemed likely that tobacco *manufacturers*, overall, obtained a net cash benefit from collecting duty of about 1.5 days per month. But even as between manufacturers the position varied; new entrants to the industry, which were also the smaller businesses, offered more generous credit terms as part of their marketing package (or were forced to accept unfavourable credit terms by powerful customers such as supermarkets).

Alcoholic Drinks. As with tobacco, the position on whether there is an overall cash flow benefit or detriment to the private sector can only be discovered by a very detailed examination of marketing; sales through a supermarket may take place, on average, before the duty payment date, whilst a specialist wine importer may keep duty-paid goods in stock for months. Unlike the tobacco industry, alcoholic drink manufacturers generally incurred cash detriments. Reported costs were greatest for distillers, averaging 17 days' net cost after commercial credit terms have been taken into account; breweries averaged 5 days' net cost, and other alcoholic drink manufacturers reported 3 days' net cost. However, the introduction of duty deferment for distillers was not fully implemented at the time to which the survey related and it is therefore certain that the cash flow detriment reported in this industry will have been reduced.

Hydrocarbon Oils. Until 1985, duty became payable as oil left the terminal. This necessarily meant a substantial cash flow detriment to the private sector. Under the 1985 reforms, duty deferment was introduced, but, because the duty point has been pulled back to an earlier stage in the production process, the U.K. industry is still at a disadvantage compared to other EC countries, where the duty point remains at the terminal. Duty deferment was seen as a *quid pro quo* for this backward movement of the duty point. Customs and Excise were reluctant to make any concession which would cause the Exchequer to suffer a cash flow loss. Because of these changes, interviewees were unable to estimate the cash flow effects of hydrocarbon oil duty, though some evidence was obtained that manufacturers were imposing more stringent credit conditions on their customers since the change. It is clear that during the negotiations on duty deferment between Customs and Excise and the industry, both sides had been keenly aware of the potential benefit to be obtained; and it is unlikely that either side would have conceded a substantial benefit to the other.

Nonetheless the distribution of road fuels, already quicker than on the Continent, appears to have speeded up since the 1985 changes, with 20 per cent more delivered direct to garages from refinery warehouses. With changes of this sort still under way, the cash flow effects of hydrocarbon oil duty remain largely conjectural.

For excises as for VAT, a notable feature, which could bring managerial benefits, was better record-keeping. One small tobacco manufacturer mentioned that the record-keeping requirements imposed because of TPD reduced the cost of employing outside accountants and it is possible that other small firms experienced similar benefits — though it would be difficult to disentangle the VAT effects from the excise duty effects.

Administrative and Compliance Costs of Main Excises, 1986-87

Table 10.3 summarises the administrative costs and estimated compliance costs of the main excise duties in 1986-87.

Table 10.3 Administrative and Compliance Costs of the Main Excises, in Relation to Revenue Yield, 1986-87

		Admin Costs		Compliance Costs		Operating Costs	
	Revenue £m.	£m.	% of revenue	£m.	% of revenue	£m.	% of revenue
Hydrocarbon oil	7,508	7.8	0.10	17.6	0.23	25.4	0.34
Tobacco products	4,768	3.7	0.08	2.7	0.06	6.4	0.13
Alcoholic drinks	4,195	30.4	0.72	13.0	0.31	43.4	1.03
Overall	16,470	41.9	0.25	33.3	0.20	75.2	0.45

An important feature of administrative costs is their reduction, since 1982-83, both as a percentage of revenue and in real terms. In 1982-83 the administrative costs of hydrocarbon oil were 0.2 per cent of tax revenue (against 0.10 per cent in 1986-87); for tobacco products the corresponding figure was 0.1 per cent (0.08); and for alcoholic drinks 1.0 (0.72). Combined administrative costs for these duties had risen only slightly from £40.4m. in 1982-83 to £41.9m. in 1986-87, implying a substantial fall in real terms. These figures reflect the withdrawal of constant Customs and Excise presence in registered traders' premises and the transfer of much of the accounting and security work to the private sector. Administrative savings have been largest in the areas of recent reforms.

Ignoring the important indirect costs, the overall compliance costs of the main excise duties are estimated to be of the order of £33m. in 1986-87, very much on a par with the administrative costs. Together these totalled £74m. or 0.45 per cent of revenue yield.

Admittedly the compliance cost estimates in this chapter are much more speculative than those for income tax and VAT, which were based on large sample surveys. But even allowing for these deficiencies, a clear picture emerges: administrative costs in 1986-87 were only one-quarter of one per cent of revenue, and compliance costs were, if anything, lower than administrative costs. Even if the compliance costs have been significantly under-estimated it would still be true that an outstanding merit of excise duties in comparison to broad-based taxes on income or consumption is that their direct costs of operation are lower, both in relative and in absolute terms.

Summary of Main Conclusions

Although the estimates of compliance cost in this chapter are somewhat speculative it is clear that both the administrative and the compliance costs of the main excises are outstandingly low, in absolute and proportional terms.

There was some evidence to suggest that smaller firms faced higher compliance costs proportionately but the effects were not as pronounced as with VAT.

The tobacco industry offers a remarkable example of the significance of the form of duty on the organisation and economics of an industry; and also an example of the economic consequences of changes in duty form.

There are no known international studies with which to compare these findings.

CHAPTER 11

OTHER TAXES

Introduction

In this chapter we look at the remaining United Kingdom taxes except for those which, for the conceptual or practical reasons outlined in Chapter 4, were omitted from the study. The justification for grouping them into one chapter is that, in absolute terms, their compliance costs are very small. However, the chapter divides very clearly into two sections. In the first section we consider the remaining taxes administered by Inland Revenue and Customs and Excise — small revenue yielders, none of which bring in as much as 1.5 per cent of total revenue from taxation. In the second section we consider local taxation, the local rates, which yield a large revenue but have exceptionally low compliance costs.

Because the compliance costs are manifestly small, comprehensive surveys, to obtain as precise a measure as possible, would not have been justified. What is presented here, therefore, is an outline of each tax, a statement of the administrative costs and an indication of the nature of the compliance costs. A rough estimate of the size of the compliance cost is then made, based on an analysis of the processes required to comply and the views of officials in the public sector and tax advisers in the private sector with whom the issues were discussed. The most extensive of the discussions took place in respect of inheritance tax, which is the one tax in this chapter where compliance costs, though small in absolute terms, were relatively high at an estimated 4 per cent of tax revenue.

I. MINOR TAXES

Stamp Duty
Outline

Because of their ease of collection (and perhaps also their importance to the taxpayer in authenticating documents) stamp duties have a long history. Recent years have seen the abolition of a number of small duties yielding little revenue.

In 1986-87 there were three main categories of stamp duty: on the sale of stocks and shares, on the sale and leasing of land and buildings, and capital duty on the raising of new capital. The combined yield was £1,860m. and the administrative cost was £5.9m.

Compliance Costs

Of the £800m. or so of revenue derived from sale of stocks and shares about £600m. in value was dealt with through the Stock Exchange 'talisman' mechanism as a part of a computerised settlement system and the compliance cost was minimal. The remaining £200m. was dealt with by the Stamp Duty Office in the same way as conveyances.

In 1986-87 there were just over a million conveyances of land and buildings, yielding £660m. The procedure is usually straightforward and, at the taxpayer's end, will normally be dealt with by a clerk in the solicitor's office. The solicitor submits, at the same time, the document and the duty to the Stamp Duty Office, listing the documents on a form designed by the Inland Revenue for the convenience of the solicitor. There were some 200,000 leases created in 1986-87, yielding £50m. revenue. Existing leases are transferred in the same manner as other conveyances, but new leases are more complex. The duty on new leases of land, buildings and other property is charged separately on the elements of rent and premium and the rental part depends on the average rent and the period of the lease, giving rise to more complicated calculations than with sales. Officials suggested that, at the Stamp Duty Office, it might take four times as long to deal with a lease as with a sale. More correspondence was involved with leases sometimes because the taxpayer (or his solicitor) got the calculation wrong. Moreover more care was required with business leases where the amount of money at issue could be large.

It follows that the compliance costs of the grants of new leases would also be higher than those arising from sales. The longer time taken, the additional correspondence and the need to employ higher grade staff, especially on business leases, would put up the compliance costs.

For grants of leases on furnished property a fixed fee of £1 is charged, which (taking compliance and administrative cost together) is barely worth collecting; but some taxpayers may like to have the leasing agreement stamped as providing authentication should there be subsequent disputes. If the agreement is for a year or more, duty is charged as on any other lease on the same terms.

Capital duty was charged at the rate of one per cent on the raising of new capital by a company. In the 1988 Budget it was abolished; but in 1986-87 it was levied on about 125,000 documents, yielding nearly £200 million in revenue. Because capital duty required a value to be put on the shares it could be time-consuming in the case of unquoted companies. However, because the rate of duty was low, protracted negotiations were unusual. Not infrequently an agreement would be made between taxpayer and Revenue that the valuation agreed was 'without prejudice'; so that, for example, neither side could use it in subsequent negotiations over other taxes such as inheritance tax or CGT. Such an agreement speeded up the outcome.

Stamp duty is a self-assessed tax and the onus is on the taxpayer to send in the documents and calculate the tax. We should expect compliance costs to be rather more than the (very low) administrative costs, where the civil servant is primarily checking and stamping. On the other hand the operations are generally so simple that the compliance cost must also be low. Considering the nature of the work, the number of documents and the charges of solicitors, a reasonable guess might be about two to three times the administrative cost, or some £15m. There is also a cash flow benefit to the Stock Exchange which serves to offset their costs in connection with stamp duty.

Inheritance Tax

Outline

Inheritance tax (IHT) is a donor-based death duty which goes back in origin to the estate duty introduced by Sir William Harcourt in 1894. It applies to individuals, close companies and trusts. From March 18, 1986 to March 16, 1987, it was levied on transfers of property at death at progressive rates in seven marginal rate (or 'slice') bands rising from 30 per cent to 60 per cent above a threshold of £71,000. The tax aggregates gifts with gifts and with the estate at death in relation to the previous seven years; but lifetime transfers between individuals (or into certain trusts for the benefit of individuals) are only charged if the transferor dies within seven years. Where gifts are immediately chargeable the rate is half that at death. Gifts within three years before death attract the death tax rate; gifts more than three but less than seven years before death are subject to a tapering rate. Transfers between spouses are wholly exempt (except where the recipient is domiciled outside the United Kingdom). There are a number of exemptions for charitable or heritage objects and special reliefs for agriculture and some business assets.

A discretionary trust is subject to a charge every 10 years on the total value of the assets.

Thresholds and rate bands are increased annually in line with the retail price index unless Parliament determines otherwise.

With lifetime transfers accounts are only required by the Capital Taxes Office for gifts that are chargeable when made; for transfers which are exempt unless the transferor dies within seven years, which are known as potentially exempt transfers (PETs), no account is required unless the gift actually becomes chargeable.

An account in respect of a deceased person has to be presented at a Probate Registry, and any tax due has to be paid before a grant of representation can be obtained, subject to certain *de minimis* limits. Where the exact value of the property is not known the executors may submit a provisional account. In general accounts must be rendered within twelve months of the end of the month in which the death or transfer occurs.

In 1986-87, including some remaining elements of the previous estate duty and capital transfer tax, the revenue yield was £995m. and the official administrative cost was £24.1m.

Compliance Costs

Particular difficulties arise in seeking to measure the compliance costs of IHT for two main reasons. Tax planning in relation to IHT may take place many years before a death; indeed, in so far as the tax planning includes taking advantage of PETs, it will be vitiated, wholly or partly, unless it takes place more than seven years before the death. Secondly, the compliance costs of IHT are the additional costs of administering an estate (or a life-time transfer) which would not have occurred had there been no tax; and the proportion of the cost of administration of the estate which IHT costs represent will vary very much with the circumstances. To take two extremes. If the whole of an estate at death was left to one person an accurate valuation would not be necessary in order to administer the estate in accordance with the wishes of the deceased. In this case all the valuation costs must be attributed to IHT. At the other extreme, if an estate was left to be divided in equal shares by value amongst a number of inheritors, the valuation would be required anyway to implement the will and the additional cost attributable to IHT is minimal.

Apart from tax planning, from a series of some ten interviews with solicitors and accountants specifically dealing with IHT, located in London and three provincial towns, the main aspects of IHT which particularly generated high compliance costs were indicated as follows: share valuations of unquoted companies; chasing up the value of PETs which became chargeable; problems associated with gifts with reservations (including uncertainty about when a gift was subject to the reservation rules given the unwillingness of the Revenue authorities to give advance rulings); queries about domicile when two countries were each trying to get their hands on the revenue; and the complications caused by frequent legislative changes.

One particular compliance cost was that in order to pay the (provisional) death duty to obtain probate the money might have to be borrowed. (Strictly speaking, the estate assets could not be used for this purpose, but 'free' assets, such as those from a trust could be). Respondents differed somewhat in their views about how significant such costs might be. Some leeway could be obtained by making creditors wait for payment; but bank borrowing could be expensive. (If the provisional payment is an under-estimate of the sum due, it should be noted that no interest is payable on overdue tax until after six months from the death).

The general consensus amongst the interviewees was that pre-death tax planning took place in about 10-20 per cent of cases in relation to estates above a value of £200,000 or so. Much of the cost of tax planning consisted of the time taken by the consultant to discover the assets and the particular needs of the client. Tax planning mainly took the form of making full use of the annual gifts exemption; the exemption where the gift constituted normal expenditure from income; the utilisation of these exemptions to pay the premiums on a life policy payable on the death of the estate owner in favour of a third party; life policies written in trust; and settlements, including discretionary trusts.

When asked what proportion of the cost of administering an estate, on average, might be attributable to IHT, the estimates of interviewees ranged from '20 per cent or less' to 40 per cent; but these estimates did not include the cost of additional professionals, such as valuers.

Inevitably the estimate of the compliance cost of IHT must be somewhat arbitrary. It has been calculated on the following assumptions based generally on the information provided by interviewees.

(1)   Pre-death tax planning was undertaken by 15 per cent of those owning estates in excess of £200,000 and the average charge for the work was £500.

(2)   IHT work accounted for 40 per cent of the cost of administering a taxable estate (including any re-arrangements for tax purposes) and administration fees were 3 per cent on the first £100,000, 2 per cent on the next £100,000 and 1 per cent thereafter. (The top figure of 40 per cent has been taken to allow for fees to other professional advisers and for IHT compliance costs in respect of estates where costs were incurred but no duty needed to be paid).

(3)   An average fee of £200 was paid for the IHT costs associated with the discretionary trusts liable for the ten-year anniversary charge assessed in 1986-87.

(4)   Any compliance costs for immediately chargeable gifts could be treated as negligible, as such gifts were very few in number under the provisions ruling in 1986-87.

Applying these assumptions to some approximate figures provided by Inland Revenue on the numbers and distribution of estates in 1986 and the numbers of discretionary trusts yields the results set out in Table 11.1.

Table 11.1 Estimated Compliance Costs of Inheritance Tax, 1986-87

£m.

Compliance Costs associated with:	
Pre-death tax planning	0.6
IHT on estates of deceased	38.4
IHT on discretionary trusts	0.1
Total	39.1

On the basis of these rough calculations, the compliance costs of IHT in 1986-87 represented 3.93 per cent of revenue yield and the total operating costs 6.35 per cent.

Car Tax

Outline

Car tax was introduced in 1973 when VAT, at 10 per cent, replaced purchase tax which had been levied at 25 per cent on the wholesale value of cars. Car tax was intended to compensate for the loss of revenue which would otherwise have occurred. The tax is levied in most cases at 10 per cent of the wholesale value and is paid in the main by United Kingdom manufacturers and the major importers, but non-registered persons importing a car are liable at the point of importation. There are approximately 135 car tax registered traders.

As with VAT, exports are relieved of tax, returns from registered traders have to be made quarterly and a grace period of one month after the end of the quarter is allowed for the submission of the previous quarter's return and payment. The premises of registered car traders are subject to inspection on similar lines to those of VAT traders.

In 1986-87 car tax raised £960m. of revenue at an administrative cost of £2m. (0.2 per cent of tax revenue).

Compliance Costs

As the yield from car tax is £960m., assuming all revenue to come from registered traders, it follows that the aggregate turnover is £9,600m. plus the value of exports or an average of £71m. plus average exports for each registered trader. Thus, we are dealing with a small number of traders, with a high average turnover. Further, car tax is somewhat less complex than VAT because there is no requirement to deduct input tax and because its coverage is so limited. These differences will be reflected both in administrative and in compliance costs, but in other respects the administrative arrangements are similar to VAT. It would thus seem reasonable to estimate the compliance costs by up-rating the administrative costs of £2.0m. by the ratio that the VAT compliance costs bear to the VAT administrative costs, i.e. 3.58 (see Chapter 8). This gives an estimated compliance cost for car tax of £7.16m., or 0.75 per cent of tax revenue.

Registered car traders get a substantial cash flow benefit. Assuming an even flow of receipts, they would, like VAT traders, be holding, on average, one-and-a-half month's tax during the collection period and one month's tax during the grace period, equivalent to 5/24T where T is the annual tax payment. The value of the cash flow benefit would be 5/24T x r where r is the rate of interest (10.5 per cent in 1986-87). This gives a cash flow benefit of £21m. for 1986-87, almost three times the compliance cost. This figure makes no allowance for non-registered traders, who get no cash flow benefit, so it is a slight over-estimation. As with VAT, the distribution of the benefit depends on trade credit terms and becomes part of the whole complex of market competition.

Betting and Gaming

Outline

Betting and gaming duties comprised a general betting duty which, in 1986-87, consisted of two distinct duties: off-course bookmaking and on-course bookmaking; a pool betting duty; a gaming licence duty (relating to premises); a gaming machine licence duty; and a bingo duty.

Table 11.2 gives the revenue, 1986-87, from each of those duties. There is no breakdown available of administrative cost between the duties. The official figure for the overall administrative cost was £6.9m., representing 0.88 per cent of revenue.

Table 11.2 Revenue from Betting and Gaming Duties 1986-87

Tax	Revenue £m.
General betting duty	346.5
Pool betting duty	254.2
Gaming licence (premises) duty	52.3
Gaming machine licence duty	74.7
Bingo duty	54.0
Total Revenue	781.7

The following paragraphs give more details about the individual duties in turn, especially the features likely to affect compliance costs.

General Betting Duty: In 1986-87 the rate of duty was 8 per cent of the stake money on off-course bets made with a bookmaker or through a totalisator; the rate on on-course bets (until abolished, March 29, 1987) was 4 per cent.

Bookmakers must register and give security to Customs and Excise of four weeks' average duty liability by means of a cash deposit equal to four weeks' average duty liability; or a bond; or a deposit account. A record of all bets must be kept on numbered slips of which the punter receives a copy. A betting duty account must be kept in a book provided by Customs and Excise and all bets entered therein by noon on the first working day following the day on which the bets were made. Monthly returns are normally required for each betting office, but arrangements can be made for composite returns. The return has to be submitted within 15 days of the end of the month to which it relates. Normally the calendar month is used, but if the accounting periods of the business are different (e.g. ending on the last Saturday of the month) businesses may be allowed to vary the period. Betting slips must be kept for six months and all other records, bank statements, etc., for six years.

The main compliance costs are obviously the cost of the security required and the strict record-keeping and retention requirements. On the other hand, the cash flow benefit of the bookmaker approximately equals in value the cost of the required security; and records of bets and customer receipts are essential to the nature of the business, so that the additional record-keeping requirements of the tax are not excessive. (Some of the large bookmakers in any case photocopy the betting slips for internal security reasons). The enforcement of a strict orderly procedure has its advantages for the business as for the Customs and Excise.

The number of registered on-course bookmakers was about 2,200 and, off-course, about 3,200 for about 10,000 betting shops. One or two large firms operate major chains of betting shops.

Pool Betting Duty. This duty applies mainly to football pools but can apply to fixed odds coupon betting and to other betting where the punter is unable to calculate in advance his exact winnings if successful. The rate of duty was 42.5 per cent of the stake money in 1986-87; promotion wholly for charities was exempt.

Pool promoters are required to make a weekly return of the total stakes and the duty, which must be remitted to Customs and Excise by the Thursday of the following week. A (free) permit is required for each of the premises used for the business. No particular form of record-keeping is laid down, but such records must be kept as will enable the duty to be calculated and verified. Coupons and tickets must be retained for three months and other documents and accounts for two years.

Well over 90 per cent of revenue is derived from two large operators and the total number of pool betting premises does not exceed ten. It is clear that the compliance costs are minimal.

Gaming licence (premises) duty. The licence is for casino-type premises; each licence covers a period of up to six months ending either on 31 March or 30 September. The duty is paid in two stages; (1) £250 on application; (2) a second payment, not later than five months after the end of the period covered by the licence, according to a progressive scale on the 'gross gaming yield' (which may be broadly defined as stakes less winnings).

In 1986-87 the rates ranged from 2.5 per cent to 33.3 per cent as follows:

Part of Gross Gaming Yield	*Rate* %
First £375,000	2.5
Next £1,875,000	12.5
Next £2,250,000	25
Remainder	33.3

Return forms supplied by Customs and Excise require information on both gross gaming yield and a general financial statement for the club's last full financial year. It is a requirement of the duty that the declaration of gross gaming yield must be certified by an independent qualified accountant.

Thus the compliance costs amount to the obligation to apply for a licence every six months and the record-keeping requirements. A collection period of six months and a grace period of five months constitutes a substantial cash flow offset.

The number of licence holders is small: 120 in the six month period to end March 1987.

Gaming Machine Licence Duty. Licences may be for a period of three, six or twelve months at rates of duty which vary according to type of machine. Licences are of two kinds — ordinary and special. Ordinary licences (for all types of gaming machine) are granted in respect of the premises and cover only the number and type of machines shown on them. Special licences apply only to small prize machines and are granted in respect of the machine (a minimum of ten special licences must be held). Compliance costs consist of the (minimal) costs of applying for licences and the more significant cost that payment has to be made with the application, so that the licensee incurs a cash flow detriment. Record-keeping is almost nil. Licences have to be displayed and special licence holders must keep a record of the location, serial numbers of model and licence of each machine with the commencement and expiry dates.

Bingo Duty. The duty applies to bingo other than 'small scale bingo', e.g. bingo in members' clubs where the stakes *or* the prizes do not exceed £400 on any one day or £1,000 in any week. The duty is chargeable as a percentage of money staked by players for their cards (10 per cent in 1986-87) plus a fraction (one-ninth in 1986-87) by which the weekly value of prizes exceeds the duty exclusive value of the stakes (the 'added prize' money).

Premises at which chargeable bingo is played must be registered with Customs and Excise and a duty account kept showing each week details such as the total amount taken as payment for bingo cards, the value of prizes, the 'added prize money' and the amount of duty. Bingo cards must have serialised numbers and a strict record kept of their use. All records must be kept for a minimum of two years. Returns are made monthly, submitted not later than 15 days after the end of the month to which they relate.

The main compliance cost is therefore the requirement to maintain strict records; as an offset, the collection period and the grace period give a cash flow benefit of (on average) one-twelfth of the annual tax paid.

There are about 900 registered bingo promoters with many more halls; some promoters are large and submit composite returns. The registered promoters divide about equally between commercial promoters and clubs.

Because of the rules in respect of the small scale bingo exception, clubs which engage in bingo but are not liable to duty because they fall below the specified levels nonetheless are required to keep similar records to liable bingo promoters, so that these records can be checked by Customs and Excise officials to validate their exemption. They thus incur a compliance cost against a nil liability and without any cash flow benefit. On the other hand, the kind of records they are required to keep are such as would be necessary in a well-run business.

Aggregate Compliance Costs

The compliance costs associated with the betting and gaming duties appear not to be excessive and, generally speaking, to involve little more work than would be required for business purposes. A reasonable guess would be that the compliance costs are of the same order of magnitude as the administrative costs, at or just below one per cent of tax revenue.

International Comparisons

There are no known studies of the compliance costs of any of these minor taxes in other countries.

However, there has been a study of the administrative and compliance costs of one capital tax elsewhere — the Irish wealth tax (Sandford and Morrissey, 1985). As the Labour Party in the United Kingdom has sought to bring in such a tax and other countries are interested in the possibility of a wealth tax, a brief review of the findings may be of interest.

The Irish introduced an annual net wealth tax on individuals and trusts in 1975 and abolished it in 1978; it was effective for three financial years. The tax was levied on individuals at a rate of one per cent above a high threshold: Ir£100,000 for a married couple; there were also a considerable number of exemptions and reliefs including the exemption of an owner-occupied house, so that the effective threshold was often much higher.

The tax was partial replacement for estate duty and was administered very much as estate duty had been (indeed, by largely the same staff). Thus the taxpayer or his agent was required to submit an inventory of his wealth and value it; this return then became the subject of negotiations with the Revenue Commissioners.

Virtually all wealth tax payers employed a professional adviser. The study of compliance costs was carried out with the assistance of a large firm of accountants who released, on a strictly anonymous and unidentifiable basis, details of their wealth tax clients and of the professional fees they paid. The study, therefore, did not have the limitations of surveys and provided a wholly reliable documented minimum compliance cost for a sample of some 5-6 per cent of individual wealth tax payers, who by comparison with national data were seen to be well representative of wealth tax payers as a whole.

Taking professional fees only, the average compliance cost: liability ratio for the sample was 18.5 per cent; the median cost:liability ratio was as high as 28 per cent. In 54 per cent of the sample, costs were at least one quarter of tax liability and in 17 per cent compliance costs exceeded liability. Although compliance costs rose with size of wealth-holding, the cost as a percentage of liability fell markedly as wealth-holding increased. Even for the largest wealth-holdings, however, compliance costs remained a significant percentage of wealth tax liability.

No official administrative costs of wealth tax were ever published, but, by inference from the number of wealth tax cases and the administrative costs of the former estate duty, the researchers estimated a minimum figure of 6 per cent of tax yield.

Part of the high costs can be attributed to the newness of the tax; but the researchers concluded that the basic reason for disproportionately high compliance and administrative costs was the form of administration used for a tax of very low rates.

Summary of Main Conclusions

Table 11.3 sums up the findings on these minor taxes.

Table 11.3 Yield and Costs of Minor Inland Revenue and Customs and Excise Duties, 1986-87

	Revenue	Administrative Costs		Compliance Costs		Operating Costs	
	£m.	£m.	%	£m.	%	£m.	%
Stamp Duty	1,860	5.9	0.32	15.0	0.81	20.9	1.12
Inheritance Tax	995	24.1	2.42	39.1	3.93	63.2	6.35
Car Tax	960	2.0	0.21	7.2	0.75	9.2	0.96
Betting and Gaming	782	6.9	0.88	6.9	0.88	13.8	1.76
	4,597	38.9	0.85	68.2	1.48	107.1	2.33

Although the figures for compliance costs cannot be regarded as other than 'gestimates', it is clear that for these minor taxes, with the exception of inheritance tax, both administrative and compliance costs are a very low proportion of tax yield.

II. LOCAL RATES

Outline

The rate is one of the oldest forms of taxation in the United Kingdom, dating from 1601, and is the only form of local taxation available to local authorities. In 1986-87 rates raised a total of £15,544m., some 11 per cent of total tax revenues.

Rateable values are determined by Inland Revenue Valuation Department for all domestic, business and commercial premises, excluding farmland and Crown properties which are exempt. In Great Britain, rates are levied by district councils in respect of all tiers of local authority (county, district and parish). In Northern Ireland the situation is rather different — each of the 26 district authorities levies a rate, and in addition a regional rate is levied by the Department of the Environment to cover services such as roads and education.

District councils in Great Britain collect *all* the rates on behalf of the local authorities. Council house tenants often pay a combined rent and rate bill. In Northern Ireland all rates are collected by the Department of the Environment and the district rate returned to the local authorities.

Administrative costs are thus incurred by Inland Revenue, district councils in Great Britain, and the Department of the Environment in Northern Ireland.

Compliance costs for the individual ratepayer are very low, except where a dispute over valuation occurs over new property, or property where there has been a change in circumstances, such as loss of amenity, downgrading of commercial areas, or a change of use in mixed hereditaments.

Administrative Costs

The official costs of valuation by Inland Revenue for the purposes of rates were £65.1m. in 1986-87.

The administrative costs incurred by the London Boroughs, the Metropolitan Districts and the non-Metropolitan Districts of England and Wales are assembled and published by the Chartered Institute of Public Finance and Accounting (CIPFA). The figures are broken down by type of authority and category of expenditure. The summary for 1986-87 for all authorities in England and Wales is reproduced in Table 11.4.

Table 11.4 Costs of Rate Collection for All Local Authorities in England and Wales, 1986-87

Expenditure	*£000s*
Employees[1]	63,095
Central Establishment Charges[2]	52,899
Computer Recharges[3]	19,416
Running Expenses[4]	18,079
Cost of Contract Services[5]	3,017
Other Expenditure[6]	7,443
Total Expenditure	165,802
Income	
Court Costs Recovered	9,605
Other Income	3,547
Total Income	13,172
Net Expenditure	**152,630**

Source: Rate Collection Statistics 1986-87, Actuals, Table 5, CIPFA.

[1] Cost of employees in the Rates Department.
[2] Apportioned cost of shared services, eg legal finance.
[3] Apportioned charges for central computer services used.
[4] Normal office expenses.
[5] Cost of services contracted out, eg bailiffs.
[6] Miscellaneous, plus grouped expenditure where some of the smaller authorities are unable to break down the costs fully.

Figures for the cost of rate collection in Scotland were made available by the Convention of Scottish Local Authorities. For 1986-87 the costs of collecting rates incurred by the Scottish local authorities were £10.9m.

For Northern Ireland, information was supplied by the Northern Ireland Office and the Department of the Environment. Staff costs incurred in maintaining rating valuation lists amounted to £2.2m. and the collection costs to approximately £5m., giving a total administrative cost for Northern Ireland of £7.2m.

Thus the total administrative cost of local rates for the United Kingdom was £236m. (as set out in Table 11.5) or 1.52 per cent of revenue yield.

Table 11.5 Administrative Costs of Local Rates, 1986-87

	£m.
Inland Revenue Valuation Costs	65.1
Collection Costs in England and Wales	152.6
Collection Costs in Scotland	10.9
Administrative Costs, Northern Ireland	7.2
Total	235.8

Compliance Costs

Compliance costs fall into two main categories: normal expenses and disputes.

The taxpayer receives a rate demand once per year and may pay in two instalments or by monthly bankers' order over a ten month period. Thus the normal expenses are very small, such as checking the rate demand and sending a cheque in the post twice per year. These might reasonably be put at about £2 per hereditament per year. The total number of hereditaments in the United Kingdom at the end of the 1986-87 financial year was 26.47m. Thus the normal expenses might be put at some £53m.

Disputes may be settled between the ratepayer and the valuation officer, usually at a site meeting; they may go to a Local Valuation Court; or they may go to the Lands Tribunal.

In 1986-87 the Valuation Office for England and Wales made 621,000 proposals to alter assessments; appeals were made in 57,600 cases but only 13,400 cases were heard in the Local Valuation Courts (though most of these probably refer to appeals on assessments made in earlier years).

In the same year, ratepayers proposed 198,000 alterations; 134,000 cases went to appeal, but of these 96,000 were withdrawn or settled without coming before the Local Valuation Courts. Only some 26,500 cases reached the Valuation Court in 1986-87.

More serious disputes cases appear before the Lands Tribunal; in 1986-87 76 cases were referred by the Valuation Office, and 279 cases by other parties. The Lands Tribunal hears about 180 cases per annum, approximately half the cases being settled out of court.

Thus, in 1986-87, in round terms, some 150,000 appeals were settled without recourse to the Courts; some 40,000 cases were heard in the Local Valuation Courts; and 180 in the Lands Tribunal.

The appeals settled outside the Courts involve the taxpayer in some minor expenses, such as correspondence, the collection of local evidence and a short site meeting, perhaps an average of £10 per case, totalling £1.5m.

Local Valuation Courts are held near the ratepayer's property and are very informal, not usually involving solicitors or land surveyors. In most cases therefore such disputes are settled at relatively low cost to the ratepayer. Even when the case is lost, no costs are awarded in the Local Valuation Court. If we assume a cost of £50 per hearing for the taxpayer, the compliance costs from disputes going to the Local Valuation Courts would amount to £2m.

Lands Tribunal cases can be very expensive, but with only about 180 cases heard per year the aggregate costs incurred by ratepayers would be low; a figure of £1-£2m. might be a reasonable guess.

These 'gestimates' give us a figure of some £5m. for disputes, which, with the £53m. normal costs, amount to £58m. as the total compliance costs, or 0.37 per cent of tax revenue.

At £294m., or 1.89 per cent of revenue, the total operating costs of local rates are below those of the other main revenue-yielding taxes — income tax and national insurance contributions, VAT and corporation tax. Rates are, however, the only main revenue-yielding tax for which the administrative costs are higher than the compliance costs — and that by a factor of four.

It should be borne in mind that 1986-87 was not a year of general revaluation for rating purposes. In such a year Inland Revenue valuation costs would be substantially higher, and compliance costs would also be higher because of an increased number of disputes.

There are some cash flow implications from the way local rates are paid. Rates are payable in two lump sums due at the beginning of April and the beginning of October. Because these payments are in advance there is some cash flow detriment to the taxpayer. Alternatively, rates may be paid in ten equal instalments when the taxpayer is unlikely to gain significant benefit or suffer significant detriment.

Summary of Main Conclusions

In 1986-87 the administrative costs of the local rates were around £236m. (1.5 per cent of tax revenue) and the 'gestimated' compliance costs were £58m. (0.4 per cent of tax revenue). The compliance costs of rates are exceptionally low for a major tax and rates are the only such tax where the administrative costs are a multiple of the compliance costs. Both administrative and compliance costs could be expected to be higher in a year of general revaluation.

Administrative and Compliance Costs of Taxation

PART III

Policy Issues

CHAPTER 12

THE BURDEN AND INCIDENCE OF ADMINISTRATIVE AND COMPLIANCE COSTS

Introduction

In this chapter we bring together the data on administrative costs and our research findings on compliance costs to examine first the total operating cost of the United Kingdom tax system in 1986-87, then the distribution of those costs, which in turn leads us on to the question of effective incidence: who really pays the administrative and compliance costs?

Size of Administrative and Compliance Costs

Table 12.1 combines the findings of Part II on individual taxes to give us a total picture of the costs of operating the United Kingdom tax system. It indicates that administrative and compliance costs combined amounted to a total well above £5 billion in 1986-87 and are of the order of 4 per cent of tax revenue. Compliance costs were over twice the level of administrative costs. For the four quarters from 1 April 1986 to end March 1987 the United Kingdom Gross Domestic Product at factor cost is estimated at £326bn. So compliance costs emerge as in excess of one per cent of GDP and tax operating costs as a whole are approximately 1.5 per cent.

Figures of 1 or 1.5 per cent may sound small; but, when the denominator is GDP, they represent a very large industry — not far short of agriculture, fishing and forestry at 1.8 per cent. These are the real resource costs of running the United Kingdom tax system. In so far as the requirement to comply with tax laws leads to a more efficient management of personal or business affairs (and for some small firms this was a result of VAT) there is a genuine resource offset to these costs. But cash flow

191

benefits are not such an offset; they transfer the distribution of the burden, but they do not reduce it.

Table 12.1 Tax operating Costs, United Kingdom 1986-87

Tax or Group	Revenue	Administrative Costs		Compliance Costs		Operating Costs	
	£b.	£m.	%	£m	%	£m.	%
Income tax, CGT and NI contributions	65.1	997	1.53	2212	3.40	3209	4.93
VAT	21.4	220	1.03	791	3.69	1011	4.72
Corporation Tax	13.5	70	0.52	300	2.22	370	2.74
Petroleum Revenue Tax	1.2	1	0.12	5	0.44	7	0.56
Excise duties (hydro-carbon oils, tobacco, alcoholic drinks)	16.5	42	0.25	33	0.20	75	0.45
Minor taxes (stamp duty, IHT, car, betting and gaming)	4.6	39	0.85	68	1.48	107	2.33
Overall Central Government	**122.3**	**1369**	**1.12**	**3409**	**2.79**	**4778**	**3.91**
Local Rates	15.5	236	1.52	58	0.37	294	1.89
Overall Central and Local Government	**137.8**	**1605**	**1.16**	**3467**	**2.52**	**5072**	**3.68**

Note: lines and columns may not add up exactly because of rounding.

The sheer size of the total of tax operating costs means that there must be considerable scope, especially in relation to compliance costs, for economies — changes which free resources for other more productive purposes or, indeed, for more leisure. From the limited international comparisons it was possible to make there is no reason to believe that the United Kingdom is unduly prodigal in the resources devoted to operating the tax system. But this does not mean that there are not many economies to be made — not least because they relate to aspects of economic activity which have often not been seriously examined.

Distribution of Compliance Costs

It is not only the size of tax operating costs that should be of concern to governments; it is also their distribution. Administrative costs are paid from taxation and it can be assumed that the distribution of taxation as a whole is in accordance with some policy of government; but this is not true of compliance costs; and one of the main findings of compliance cost studies is that the burden is far from evenly spread.

Personal Taxation

The Poor. In Chapter 1 we wrote about the psychic or psychological costs of taxation. Because, by their nature, psychic costs are so difficult to measure, when, in Part II, we sought to quantify compliance costs, psychic costs slipped out of our reckoning. It is time, now, to pull them back in. The psychic costs of taxation — stress and anxiety occasioned by having to deal with personal tax affairs they do not understand — fall disproportionately on certain sectors of the population, in particular the poorer pensioners, widows and divorced or separated women. Sometimes they seek professional tax advice they can ill afford, typically going to a bank (see Chapter 5); then the disproportionate burden of psychic costs is transmuted into a disproportionate burden of financial cost.

This aspect of compliance cost was the subject of research at Bath University by Sandford (1973) and especially by Lewis *et al* in the 1980s and was summarised in Sandford and Lewis (1986). In the early 1970s a study was made of tax enquiries submitted through newspapers to Press Inquiry Bureaux and the subject of visits to Citizens Advice Bureaux (CABs). It was estimated that in 1970 around 40,000 questions on taxation were put to the inquiry bureaux of press companies based in England and Wales and some 25,000 to CABs.

Over 1,000 tax enquiries submitted to the Westminster Press Bureau were analysed in detail over a five-month period in 1971. It was found that over two-thirds of the letter writers whose age could be identified were retired or nearing retirement and that correspondents were mainly on low incomes. Those nearing retirement especially asked questions on the effect of retirement, or post-retirement employment, on their tax payments. Those who had retired were particularly anxious about the taxation effects of pension changes, sought explanations of the age reliefs, and advice on their investments. Other less numerous enquiries concerned problems faced by those whose marital status had been changed by the death or divorce of a spouse, and the particular complications of CGT (which at that time had a low threshold and no indexation).

The main findings from the Westminster Press enquiry were amply confirmed by a less detailed investigation of enquiries to the John Hilton Bureau (serving two national newspapers, the *News of the World* and *The Sun*) and the evidence from CABs. Interviews were held with the main tax adviser in ten CABs, selected to span a range of different types of community, e.g. urban, rural, working class, retired. References to people who were 'flustered', 'muddled' or 'in a tangle' were frequent. Tax enquirers are 'among the most puzzled we get' was a typical comment.

The more recent study by Lewis replicated (as far as possible) the earlier study of the tax enquiries to the Westminster Press Bureau; the later researchers also visited a series of CABs in the Wessex region and monitored a money phone-in programme on Radio Bristol.

Between November 1982 and April 1983, 1,095 letters containing tax queries to the Westminster Press Bureau were analysed. An even larger proportion of correspondents than in the earlier study was retired (72 per cent against 62 per cent); and also the later study showed a higher percentage of widows (22 per cent against 11 per cent). This difference between the two surveys may be partly accounted for by the increase in the retired people in the country, both in absolute terms and proportionately, together with the greater longevity of women. The majority of the enquiries came from people with incomes under £90 per week, with 29 per cent having incomes under £60. Widows made up the majority (57 per cent) of those on the lowest incomes.

Ninety-eight per cent of the letters referred to income tax; the remainder to CGT, capital transfer tax or some combination of these three.

Some 20 CABs in Wessex and an Age Concern Group in Plymouth took part in a six-week survey towards the end of 1982 and detailed questionnaires were completed on a total of 49 enquiries. Of the enquirers over half were women; one-third of the total enquirers were widowed; 88 per cent (43 out of 49) were 60 years or older.

The 49 enquirers had 101 sources of income amongst them: state retirement pension, 32; occupational pensions, 25; building society interest, 15. A further 14 received some other state benefit or pension. Only 6 had earnings from employment, trade or business.

To quote from Sandford and Lewis (1986).

'Members of CAB staff dealing with tax problems were particularly asked to comment on pensioners' tax difficulties. Their remarks were concentrated in eight main areas and can be summarised as follows:

(1)   Pensioners do not appreciate that, on their tax returns, details of income refer to the previous year while allowances claimed are for the current year.

(2)   Many pensioners do not understand that although their state pension is not taxed at source it is still taxable. This means that a large proportion of personal allowances is absorbed by the state pension so that any code number applied to a further source of income, for example part-time earnings, reflects this fact and a second income appears to be taxed very severely. In this respect building society interest may also cause confusion. Many taxpayers seem to think that they need not disclose building society interest because it is 'taxed at source'. They do not understand that building society interest can affect the calculation of age allowance.

(3)   The Inland Revenue do not always make it clear that they are often willing to recover arrears of tax by adjusting the taxpayers' code number for the following year.

(4)   Pensioners with straightforward affairs do not receive a tax return annually and so are often not aware of their obligation to inform Inland Revenue of changes in circumstances and income.

(5)   People are frightened of the consequences of completing tax returns wrongly. This fear is accentuated when pensioners are not numerate or have poor eyesight. An associated

problem is the difficulty that many pensioners have of relating the information required to the appropriate section of the tax return — exacerbated by the fact that many items on the tax return do not apply to them.

(6)   Many pensioners have difficulty in calculating their annual amount of state pension, particularly as pensions are up-rated in November, roughly half-way through the tax year; the exercise would be much easier if the tax year and benefit year coincided.

(7)   Many CABs identified notices of coding as a special area of confusion. Many pensioners do not know if their code number is correct; nor do they understand why it changes or the implications of a change for them.

(8)   A main area of concern was the position of the newly widowed. New widows were often unaware of the workings of the tax system. They are not used to completing official forms and so have many difficulties when, on the death of their husbands, they are faced, for the first time, with the complexities of the tax system.'

It should be recognised that most elderly people get their information from Inland Revenue rather than outside agencies and that the Revenue acknowledges a duty to provide an information service to the public. Nonetheless, the problem of the low-income perplexed pensioner who may suffer considerable stress and anxiety as a result of the tax system is very much with us. Nor will it go away. With the numbers of pensioners rising and their average age increasing, it will become more acute. The number of widows will also rise for demographic reasons, whilst the increasing numbers of divorces will add to the problems of women battling with tax problems for the first time. Moreover the computerisation of Revenue work in distant centres will aggravate these problems.

Capital Gains Tax and Inheritance Tax. It is not only in respect of income tax and not only on the poorest that the compliance costs of personal taxation may fall inequitably, even though the most severe problems probably lie there. The compliance costs of CGT are essentially uneven in their incidence and the same amount of expensive delving into the past may be necessary whether the tax liability (and the capacity to pay of the taxpayer) is large or small. It may even be necessary to incur substantial compliance costs to establish a nil liability. For the small taxpayer the compliance costs can be disproportionately high. With much tax work for CGT and IHT there are economies of scale which mean that the compliance costs are regressive, e.g. it is likely to take only the same time to value a large shareholding as a small shareholding in a private company. With IHT this fact is recognised in the scale of charges used by banks and solicitors for administering an estate. Moreover the study of the Irish wealth tax (see Chapter 11), administered on the same lines as IHT, revealed a marked regressiveness in the impact of compliance costs.

Business Taxes

It is, however, in relation to taxes on business, that the burden of tax compliance is most evidently inequitable. The regressiveness of the compliance costs of business taxes and the extent of that regressiveness is perhaps the most significant finding of the research. Whether it be VAT, the costs to employers of collecting PAYE and NI contributions, corporation tax or, indeed, income tax on the self-employed, the burden of compliance falls disproportionately on the small; which is another way of saying that there are substantial economies of scale in tax collection and remission.

This conclusion is not new. It is a common element in all the earlier literature on compliance costs. But it has not hitherto been as fully documented. Moreover, whereas in Part II we looked at the business taxes individually the VAT 2 study gives us the means to analyse the combined burden of VAT, PAYE and corporation tax on a number of companies and to compare the impact of these different taxes.

A total of 54 respondents amongst the companies to the VAT 2 survey gave complete information covering VAT, PAYE, corporation tax and also the costs of deducting interest at source. The number is too small to cover adequately all the size ranges and thus the companies have been grouped into three size bands only: 'small' — up to £100,000 p.a. taxable turnover; 'medium' — £100,000 p.a. to £1m. p.a.; and 'large' — over £1m. Table 12.2 gives the mean compliance costs for each tax individually and together.

It should be recalled that this is not the full range of taxes which businesses face. Local rates, possibly excise duties, occasionally stamp duties will also have to be complied with. But the taxes in Table 12.2 are those attracting the biggest compliance costs. Taking these three taxes together, it can be seen that even the small businesses face a cost of well over £1,000 p.a. simply to comply with taxation.

Table 12.2 Mean Compliance Costs of VAT, PAYE and Corporation Tax, 1986-87

Mean Compliance Costs

Size	Number of Respondents	VAT £	PAYE £	CT (plus interest deduction) £	Total £
Small	9	436	470	262	1,168
Medium	28	999	640	431	2,070
Large	17	1,697	2,509	2,841	7,047

It is interesting that, for the small and medium sizes, corporation tax represents the least burden; but it is the heaviest of the three for the larger firms (40.3 per cent of their compliance costs), which was in line with our analysis in Chapter 9.

Table 12.3 shows the composition of compliance costs, taking the three taxes together.

Table 12.3 Composition of Compliance Costs of VAT, PAYE and Corporation Tax, Taken Together, 1986-87

Averages

Size	Number of Respondents	In-house staff costs Directors £	Accounts £	Other £	Outside Advisers £	Other Costs £	All Taxes £
Small	9	693	8	22	334	111	1,168
Medium	28	464	288	386	850	82	2,070
Large	17	1,121	1,732	1,806	1,377	1,012	7,047

Nearly 60 per cent of small firm costs are directors' time; and most of the remainder (29 per cent) represents fees to outside advisers. The heaviest users of outside advice (proportionately) are the medium-sized firms, for whom fees to outside advisers represented 41 per cent of their compliance costs. With the large firms, costs are more evenly spread amongst the various categories, but they use in-house staff more heavily than other companies, with accounts staff and other staff (which includes computing staff) each accounting for about a quarter of their compliance costs.

Finally, Table 12.4 expresses compliance costs as a percentage of taxable turnover and shows the markedly regressive pattern for each tax and all the taxes taken together.

Table 12.4 Compliance Costs as a Percentage of Taxable Turnover, for VAT, PAYE and Corporation Tax, 1986-87

Costs as Percentage of Taxable Turnover

Size	Number of Respondents	VAT	PAYE	CT (plus interest) deduction)	All Taxes
		%	%	%	%
Small	9	1.48	1.39	0.79	3.66
Medium	28	0.28	0.19	0.15	0.62
Large	17	0.05	0.08	0.04	0.17

Thus, for every £1,000 of goods sold by companies with a turnover below £100,000 the average compliance cost, taking all the taxes together, is £37. For companies with a turnover above £1m. the corresponding figure is £1.70. Had we been able to take narrower bands, e.g. £20,000-£50,000 at the lower end, and over £10m. at the upper end, there is no doubt that the discrepancies would have been still more marked as we know from analysing the individual taxes.

Although it would have been incorrect to take account of cash flow benefits in considering the overall resource costs of operating the tax system, cash flow benefits should be taken into account in considering the distribution of the burden. Taking businesses as a whole the existence of cash flow benefits is a major offset to compliance costs. On our reckoning, in aggregate, the cash flow benefits exceeded the compliance costs to employers of collecting and remitting PAYE and to companies of collecting and remitting corporation tax and substantially reduced the net compliance costs of VAT. The estimates of cash flow benefit in Part II should be treated with extreme caution, both because of the debatable assumptions in respect of PAYE and corporation tax and because of the sensitivity of the estimates to the level of interest rates. However, there is no gainsaying the importance of the cash flow benefits in reducing the compliance cost burdens to the private sector.

However, they do nothing to reduce the regressiveness of compliance costs. As a result of cash flow benefits net compliance costs are frequently negative for the larger firms; but they remain positive and substantial for small firms. Indeed, largely because of the bigger market power of the large firms in drawing the cash flow benefit of VAT to themselves, the VAT 1 study concluded that the existence of the cash flow benefit actually increased the regressive impact of compliance costs (Sandford *et al*, 1981, p.100).

Effective Incidence of Compliance Costs

All this brings us to the question, who really pays the compliance costs? What is their effective incidence?

If compliance costs were spread evenly over businesses in proportion to their size we would expect the effective incidence of the compliance costs to be identical to the incidence of an extra tranche of tax. This does not mean that it is unimportant. It would give rise to distortion costs of consumption and production additional to those already present. (The subject of compliance cost and the 'excess burden' of taxation is explored by Professor Collard in Appendix E). With a general consumption tax, like VAT, we would expect the bulk of the additional tax (i.e. the compliance cost) to be passed forward to the consumer.

But compliance costs are not evenly spread. They fall disproportionately on small firms. It follows that, where small firms are competing in the same market with large firms (as in most retailing, for example) they are being put under a state-created competitive disadvantage. They cannot pass on their compliance costs to the same extent as the larger firms (whose net compliance costs may, indeed, be nil or negative). They have to take a cut in their rate of profit or, in the case of small proprietors perhaps in their leisure. Compliance costs then become a factor helping to push small firms out of particular markets.

For some small businessmen there may be a further effect. They may strongly resent what they, not unreasonably, regard as unfair treatment from the state. In both the VAT 1 and the VAT 2 surveys, whilst a substantial proportion of VAT traders 'did not mind doing VAT work', there was a minority who strongly resented it: 30 per cent in 1979; 24 per cent in 1987. Surveys of the government-imposed burdens on small business have all found VAT appearing at the top of the list (e.g. Appendix 3, *Burdens on Business*, DTI, 1985). Moreover, written-in comments on the Bath VAT surveys attest to the opposition to VAT amongst some traders.

Where this resentment is fierce, it may boil over in, or provide an excuse for, illegal action in the form of tax evasion. A trader can come to think such action justified as correcting an imbalance of treatment by the state. Such an outcome is, to say the least, unhealthy.

The considerations of this chapter lead us naturally to the consideration of government policy on administrative and compliance costs which we consider in the next chapter.

CHAPTER 13

POLICY ON ADMINISTRATIVE AND COMPLIANCE COSTS

Introduction

The prime purpose of this chapter is to stress the importance of compliance costs as an objective of policy and to try to lay down some guidelines and principles, relating to tax operating costs, of assistance to policy-makers. We have not attempted a tax by tax analysis of particular ways in which compliance costs (or administrative costs) might be reduced or offset. Our study, covering such a wide field, was not sufficiently detailed to make such a tax by tax scrutiny possible; nor, indeed, because of conflicting objectives, is the problem of reducing compliance costs as simple as such an approach might imply.

We start with administrative costs.

Policy on Administrative Costs

Policy Objective

What should be the policy objective with respect to administrative costs?

At first blush, the appropriate policy objective might appear simple (at least in expression): to minimise administrative costs for any given tax revenue; or, alternatively, to maximise revenue from any given administrative cost. However, there are difficulties with this formulation, both in relation to tax structure and in relation to compliance costs.

As was discussed in Chapter 1 in examining the deficiencies of the ratio of tax cost:revenue yield as a measure of efficiency, a similar revenue may be obtained in either of two ways: by lower tax rates and more intensive enforcement; or higher tax rates and less intensive enforcement. The second method might well generate less administrative costs but is not necessarily to be preferred. In practice there are not just two options but a whole range of possibilities of raising the same revenue from different combinations of tax rates and levels of enforcement. In fact the choice of combination is more a policy matter for government than for a tax department and the objective of administrative policy is best phrased by reference to a given tax structure.

The second difficulty with the statement of objective relates to compliance costs. In practice there is a significant element of transferability between administrative costs and compliance costs. It is therefore often possible to reduce administrative costs by changing administrative structure or practice in a way which puts more work or cost on the taxpayer (e.g. by substituting self-assessment for revenue assessment). Moreover, even with a given administrative structure, a heavy-handed application of the rules (e.g. an increase in investigation cases carried out in an unpleasant way) may increase compliance costs not only amongst tax evaders but also amongst honest taxpayers. Honest taxpayers subject to investigation incur higher costs as do those who, because of the *possibility* of investigation, spend undue time to ensure that their records are meticulous. Such costs may be both psychic and financial.

Thus, administrative costs should not be seen in isolation from compliance costs. Minimising tax operating costs would be a more valid objective than minimising administrative costs. But even this statement of objective is not satisfactory. As we emphasised in the previous chapter, compliance costs are often inequitable and regressive in their incidence; they may generate psychic costs; and they may also give rise to resentment. Unless it can be shown that the private sector is more efficient in carrying out a particular tax collection function, in the trade-off between administrative and compliance costs there is a strong case for bending in the direction of more administrative costs and less compliance costs. Where the private sector is indisputably more efficient, there is a case for compensation.

Perhaps the best that can be done is to suggest that the objective might be phrased in terms of minimising operating costs in obtaining a given revenue from a given tax structure; or, alternatively and perhaps more realistically, obtaining the maximum revenue that is properly due, with given operating costs from a given tax structure.

Figure 6

Line of Maximum Revenue Potential (MRP) — Tax base x tax rate(s).

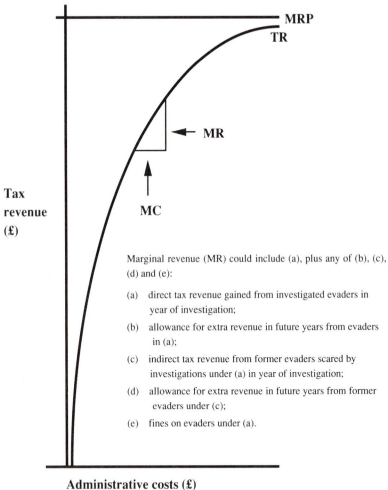

Administrative costs (£)

Relationship of Tax Revenue and Administrative Cost
(Applicable to an individual tax or the tax system as a whole)

What Resources for Tax Administration?

A vital practical issue is how many resources should be applied to tax administration; and, within tax administration, how should such resources be allocated as between taxes; and to each function in relation to one (or more) taxes.

The attached diagram (similar in principle to that in Chapter 1, and, in respect of which, the authors acknowledge their debt to Dean, 1975) represents the relationship between tax revenue and administrative costs in respect of a particular tax or the tax system as a whole. The logic of the shape of the curve relating total revenue (TR) and cost is that some administrative cost in the form of overheads has to be incurred without generating any tax revenue. Thereafter additional costs at first give a high return in yield, but the yield diminishes (marginal tax revenue rises more slowly) the nearer the line of maximum revenue potential (i.e. tax base x tax rate) is approached. The gap between the total revenue curve and the line of maximum revenue potential (MRP) represents uncollected tax. The smaller the gap, the higher the tax enforcement cost of reducing it further. (The MRP line should not be regarded as absolutely fixed; the development of successful avoidance devices would lower it; the successful stopping of avoidance devices would raise it).

The initial response to the question of what resources should be put into tax administration might be that resources should continue to be employed up to the point at which marginal cost (MC) equalled marginal revenue (MR). (If the axes were on the same scale this would be where the total revenue curve was at 45 degrees). Up to that point, additional enforcement would generate more revenue than cost; thereafter, the addition to cost would exceed the addition to revenue.

However, there are reasons to suggest that equating MC and MR is not the right criterion.

First, it is important to appreciate that the revenue, which is the outcome of the application of real resources, simply represents a transfer of income. Resources applied to tax administration do not generate new goods or services. Any implied analogy with the output of a business, where MC = MR is the appropriate criterion, is therefore false. The rule of equality of MC and MR does not tell us what total resources should be applied to tax administration — though that is not to say that the *relationship* between MC and MR is not a relevant consideration.

Secondly, there is the point we have already made in the previous section of this chapter. Looking at administrative costs ignores compliance costs which are likely to have risen with the increased enforcement levels. However, if there are arguments for applying less resources than would equate MC with MR there is also a case for applying resources beyond that point. The gap between TR and MRP represents the extent of evasion. It can be argued that tax evaders should be pursued as criminals should be pursued — they steal from the rest of the community. No-one argues that police expenditure on catching criminals should be related to the loot that can be recovered from them. (In that case plain murderers would not be pursued at all!) Additional expenditure is, therefore, justifiable (beyond the point of MC = MR) in terms of bringing criminals to justice.

The total resources to be allocated to a revenue department is a decision for the government which should take these matters into account, although it will also be influenced by other political considerations. There can be no hard and fast rule. For a revenue department the more practical issue is, how, given its total budget, should the resources be allocated within it.

Here the marginal principle is relevant. It can much more strongly be argued that resources should be so allocated that the ratio between administrative cost and revenue is the same, at the margin, for all taxes and sections of taxes. If this is *not* so, then additional revenue can be gained for the same cost by transferring resources from where the cost:yield ratio is high to where the cost:yield ratio is low and continuing so to do until the ratios equalise. (It should be stressed that we are talking about *marginal* cost and revenue. The average cost of tax A may be much higher than of tax B, but it may still pay to transfer resources at the margin from B to A). However, remembering that the objective of tax administration should relate to operating costs rather than just administrative costs, the qualification about the effect on compliance costs remains relevant. If a marginal reallocation of resources in administration increases compliance costs, for the purpose of comparing cost:yield at the margin between taxes, any increase in compliance cost should be added to administrative cost; or, more generally, the marginal operating cost:marginal revenue is a more relevant ratio than the marginal administrative cost:marginal revenue. Whilst all this may be fine in theory, there are a number of practical difficulties:

(1)   The problem of allocating costs of services jointly supplied, e.g. where valuations are used for more than one tax; where tax officers are employed on several taxes, etc.

(2)   The problem of what components to include in marginal revenue arising from enforcement activities and how to treat them:

    a)   Clearly the extra tax directly collected should be included; but should an allowance be made for the present value of the tax revenue expected from its continuance in future years?

    b)   Ideally, extra tax arising from the evasion-deterrent effect of extra enforcement should be included, but this is exceptionally difficult to measure.

    c)   Should fines as a result of enforcement activities count as part of marginal revenue?

(3)   The full application of the principle would require an exceptionally detailed breakdown of costs and exceptional flexibility in the application of resources.

(4)   A particularly difficult problem arises where the introduction of, or a change in, one tax generates additional revenue from another tax; e.g. a CGT discourages the holding of assets for capital gain relatively to income-yielding assets, and thus increases income tax revenue. Such a revenue addition should be set against the costs of CGT rather than income tax.

(5)   Measuring the marginal compliance cost (to arrive at marginal operating cost) may be even more difficult than measuring marginal administrative cost.

In practice the MC:MR relationship may be more readily applicable to certain branches of revenue activity (e.g., in Inland Revenue, the Enquiry Branch or the PAYE audit) than to others. But even if the marginal relationship can be difficult to apply, keeping the principles in mind can be helpful.

United Kingdom Practice

For some years, especially since the development of the Financial Management Initiative (FMI) Inland Revenue and Customs and Excise have been taking various measures to improve departmental efficiency, setting performance targets, developing 'in depth' investigations and generally seeking to concentrate resources in directions in which it is believed revenue is most at risk.

Whilst, as indicated in Chapter 1, the United Kingdom is well in advance of most countries in analysing administrative costs, it still has some way to go. In particular, the revenue departments have not developed the degree of sophistication of some aspects of the United States Internal Revenue Service (IRS). By analysing a series of special audits, the IRS has developed a technique known as discriminant function analysis (DIF) designed to identify the returns that are likely to yield most revenue from an audit. The higher the DIF score the more likely that investigating the return will yield additional revenue. The DIF scores are then used to select returns for routine audits. Audit rates and yields in respect of individuals in different income brackets, and corporations of different sizes, are also analysed by the IRS together with the estimated average and marginal yield for each category and the ratio of marginal yield to marginal cost.

Apart from the problems of measurement, which we have already discussed, it must be recognised that there may be philosophical problems in applying, with full rigour, a policy of concentrating resources where they are expected to yield most tax. Indeed, the Committee on the Enforcement Powers of the Revenue Departments (Keith, 1983) was concerned that the policy then being pursued by Inland Revenue of concentrating on small businessmen was being perceived as unfair and that it was important that it should be considered even-handed amongst potential evaders in order to uphold the integrity of the system and be seen to operate equitably. Thus the perception of equity may restrict the application of the marginal approach.

It could be argued that the existence of two revenue departments in the United Kingdom, rather than one, restricts the application of the marginal approach because it reduces the flexibility with which resources can be applied. This argument had particular force as long as 'on the ground' co-operation between Inland Revenue and Customs and Excise was restricted. These restrictions have now been reduced. The Financial Secretary to the Treasury recently announced that as from 1 April 1988 Inland Revenue and Customs and Excise would be extending, nationwide, their arrangements for exchange of information at local level. In practice close co-operation between departments may be able to give as much, or almost as much, flexibility as would obtain between separate divisions within a large department.

Policy on Compliance Costs

Four criteria may be laid down in respect of government policy on compliance costs. Governments should (1) explicitly recognise their importance; (2) resist the temptation to reduce administrative costs at the expense of compliance costs; (3) seek to minimise compliance costs, especially for small businesses, and (4) be more prepared to compensate for compliance costs. Let us explore these aspects more fully under the headings of recognition, allocation, minimisation and compensation.

(1) Recognition

As we indicated in Chapter 2, there has for long been a neglect of compliance costs by economists, administrators and governments and they are too important, both because of their size and their distributional effects, to be ignored. Whilst in recent years there has been a growth in interest in compliance costs it is vital that they should be an automatic and continuing ingredient in the tax policy-making process. Explicit recognition of the importance of compliance costs is the first step to this goal.

In this respect the United Kingdom leads the field. The revenue departments helped to finance the research for this book and have given the researchers every assistance without seeking in any way to impair their independence. The Government has published three White Papers (Cmnd. 9571, 1985, Cmnd. 9794, 1986 and Cmnd. 512, 1988) concerned with lifting the burdens of regulation, including tax regulation, from businesses and in pursuance of this object Customs and Excise and Inland Revenue have established their own departmental Deregulation Units. In July 1986 the Government published, through both revenue departments, a Taxpayers' Charter, which stated: 'In particular it recognises the need to minimise costs incurred by taxpayers in complying with the law'. A compliance cost assessment is now prepared for every tax change where it is deemed to be relevant and departmental Press Notices about changes in tax regulations now regularly include a paragraph on the compliance cost implications. Few, if any, other Governments have so clearly recognised in their statements the need to consider compliance costs. But there is still some way to go in the direction of explicit recognition (and even more in translating words into actions, as we indicate below).

In terms of recognition the ideal would be a tax cost budget, published as part of the annual Budget Statement, which included a quantitative estimate of both the administrative costs and the compliance costs associated with projected tax changes. To some extent this already happens on the administrative side when the Chancellor states that a particular tax change will save 'X00' staff; but it is vital also to include compliance cost, especially where the reduction in public sector cost is at the expense of higher private sector costs. Only if both are included can one judge the efficiency of the change. The difficulties of estimation are obvious; but if the attempt was made, whilst early estimates would often be wide of the mark, growing experience and the ensuing development of more sophisticated techniques would, as with the estimation of the revenue effects of tax changes, bring increasing accuracy.

(2) Allocation

We have already stressed the element of transferability between administrative costs and compliance costs. Where a new tax or a major change in the tax structure is under consideration, how responsibilities for operating the tax are divided between the public and private sectors should be a major consideration. Governments concerned with the growth of public expenditure, or with the increase in taxation which goes with it, are under constant temptation to take measures which reduce public sector costs at the expense of private sector costs. Moreover, revenue departments, under pressure to fulfil departmental goals and improve performance indicators, face the same temptation. For reasons already indicated above the temptation should be resisted unless it can be clearly shown that the alternative arrangement is more efficient — in which case compensation should be considered.

The United Kingdom Government and its revenue departments, for all their stated concern with compliance costs, have not been immune to this temptation. In recent years there have been a number of measures which have reduced administrative costs at the expense of compliance costs. The major changes in the administration of the excises, described in Chapter 10, are one example; another is the requirement placed on the banks to pay interest net rather than gross (Chapter 7). In these cases there is almost certainly an efficiency justification.* In other cases such

---

* Even more important as an example of the transfer of costs from the public to the private sector, but not strictly within our terms of reference, is the additional requirements placed on employers in respect of the payment of sickness and maternity benefit.

justification is lacking. A trivial but very clear example is the recent decision of Inland Revenue to cease sending stamped addressed envelopes with tax return forms, leaving the cost of postage to the taxpayer.

More subtly, there is a potential conflict between the efficiency objectives being pursued by the revenue departments and the objective of minimising compliance costs. An example is the policy of Customs and Excise in cutting back on educational visits to VAT traders. It can be expected that such educational visits reduce compliance costs. To cut them back reduces administrative costs at the expense of compliance costs and, indeed, was one suggested reason that VAT traders were turning more to accountants for help with VAT compliance work (see Chapter 8). Further, there was a widely held view amongst accountants interviewed that both Customs and Excise officers and Inland Revenue inspectors had become less helpful than a few years ago, a change in attitude explained partly, at least, in terms of the pressure for performance and the stricter timetables they faced. Finally, there was concern expressed by a number of tax advisers that back duty cases and PAYE audits were being conducted in a heavy-handed way which put up compliance costs, both psychic and financial.

In a recent survey on this issue (Kempton, 1988), accountant respondents were concerned about the health of clients subjected to an in-depth investigation. One wrote that 'The mental stress caused to an innocent person is incalculable and can never be compensated'. Another referred to 'nervous disorders inflicted on clients due to in-depth investigations', whilst a third argued that 'the Revenue must realise that such cases if prolonged can have serious effects on the health of the taxpayer'. On the question of financial cost, to quote the study: 'The general thrust of comments received was that innocent or nearly innocent taxpayers are frequently caught up in investigations and have to incur substantial professional fees as well as loss of earnings in order to establish their innocence'.

It might be added that interviewees amongst professional advisers in the present study sometimes expressed concern that the quality of Revenue staff was often not as high as it should be; and there was a widespread acceptance that pay levels for the Service were far too low to attract and keep the right number of the right quality staff.

The objectives of catching evaders and of increasing efficiency, as implemented through the Financial Management Initiative, are to be applauded. But there is clearly a danger that the narrower objective of minimising administrative costs is pursued at the expense of the wider and more relevant objective of minimising tax operating costs. If administrative departments are under pressure, concern for compliance costs may go out of the window.

(3) Minimisation

As an important objective of policy a government should seek to minimise compliance costs especially for small businesses, which face disproportionately large costs and whose competitiveness is therefore reduced. In saying this it is fully appreciated that minimising compliance costs is only one policy objective amongst many and that it should neither be pursued exclusively nor given priority. As a policy objective minimising compliance costs cannot be pursued without regard to the effect on administrative costs and it will often conflict with equity or with a concern for neutrality or efficiency in resource use and it will often have to give way. But it is important that it should be given due weight in policy decisions.

Compliance costs enter so many aspects of the taxation process that we can only list out the points in summary form, together with a few comments arising from the study. It is convenient to group the points under the headings of temporary compliance costs, regular costs and costs arising from the inter-relationships between taxes. Many of the points are obvious, but it is useful to include them in a comprehensive check list.

Temporary Compliance Costs

Stability. Temporary compliance costs relate to 'once and for all' start-up costs and to learning costs. Many respondents and interviewees emphasised the importance of stability in taxation in order to minimise temporary costs and, in Chapter 8, arising from Bannock's study, it was suggested that one reason that the attitude to VAT was more favourable in Germany than in the United Kingdom was the greater stability that the German tax had enjoyed.

The Consultation and Legislative Process. One reason for stability is that government 'gets it right' in the first place; thus the whole process of consultation and of the enactment of tax legislation is relevant to compliance costs. The processes and deficiencies of the United Kingdom methods have been considered elsewhere at some depth for the period 1964-74 (Robinson and Sandford, 1983) and for the period 1979-87

(Gammie, 1988). The subject will not be pursued here except to say that the methods leave considerable scope for improvement.

Education Campaign. When a new tax is introduced, or a major change in a tax projected, a good 'education campaign', with clear literature, TV programmes, videos and the like, can be of considerable benefit in minimising learning costs for those who have to comply. (The manner in which VAT, known as GST — Goods and Services Tax — was introduced in New Zealand in 1986, is particularly interesting for its ingenious educational features).

Frequency and Timing of Changes. Compliance costs are minimised if the frequency of tax changes is minimised and if the timing takes account of the convenience of the taxpayer, e.g. that changes in VAT rates apply from the beginning of a month, rather than instantaneously, to allow time for re-pricing and to tie in, as far as possible, with the period of accounts.

Regular Compliance Costs

Tax Structure. Compliance costs are minimised if a tax is as simple as possible — e.g. single rate, minimum borderlines, high threshold, convenient form of threshold, minimum of special exemptions, reliefs and provisions. Examples from the study are many. Although the higher rate of VAT in the United Kingdom, from 1974-79, applied to only a comparatively small range of goods, it probably raised overall compliance costs by 8 or 9 per cent; the change in VAT rating in the construction industry reduced compliance costs by improving a borderline; the low income threshold for certain payments in kind, which has remained unchanged for a considerable period, was complained about by accountants as increasing compliance costs of income tax; a CGT threshold based on disposals rather than (or alternative to) actual capital gains can remove for many the need to incur substantial compliance costs to demonstrate a nil liability; and the Business Expansion Scheme was given by interviewees as an example of recent complications in income tax. One special aspect of structure was the way the income tax unit — with the husband responsible for the wife's tax affairs — left the widow unprepared for the complexities of tax. The proposals for independent taxation of husband and wife will gradually change that situation.

Provision of Information and Advice. Compliance costs are minimised if tax literature is free, readily accessible, readable and easily comprehensible; and if tax offices and tax officers freely give advice to taxpayers in language they can understand.

Tax Forms. Similarly, tax forms should be designed to be as short, simple and clear as possible. Where feasible businesses should be allowed to use their own forms and computer print-out. The PAYE study showed significantly lower costs of compliance for firms using their own (Inland Revenue approved) forms than those using standard forms. The re-design of the VAT form in 1978 appears to have been one factor reducing VAT compliance costs. In this area much progress has been made in the United Kingdom. Inland Revenue have established a forms design unit and the attractiveness and readability of the tax forms and tax literature of the two revenue departments have increased markedly and must have benefited compliance costs.

Payment Arrangements. The method and timing of returns and payments should be convenient to the taxpayer, e.g. tying in with the period of business accounts. Requirements that discriminate against small firms should be avoided. On the first point, in interviews with representatives of the National Association of Warehouse Keepers, the complaint was made that they faced additional compliance costs because payments for customs duties related to the calendar month whereas the excise month ran from the 15th to the 14th. (It was said that the Treasury blocked harmonisation because the current system provided a more even cash flow). On the second point the form of bond required (e.g. from tobacco manufacturers) consisting of a fixed sum, the same for all firms, plus a proportion of the monthly take, is necessarily harder on small businesses.

Certainty. Adam Smith stressed the importance of certainty of payment in his famous canons of taxation and several interviewees, especially in relation to the provisions on gifts with reservations under IHT, held that uncertainty increased compliance costs. Uncertainty may be a product of obscure legislation. In the IHT example the interviewees regretted the unwillingness of the Inland Revenue to give advance rulings.

Appeal Mechanisms. Simple and low cost appeal mechanisms for non-frivolous appeals help to minimise compliance costs.

Taxpayer Benefits. Besides policies seeking to minimise gross compliance costs, any policy which enables taxpayers to maximise legitimate benefits from compliance helps to minimise net compliance costs. The surveys revealed that many small traders did not use VAT records to improve management nor appreciate that they got a cash flow benefit. A government-produced or sponsored booklet on 'Making the

Most of VAT' would be helpful. Another useful measure would be to encourage the use of interest-bearing tax reserve certificates of small denominations; a small businessman, setting aside the tax on his product as it accrued, would avoid difficulties in meeting his tax liabilities when payment time arrived and would appreciate the cash flow benefit of collecting VAT.

Relations between Taxes

Fewer Taxes. As a general rule, the more taxes there are, the higher compliance costs are likely to be. Fewer taxes with broad bases which minimise exemptions and reliefs and the difficult borderlines to which they give rise are likely to mean less compliance costs, as are fewer taxes at higher rates than many taxes at lower rates (though this option may well conflict with other objectives). When Sir Geoffrey Howe altered the balance of taxation in 1979 he was moving in this direction — by raising the standard rate of VAT and at the same time raising income tax thresholds, which took a number of income tax payers out of the system.

Common Base. A common base, common definitions and common procedures for taxes can reduce compliance costs. Thus many of the respondents to the PAYE survey considered that compliance costs would fall if PAYE and NI contributions were amalgamated to a common base.

Common Valuations. The use of valuations common to a number of taxes can reduce both administrative and compliance costs. One reason why many of the countries on the continent of Europe operate annual wealth taxes much more economically than the Irish wealth tax (considered in Chapter 11) is the existence of common, administratively determined, values for wealth taxes, local property taxes and death duties.

Harmonisation of Processes. Harmonisation of processes can reduce compliance costs, e.g. the use of accounting controls rather than physical controls for excise duties on goods also subject to VAT. The example, (above) of different payment periods for customs duties and for excise duties also illustrates the point.

Borderlines Between Taxes

Just as difficult borderlines within a tax create compliance costs, so borderlines between taxes, which encourage taxpayers to transfer between them, add to compliance costs as well as causing economic distortion. Thus several interviewees pointed out that the removal of the upper limit on NI contributions encouraged payment in kind (not subject to national insurance contributions) as against salary increases; for similar reasons, the reduction in corporation tax and income tax rates, encouraged the payment of dividends by private companies instead of increasing directors' remuneration. The more neutral the tax system, the less the likelihood that it will cause changes in taxpayer behaviour leading to economic distortion and often an accompanying increase in compliance costs.

(4) Compensation

Where compliance costs represent a particular burden which is not susceptible to reduction, compensation should be considered.

The most serious effect of compliance costs is the disproportionate burden put on the small businesses which are placed at a competitive disadvantage. As that disadvantage is state-created there is a strong argument for compensating action by the state. It is sometimes argued that there is no such obligation on the state because the disadvantage is but a reflection of the economies of size and simply mirrors an economic reality applying throughout the market. Thus, proportionately, the disadvantage of the small firm is no more in tax compliance work than in its ordinary line of business. This argument is false. Many small firms have established themselves in market areas where there are no economies of scale, or where such economies are very limited, like bespoke tailoring, many specialist service activities and craft industries. In obliging them to undertake tax compliance work the state is forcing them into a form of economic activity different from that which they have chosen, and where economies of scale are very pronounced. There is a real state-created disadvantage.

There are many ways of trying to compensate small firms. The German and Dutch systems in respect of very small VAT traders (see Chapter 8) are examples. The difficulty is to devise a mechanism which is itself fair.

A starting point is to recognise that with the main United Kingdom taxes on business there is already a substantial compensation process through the cash flow benefit. However, as it operates in the United Kingdom, that benefit over-compensates the big firms and under-compensates the small.

The simplest and most obvious method would seem to be to follow the example of a number of other countries and adopt differential payment periods, for businesses of different sizes, both for VAT and for PAYE, i.e.

reduce the collection and/or grace periods for larger firms and increase them for small. The benefit to small firms is not only that they would have a longer collection and (perhaps) grace period; but the fact that their competitors, who have low or negative net compliance costs, would have shorter periods. It is the relativity that matters in the market situation. The beauty of the solution from the government's viewpoint is that it is costless — indeed, depending on where the lines were drawn it would generate a once and for all cash benefit to the government, enabling it to reduce the public sector borrowing requirement (or increase repayments of public debt), with a reduction of subsequent interest payments. The United Kingdom, in fact, is very generous in the payment periods allowed to large firms and some reduction would only put them in a similar position to such firms abroad. (For details on the differential payment periods for VAT in a number of European countries, see Godwin and Sandford, 1983).

Income tax collection lags have been documented for various OECD countries (OECD, 1983). It is noteworthy that, in the United States, employers are required to pay over withheld income tax together with payroll taxes 'at a frequency that presently ranges from once per calendar year quarter to eight times per month, depending on the size of the withheld tax liability of all employees working for the employer'.

The circumstances in which direct compensation payments might be made from the Exchequer are always likely to be rare; but a case can be made for them in at least two circumstances. One relates to the discussion earlier in this chapter about the effect of in-depth investigations on the compliance costs of the honest taxpayer. There is an argument for much wider provisions than at present exist to enable the innocent taxpayer to secure compensation for costs incurred in facing an in-depth investigation, irrespective of whether the investigation was prompted by reasonable grounds for suspicion. Whilst such provisions would not be without difficulty, the matter should be examined sympathetically by Inland Revenue. The extension of in-depth investigations would receive wide support from the accountancy profession if a satisfactory compensation system could be devised (see Kempton, 1988, pp.331-7).

A second circumstance where compensation would seem eminently justified is where the government specifically transfers a function from the public to the private sector because the private sector can do it more efficiently, leading to a fall in total operating costs. In that case the state could fully compensate the private sector and still be left with a positive saving. As a minimum, the state should compensate for the substantial temporary costs involved. There are some somewhat half-hearted attempts to do this in the United Kingdom, as when the banks and building societies received a minimal sum towards postage and envelopes when they had to inform customers with mortgages of the change to the MIRAS system.

Concluding Observations

These final observations are directed particularly to the detail of the United Kingdom tax system; but the concluding sentence applies to all tax systems.

In the United Kingdom since the year 1986-87 a number of important developments affecting administrative and compliance costs have taken place or are projected.

Affecting the compliance costs of all or almost all the United Kingdom taxes is something of an explosion in the salaries of accountants as a consequence of the 'Big Bang' of October 1986. The impact was barely felt in our estimates of accountancy charges for 1986-87; but casual empiricism suggests a major increase since then, which would push up aggregate compliance costs substantially.

Another general influence is the increased use of computers and electronic data. The VAT 2 survey revealed no conclusive evidence that businesses using computers for VAT and other tax work had lower compliance costs than similar businesses that did not; but the long term effect must surely be to reduce compliance costs.

On income tax, perhaps the most significant change is the projected separate taxation of husband and wife, which we can expect, in the long run, to do something to help the situation of the perplexed widow.

The changes to CGT, in making 1982 rather than 1965 the base year, will do a little to reduce compliance costs but CGT will always be a high compliance cost tax. Applying income tax rates to CGT will remove the advantage of switching income into gains, once the threshold level of CGT has been reached.

The consensus amongst accountants interviewed was that the proposed 'Pay and File' system for corporation tax would have little effect on compliance costs, but it would impose a stricter timetable on business.

The projected community charge — a form of poll tax to replace the local domestic rate — will make little difference to the compliance costs of local taxation (which were minimal for local rates) but is likely to result in a substantial increase in administrative costs.

The most extensive changes and projected changes relate to VAT. We have already looked at some of the VAT changes post 1986-87 in our explanation of the paradox presented by the apparent discrepancy between the survey findings and the views of VAT advisers.

But in addition to the changes, as in the partial exemption rules, which put up compliance costs, a series of measures was proposed in the 1987 Budget for easing the burden of compliance on small firms, including a cash accounting proposal (to come into effect, for those who wished to take advantage of it, in October 1987) and an annual accounting option as from the summer of 1988. It should be noted, however, that traders adopting annual accounting are required to make nine direct debit payments on account during the year and a tenth balancing payment with the return; and the intention was that the scheme should be neutral in cash flow terms, though offering a real simplification to those traders who chose to use it.

The biggest projected changes to VAT are likely to come as part of the proposals to establish a single internal market by 1992 within the European Community (European Commission, 1987). The Commission had proposed that, from 1 January 1993, intra-Community trade should be treated for VAT purposes just like internal trade and not zero-rated. It was further proposed that all Member countries should adopt two rates of VAT, a standard rate and a reduced rate (roughly covering the goods at present zero-rated in the United Kingdom). Member countries would be free to choose the exact percentage from within a band of 14-20 per cent for standard rate and 4-9 per cent for reduced rate. All products except for a limited exemption list would be subject to one or other of these rates except for extra-Community exports which would continue to be zero-rated.

The implications of implementing such proposals for the administrative and compliance cost of the United Kingdom VAT would be considerable. If the zero rating of domestic products were abolished, the number and proportion of refund traders would drop to a very low figure, which would reduce administrative costs and probably compliance costs (as there would be far fewer monthly returns submitted). Even at the minimum permitted rates VAT revenues would increase significantly reducing the cost:yield ratios. Other proposals from the Commission, for a clearing house, to allow for compensating payments to net importing countries, would generate additional compliance costs.

As well as the approximation of VAT rates, the Commission has proposed the equalisation of the main excise duties, operating through a system of linked bonded warehouses. In the face of opposition from several countries, most prominently the United Kingdom, the Commission is having to re-think its plans for VAT and excises, so that the ultimate shape that these taxes will take remains unclear.

What is clear, however, both from the studies outlined in Part II of this book and the recent and projected changes in taxation, is that compliance costs are affected by every aspect of tax policy, whether it be the introduction of a new tax; or a change in tax structure (such as a reduction in the number of rates of VAT or a widening of the income tax base); or an alteration in the balance of taxation (for example, by raising indirect tax rates to pay for an increase in the income tax threshold); or changes in the method of administration (like moving from revenue- to self-assessment, adopting a scheme of mortgage relief at source, or introducing a VAT clearing house). What is important is that the significance of compliance costs should be fully recognised and that they should be consistently taken into account and given due weight in tax policy-making.

Administrative and Compliance Costs of Taxation

APPENDICES

APPENDIX A

**SUMMARIES OF PREVIOUS
RESEARCH STUDIES ON
COMPLIANCE COSTS**

1. Corporate Taxation

Title and Method	Authors	Reference	No. of responses	Response rate (%)	Respondents	Findings
1 The cost to business concerns of compliance with tax laws — mail questionnaire survey	**R.M.Haig**	*Management Review* November 1935, 232-333	160	10	Large US corporations with annual average sales of $17m.	Total compliance costs were 2.3% of tax liability. Size of costs was influenced by the number of states traded in. High compliance costs possibly imply low administrative costs.
2 Costs of tax administration Examples of compliance expenses — case studies and interviews.	**J.W.Martin**	*Bulletin of the National Tax Association*, April 1944, 194-205	5	100	Large and medium sized US corporations	Compliance costs were highly variable, being influenced by the type of business, type of tax, state policy and level — federal , state or local — and possibly by size and efficiency of firm. There was a floor to compliance costs, so they were proportionately higher for small firms.
3 The tax on taxes — mail questionnaire survey	**J.B.May and G.C. Thompson**	*Conference Board Business Record*, April 1950, 130-3	125	?	US manufacturing companies	Compliance costs were 1.5% of tax liability and 0.1% of sales. Differences between state tax laws cause high costs.
4 The high cost of compliance — mail questionnaire survey	**S.M.Mathes and G.C. Thompson**	*Business Record*, August 1959, 383-8	222	?	US manufacturing companies	Compliance costs appeared to be increasing and this trend was likely to continue.
5 Compliance costs and the Ohio axle mile tax — case studies	**C.V.Oster and A.D. Lynn**	*National Tax Journal*, April 1955, 209-14	11	61	Ohio trucking companies	Compliance costs of this tax were 10% of tax liability. They were highly variable with the predictability of operations, low costs being incurred where operations were very predictable and vice versa.

1. Corporate Taxation

Title and Method	Authors	Reference	No. of responses	Response rate (%)	Respondents	Findings
6 The cost of tax compliance — mail questionnaire survey	**M.H.Bryden**	*Canadian Tax Foundation* Paper 25, July 1961	125	25	Corporate supporters of CTF - nearly 50% manufacturers	Compliance costs were highly variable even between similar firms. They were proportionately higher for small firms. Costs of minor taxes were very high compared to liability.
7 Corporations' federal income tax compliance costs — case studies	**K.S. Johnston**	Ohio University Bureau of Business Research Monograph 10, 1961	6	100	Firms in Columbus, Ohio	There were economies of scale in compliance procedures — costs are proportionately higher for smaller firms
8 Administrative and compliance costs of state and local taxes	**J.H.Wicks and M.N. Killworth**	*National Tax Journal*, September 1967, 309-15	74	?	Employers in Montana	Employers' costs of withholding income tax averaged 8.3% of taxes withheld.
9 *Development of methodology for estimating tax-payer paperwork burden* — mail questionnaire survey	**Arthur D. Little Corporation**	*Final Report to Department of the Treasury*, IRS, Washington, 1988	1474	37	Partnerships and Corporations and their paid preparers	Business compliance costs of U.S. federal income tax in 1983 amounted to 2748 million hours.

2. Business Taxation Excluding Corporate Taxation

Title and Method	Authors	Reference	No. of responses	Response rate (%)	Respondents	Findings
10 A measurement of the cost of collecting sales tax monies in selected retail stores — time studies and interviews	**M.P. Matthews**	Salt Lake City: Bureau of Economic & Business Research, University of Utah, 1956	7	100	Utah retail stores	Compliance costs were highly variable, with selling costs higher than administrative costs. Average transaction size is the principal determining factor, but store policy also had an influence. Compliance weighed heaviest on smaller firms.
11 Retailers' costs of sales tax collection in Ohio — time studies and interviews	**J.C.Yocum**	Ohio University Bureau of Business Research, 1961	526	?	Ohio retail stores over \$50,000 in second half of 1959	Compliance costs were influenced by size of firm, average transaction size, and ratio of taxable to gross sales. They were proportionately greater for small firms
12 The burden of compliance—mail questionnaire plus survey follow-up interviews and time studies, plus supplementary interviews	**F.J.Muller**	Seattle Bureau of Business Research, 1963	198 by questionnaire - Follow up of 75 - by interview	80 25	Small businesses in Washington State	Economies of scale existed in sales tax compliance costs, particularly in administering the system. Indirect costs were also significant, and costs in stress were often high. Payroll taxes were also investigated, with similar findings.
13 The disguised tax burden. Compliance costs of German businessmen and professionals — opinion poll interviews	**B. Strumpel**	1963 *National Tax Journal*, January 1966, 70-77	1009	?	German businessmen with less than 100 employees each	Owners spent an average of 18 hours per month on tax work and their employees a further 4 hours. Cost of tax advice was 60 Dm per month. Compliance costs were regressive; other taxpayers did not incur significant costs.
14 German Added Value Tax - 2 years after — questionnaire survey	**R.J.Niehus**	*Taxes*, September 1969, 554-55	?	?	?	66-70 per cent of German businesses surveyed said the VAT law caused more book work, often much more than a ten percent increase.

2. Business Taxation Excluding Corporate Taxation

Title and Method	Authors	Reference	No. of responses	Response rate (%)	Respondents	Findings
15 Value Added Tax, the cost to the businessman — simulation exercise	P.A.Barker	*Journal of Accountancy,* September 1972, 75-9	6	100	Selected Indiana Firms	Compliance costs of a hypothetical VAT are related to the number of sales and purchases invoices handled, and to average transaction size. Manufacturers handle the greatest number of invoices and incur the highest costs.
16 VAT — compliance costs to the independent retailer — interview survey	M.Godwin	*Accountancy,* September 1976, 48-60	29	44	Independent Bath retailers	Compliance costs were related to the scheme of accounting selected for VAT, and this in turn depends on the rating of goods sold. Frequent changes in the tax increase compliance costs.
17 Compliance costs of the Value Added Tax — simulation exercise	S.K.Parker	*Taxes,* June 1976, 369-80	6	-	Non-retail businesses	Indicated that a hypothetical VAT on either the invoice or the accounts basis could be operated without major accounting changes in any of the surveyed firms. Total compliance costs amounted to less than 1 percent of sales. Compliance costs were regressive.
18 *Costs and benefits of Value Added Tax* — mail questionnaire survey with follow-up interviews and supplementary interviews.	C.T. Sandford, M.R.Godwin P.J.W. Hardwick and M.I. Butterworth	Heinemann Educational Books, London 1981	2857	31	UK VAT registered traders; additional follow-up interviews with respondents and with tax advisers.	VAT compliance costs are strongly regressive in relation to turnover. Large cash flow benefits accrued, mainly to the benefit of the largest firms. Comprehension problems with VAT regulations were widespread.
19 Simplifying VAT for small traders — interview survey	M.R.Godwin and C.T. Sandford	*Accounting and Business Research,* Autumn 1983, 279-288	-	-	Tax officials, accountants and academics in West Germany, the Netherlands, Belgium and at the EEC	Several schemes are in operation including tapering and forfeit schemes, but variable tax return periods offer the best prospect for reducing compliance costs.

2. Business Taxation Excluding Corporate Taxation

Title and Method	Authors	Reference	No. of responses	Response rate (%)	Respondents	Findings
20 PAYE — Cost or benefit to employers? — mail questionnaire survey with follow-up interviews	**M.R. Godwin, P.J.W. Hardwick and C.T. Sandford**	*Accountancy*, November 1983, 107-112	783	30	UK employers	PAYE compliance costs are about 1% of yield, and are regressive; cash flow benefits accrue, mainly to the largest firms.
21 A comparative analysis of sales tax compliance costs for retail businesses — telephone interviews and time studies	**Peat Marwick, Accountants**	Mimeo, Small Business Administration, Washington DC, 1985	80	27	US retail sales taxpaying traders in several states	The extent of exemptions and the rate of tax affect compliance costs significantly; filing returns is the area where economies of scale are greatest; variable return periods offer the greatest scope for reducing cost inequities.
22 PAYE/PRSI and operating costs — mail questionnaire survey	**R.J. Leonard**	Unpublished M Litt thesis, Trinity College, Dublin, 1986	119	40	Members of the Federated Union of Employers in Ireland	Compliance costs average 2.7%, distributed regressively. Cash flow benefits accrue mainly to the largest firms.
23 The compliance costs of VAT for smaller firms in Britain and Germany — mail questionnaire survey	**G.Bannock and H. Albach**	Graham Bannock and Partners, London 1987	262(UK) 197(Germany)	44(UK) 25(Germany)	VAT registered small and medium sized traders	Costs tend to be higher in the UK than Germany. German traders used accountants more frequently than UK traders. Less hostility to VAT in Germany than in the UK.

3. Personal Taxation

Title and Method	Authors	Reference	No. of responses	Response rate (%)	Respondents	Findings
24 Taxpayer compliance costs from the Montana personal income tax — questionnaire survey	**J.H. Wicks**	*Montana Business Quarterly*, Fall 1965, 36-42	106	33	Parents of economics undergraduates	Compliance costs were a function of occupation. A few respondents reported very high costs. Response was biased towards higher cost taxpayers — low compliance cost taxpayers did not reply.
25 Taxpayer compliance costs from personal income taxation — questionnaire survey	**J.H. Wicks**	*Iowa Business Digest*, August 1966, 16-21	118	31	Parents of college students	Similar to the above. The self-employed incurred the highest compliance costs. Costs were not related to income or to size of tax payment.
26 Administrative and compliance costs of state and local taxes — questionnaire survey	**J.H. Wicks and M.N Killworth**	*National Tax Journal*, September 1967, 309-15	421	42	Montana income taxpayers	Average compliance cost of the Montana income tax to the personal taxpayer was 20.7% of liability.
27 *The hidden costs of taxation* — opinion poll interviews, follow-up mail questionnaire survey plus some interviews	**C.T. Sandford**	Institute for Fiscal Studies, 1973	2773 for short questionnaire, 137 follow-up	78 for questionnaire, 41 for follow-up	UK personal taxpayers, with re-survey of those paying for tax advice or spending at least 8 hours p.a. on tax work	UK personal taxpayers' costs increased between 1965 and 1970. The self-employed constitute half of the high cost taxpayers. Compliance costs were inequitable and regressive. Total operating costs of personal direct taxation were between 3.8 and 5.8% of revenue, whereas administrative costs were less than 1.5%.
28 Accountants and the tax system — interview survey	**C.T. Sandford and P.N. Dean**	*Accounting and Business Research*, Winter 1971/2, 3-37	82	37	UK accountants	Capital gains tax involves high costs. Much tax work is not billed as such. Compliance costs are regressive and rising.

3. Personal Taxation

Title and Method	Authors	Reference	No. of responses	Response rate (%)	Respondents	Findings
29 *The Irish wealth tax: a case study in economics and politics* — study of client records of a major accounting firm	**C.T. Sandford and O. Morrissey**	Economic and Social Research Institute, Dublin. 1985	-	-	5-6% of Irish wealth tax payers	Compliance costs averaged 18.5% of liability; administrative costs were at least 6% of yield. The form of administration was too cumbersome for a tax imposed at low rates.
30 The compliance costs of the US individual income tax system — mail questionnaire survey	**J.R. Slemrod and N. Sorum**	*National Tax Journal*, 37, 4, 461-474, 1984	600	33	Minnesota income tax payers	Compliance costs exceeded 7% of total federal and state income tax revenue. The self-employed incur high costs.
31 The compliance costs of itemis-ing deductions: evidence from individual tax returns — documentary analysis	**M.M.Pitt and J.R. Slemrod**	Mimeo 1988	13,409 returns from the U.S. Treasury tax file.			Privately borne cost in 1982 of allowing itemised Deductions estimated at $1.44bn. An increased standard deduction enhances progressivity, diminishes horizontal equity and saves resource costs
32 The administrative and compliance costs of personal income taxes and payroll taxes, Canada, 1986 — opinion poll interviews with mail questionnaire survey of employers	**F. Vaillancourt**	Canadian Tax Foundation. 1989	2040 residents 385 employers	quota sample - refusals not indicated 10	Residents and employers in 10 Canadian provinces	For personal taxpayers, average compliance cost was 2.5% of taxes collected; for employers, it was 3.6%. Costs of unemployment insurance were high.
33 *Development of methodology for estimating tax-payer paperwork burden* - (1) Diary check (2) Mail question	**Arthur D. Little Corporation**	*Final Report to Department of the Treasury*, IRS, Washington, 1988	(1) 750 (2) 6,200	? 65	U.S. individual federal income tax payers	Average burden for individuals, 1983 was 26.4 hours, aggregating to 1.59 billion hours.

APPENDIX B

Technical Aspects of the Personal Taxpayers' Study

(i) The Personal Taxpayers' Survey

The empirical part of the personal taxpayers' study consisted primarily of a mail survey of taxpayers. Information was sought on the time spent on tax work by the respondent and the respondent's spouse; on fees normally paid to professional advisers, and any other costs incurred; and on abnormal expenditures on specific tax problems; all questions related to the tax year 1983-84. The Inland Revenue selected a sample of 4,241 income taxpayers, stratified to the research team's specifications (within the constraints dictated by the administrative classifications and procedures used by Inland Revenue), and mailed the questionnaires in such a way as to safeguard the anonymity of respondents.

In addition to the data obtained by questionnaire, the Inland Revenue also supplied data from the Survey of Personal Incomes (SPI) covering respondents' sources and size of income. Particular care was taken to ensure that it was impossible for the researchers to identify any individual from the data supplied. Questionnaire and SPI data were matched by code numbers; the researchers never saw the names and addresses of sample members, and the Inland Revenue had no access to the completed questionnaires. Thus anonymity and confidentiality were maintained; respondents were not even given the option of identifying themselves.

Response

In the personal taxpayers' survey, 1,776 usable replies were received, and a further 56 unusable responses were received as set out in Table B.2. Deducting the 142 sample members classed as 'out of frame' from the gross sample left a net sample frame of 4,099. The 1,776 usable responses thus represent a response rate of 43.3 per cent, a high percentage for a survey of this kind. Stratification details were provided by the Inland Revenue which enabled the researchers to calculate the response rates for each stratum. These are set out in Table B.1.

231

Table B.1. Personal Taxpayers' Survey: Response Rates by Inland Revenue Stratum

	Response rate (%) — N of respondents in brackets	*Sampling Fraction*
Schedule D cases		
A) Income greater than £45,000 (1982-83)	37.4 (110)	1 in 30
B) Other higher rate and/or surcharge cases	37.6 (216)	1 in 500
D) Remainder of Schedule D cases	28.6 (355)	1 in 2,000
Schedule E cases		
T) Income greater than £45,000 (1982-83)	45.3 (169)	1 in 30
S) Other higher rate and/or surcharge cases	55.2 (672)	1 in 600
F) Other cases with income of £9,500 or more	53.7 (65)	1 in 10,000
P) Other cases with income below £9,500	40.4 (57)	1 in 120,000
Repayment claim cases		
R) Taxpayers with some investment income who made a repayment claim during 1982-83	47.0 (127)	1 in 2,000
Other		
L & K) Unemployment and supplementary benefit cases, and those leaving the PAYE system	23.0 (2)	1 in 333,333

For the analysis of costs as a percentage of income, self- employed taxpayers who had made losses, or whose incomes were near zero, were excluded. For consistency, they were also excluded from certain other analyses as well.

The overall response rate was appreciably higher than for comparable surveys and the sample coverage of higher rate taxpayers, and of all Schedule D taxpayers was satisfactory (though it is apparent from the table that the response from Schedule D cases was lower than that for Schedule E cases in all strata). Co-operation with Inland Revenue enabled us to omit detailed income questions from the questionnaire, with a beneficial effect on response.

However, it may be seen from Table B.1 that the sampling fractions in Strata L, K and P, which together contribute 78 per cent of all tax units, are extremely low. On general evidence, compliance costs in these categories were expected to be low, and in order to keep costs within bounds, the sample sizes in these strata were deliberately kept down in the planning stage. In the event, the size of sample drawn at local level by Inland Revenue was for technical reasons even lower than had been agreed. These are the low compliance cost strata, and thus of relatively little significance; nonetheless the reliability of the grossed-up figures is somewhat reduced.

Table B.2 Personal Taxpayers' Survey: Out of Frame and Unusable Responses

	N
Gone away (out of frame)	109
Deceased (out of frame)	18
Ill (out of frame)	1
Not known at address (out of frame)	12
Address does not exist (out of frame)	2
Questionnaire inadequately completed	56

(ii) The Regression Analysis of Personal Taxpayers' Costs

Our findings are that compliance costs fall into two categories, a distinct 'high compliance cost' group whose income is derived at least in part from sources other than employment, and a relatively low cost majority. Factors associated with high compliance costs may include the schedule under which income is taxed (which depends on the type(s) of income received); the number of different types of income; the allowances claimed (if any); and whether or not professional tax advice is required.

Regression analysis was used to determine whether these factors affected compliance costs significantly. Stepwise regression was selected, using the SPSSX default criteria as follows:

The equation is computed. The independent variable with the largest probability of F is then removed if that probability exceeds 0.10. The equation is recomputed without the removed variable, and the rest of the variables are examined for removal. Once no more independent variables need to be removed, remaining variables are examined to see if they satisfy positive requirements for entry. The variable with the smallest probability of F is entered if that probability is less than 0.05 and tolerance criteria are satisfied.

Tolerance of the variable being considered for entry (i.e. the proportion of the variance of that variable not accounted for by other variables in the equation) must be better than 0.01, and entry into the equation of the variable being considered must also not reduce the tolerance of variables already in the equation below 0.01 (this latter condition is called the 'minimum tolerance' criterion). Once an additional variable has been entered, all variables in the equation are again examined for removal. This process continues until no variables in the equation need to be removed and no variables not in the equation are eligible for entry, or until the maximum number of steps, which is twice the number of independent variables, has been reached.

A total of four regression equations were run; for all Schedule D respondents; all Schedule E respondents; all respondents employing a tax adviser; and all respondents *not* employing a tax adviser. Variables included were: individual types of income; whether an adviser had been employed; total and taxable income levels; whether any difficulties, problems, or claims for repayment had been made; levels of any capital allowances or stock relief; and whether the respondent was a qualified accountant or otherwise capable of dealing with tax affairs.

The results of the regressions are given in Table B.3. As a stepwise technique was adopted, variables (except the constant term) were only included if they were statistically significant. Factors tending to increase compliance costs, and those factors tending to reduce compliance costs, have been listed separately for each equation.

Table B.3 Regression Results from PITS

Dependent Variable: **Total Compliance Cost**

Coefficients which are not significant at the 95 per cent level are marked thus '*'.

Equation I: All Schedule D Respondents

Adjusted R-squared = 0.31

Constant = -91.0*

Variables in the equation:	**Coefficient**

(a) Increasing compliance costs:

Total Income	0.009
Value of Main Capital Allowances	0.041
Use of an Accountant	571.1
Presence of Capital Gains	791.8
Presence of Professional Fees	420.1
Presence of Royalties	1,025.7

(b) Reducing compliance costs:

Presence of Building Society Interest	-294.3

Equation II: All Schedule E Respondents

Adjusted R-squared = 0.36

Constant = -133.29

Variables included in the equation: **Coefficient**

(a) Increasing compliance costs:

Number of Income Sources	44.3
Use of an Accountant	395.9
Presence of Business Profits	297.1
Presence of Directors' Fees	235.1
Presence of Overseas Earnings	279.1
Presence of Non-State/Occupational Pension	230.0
Presence of Unusual Difficulties	53.9

(b) Reducing compliance costs:

Presence of Investment Income not taxed at source	-164.8

Equation III: All Respondents using a Tax Adviser

Adjusted R-squared = 0.20

Constant = 258.5

Variables included in the equation: **Coefficient**

(a) Increasing compliance costs:

Number of Own Income Sources	125.2
Total Income	0.044
Value of Main Capital Allowances	0.043
Presence of Non-State/Occupational Pensions	542.3
Presence of Royalties	787.3

(b) Reducing compliance costs:

Taxable Income	-0.04
Presence of Building Society Interest	-299.4
Presence of Wage Income	-253.2
Presence of State Pension	-346.6

Equation III: All Respondents not using a Tax Adviser

Adjusted R-squared = 0.39

Constant = -7.67*

Variables included in the equation:	**Coefficient**

(a) Increasing compliance costs:

Taxable Income	0.002
Presence of Capital Gains	171.0
Presence of Directors' Fees	218.0
Presence of Professional Fees	141.3
Presence of Overseas Earnings	278.5
Subsidiary Capital Allowances	2.4

(b) Reducing compliance costs:

None

The regression analysis suggests that for all respondents, costs are related to income and often to professional status: it was to be expected that these variables would influence respondents' valuations of time. However, there are clear differences between schedules. For Schedule D taxpayers other important factors also include the value of capital allowances claimed, and liability to capital gains tax. Clearly both claiming capital allowances, and determining liability to capital gains tax, are matters which may involve self-employed taxpayers and their advisers in drawn-out and costly negotiations with Inland Revenue.

These factors did not affect Schedule E taxpayers: for this group, the presence of business profits as well as income from employment was consistently significant. This confirms that the important factor for Schedule E taxpayers is whether they also have non-Schedule E income sources. The number of income sources was also important, as was the presence of unusual difficulties.

None of the following factors was found to have any significant impact on costs: maintenance, unemployment benefit, untaxed benefits or benefits in kind, or trust income; presence of problems or claims for repayment of tax; level of claims for stock reliefs; and whether the respondent was qualified or capable of coping with tax affairs.

While the above results are not outstanding, there is some evidence of a clear relationship between costs and total income for taxpayers whose costs exceed 1 per cent of income. The correlation coefficient between costs and total income for all respondents is only 0.29. Further analysis of Schedule D respondents found that those whose costs exceeded 1 per cent of income were typically self-employed, using a tax adviser, and reporting difficulties with the return for and/or other problems in their dealings with Inland Revenue. Schedule D respondents whose costs were lower than this were often retired; widowed, separated, or divorced; and did not employ an accountant. An unusually high proportion of our female respondents fell into this category.

However, when taxpayers whose costs exceed one per cent of total income are selected, the correlation between costs and total income rises to 0.56, and when taxpayers whose costs exceed 2 per cent are selected, it rises to 0.71. The improvement is particularly marked in the case of Schedule D taxpayers: for all Schedule D respondents, the correlation is 0.32; for those whose costs exceed 1 per cent it improves to 0.63; and for those whose costs exceed 2 per cent of total income it rises to 0.73.

(iii) Timing of Tax Payments for the Self-Employed (Schedule D Cases I and II)

Tax is chargeable on the profits of the accounting period ending in the year preceding the year of assessment. It is payable in two equal instalments on 1 January in the year of assessment and the following 1 July. For a firm with an accounting date ending 31 December the position will be as follows:

Accounting period   1 January to 31 December 1985

Year of assessment   6 April 1986 to 5 April 1987

Tax due   1 January 1987 and 1 July 1987

But this does not mean the overall lags in payment are as long as this implies. There are special rules for the opening and closing years. In the first year a taxpayer is liable on actual income (prorated from the accounts if necessary), in the second year on the profits of the first 12 months of trading and in the third year on the profits of the accounting period ending in the previous tax year. Alternatively he may elect to have his tax bills for both the second and third years (but not one or the other) based on his actual earnings in those years. Conversely, on cessation, the last year's income is taxed on an actual basis and in the two preceding years the taxpayer pays the higher of actual and preceding year profits.

Thus for a new business payments will be as follows:

Actual Profits

1 January — 31 December 1985 Profits 1,000
1 January — 31 December 1986 Profits 2,000
1 January — 31 December 1987 Profits 3,000

Taxable Income

1984-85 1/4 x 1,000 = 250
         and
The lower of
1985-86 — 1,000} Commencement rules.
1986-87 — 1,000}

        or

1985-86 (3/4 x 1,000 + 1/4 x 2,000) = 1,250 } Alternative actual
1986-87 (3/4 x 2,000 + 1/4 x 3,000) = 2,250 } basis

On cessation the position will be:

Actual Profits

1 January — 31 December 1984	8,000
1 January — 31 December 1985	10,000
1 January — 31 December 1986	12,000
1 January — 31 December 1987	16,000

Taxable Income

The higher of
1985-86 — 8,000} Previous year basis
1986-87 — 10,000}

     or

1985-86 (1/4 x 12,000 + 3/4 x 10,000) = 10,500} Actual profit
1986-87 (1/4 x 16,000 + 3/4 x 12,000) = 13,000} basis
1987-88 (3/4 x 16,000)   = 12,000

(iv) Facsimile (half size) of Personal Taxpayers Questionnaire

Confidential

Bath University Centre for Fiscal Studies

Study of the Costs incurred by Personal Taxpayers, 1984

All the questions relate to the past income tax year, that is 6 April 1983 to 5 April 1984.
Married persons should enter details for their spouse where a column or space is provided.

A Personal details

Please indicate by ticking the appropriate boxes whether you are:

Male ☐

Female ☐

Single ☐

Married ☐

Separated, divorced or widowed ☐

Aged 16–24 ☐

Aged 25–49 ☐

Aged over 50 but below retirement age ☐

Over retirement age ☐

	Self	Spouse
In full-time employment	☐	☐
In part-time employment	☐	☐
Director of a public company	☐	☐
Director of a private company	☐	☐
Self-employed	☐	☐
Retired	☐	☐
A full-time student	☐	☐
Unemployed	☐	☐
Not seeking paid employment e g full-time housewife	☐	☐
In some other category (please state)	☐	☐

B Income details

Various forms of income and capital gains are described below

Please tick all those which describe your sources of income *for the past year.*

	Self	Spouse
Salaries, wages, tips, commissions	☐	☐
Business profits/partnership income	☐	☐
Professional and consultant fees	☐	☐
Director's fees	☐	☐
Rent	☐	☐
Building society interest	☐	☐
Investment income (tax not deducted at source)	☐	☐
Investment income (tax deducted at source)	☐	☐
Benefit in kind e g car, rent free accommodation	☐	☐
State pensions	☐	☐
Occupational pensions	☐	☐
Other pensions	☐	☐
Maintenance payments e g alimony	☐	☐
Unemployment benefit	☐	☐
Child benefit, maternity benefit or other untaxed benefit	☐	☐
Capital gains	☐	☐
Overseas earnings	☐	☐
Trust income	☐	☐
Royalties	☐	☐
Other (please state)	☐	☐

C Taxation

1 Do you have regular difficulties in completing your tax return?   yes ☐ no ☐

If yes, please say whether the problem is in the income tax and/or capital gains section and describe it briefly.

2 Did you have any problems with the Inland Revenue during the past year?   yes ☐ no ☐

If yes, describe them briefly.

3 Have you made a claim for a repayment of tax during the past year?   yes ☐ no ☐

If yes, please give the reason for your claim, the sum involved and the time it took to settle your claim (in weeks).

Sum involved: £ ____

Number of weeks taken to settle claim: ____

Reason for claim:

4 Please show below the amount of time you (and your spouse) spent on your tax affairs in the past year. If you get someone else to deal with your tax affairs, please state the amount of time you spent preparing information for them, seeing them, etc.

Time spent on income tax (in hours):
Self ____   Wife ____

Time spent on capital gains tax (in hours):
Self ____   Wife ____

The hourly value of this time to me was approximately:
Self £ ____ per hour   Wife £ ____ per hour

5 Did you have to pay any incidental expenses in connection with your tax affairs—e g travel, telephone calls, postage?   yes ☐ no ☐

(Do not include advisers' fees here - see Q8).

If yes, describe the expenses and say how much you paid.   Sum involved: £ ____

Description of expenses:

6 Did you pay for professional advice on your tax affairs?   yes ☐ no ☐

If **yes**, answer questions **7** to **10**

If **no**, answer only questions **11** and **12**

This page is only for taxpayers who pay an adviser to do income tax/capital gains tax work

7 Why do you employ a tax adviser?
Please tick your reason(s)

I can't find/afford the time to deal with tax myself ☐

Changes in my circumstances have made me seek advice ☐

The tax forms are too complicated to understand ☐

My income comes from too many sources for me to cope with it easily ☐

I want to be sure of getting all the allowances I am entitled to ☐

I feel happier knowing my returns are accurate ☐

I have been wrongly charged in the past and I don't want it to happen again ☐

I wish to take every opportunity the law allows to cut my tax bill ☐

My adviser saves me more than I pay him ☐

Discussions with my tax adviser help me with other financial matters ☐

Inland Revenue suggested I use professional advisers ☐

Other (please state) ☐

8 Who gives you professional advice on your tax affairs?
(please tick below)

Accountant/accountancy firm ☐

Solicitor/Barrister ☐

Bank manager/bank tax department ☐

Valuer ☐

Other ☐

How much were you charged in the past year?

£ _____

9 Did this amount include payment for work other than your personal tax affairs (e g VAT, payrolls, etc)?   yes ☐ no ☐

If yes, give an estimate of the proportion of the fee that arose solely for:
Income tax work

£ _____

Capital gains tax work

£ _____

10 Did these fees include costs of any *exceptional* difficulties?   yes ☐ no ☐

If yes, please describe the difficulty and give an estimate of the extra fees charged.

Extra fees charged: £ _____

Description of difficulty:

Please go to question 12

244 Administrative and Compliance Costs of Taxation

This question is for taxpayers who do not pay for personal tax advice

11 Please tick below your reason(s) for *not* paying for professional advice

My tax affairs are simple ☐

I am professionally qualified to handle tax affairs ☐

Athough not professionally qualified, I am capable of handling my own tax affairs ☐

It is as easy to do it myself as it is to give the information to someone else ☐

I have a relative/friend who helps me without charge ☐

I get help from the Inland Revenue staff ☐

I can get help from Inland Revenue leaflets ☐

I can get help from other books, etc ☐

I can get help from Citizens' Advice Bureaux ☐

I can get help from Press Enquiry Bureaux ☐

I wish to keep my tax affairs private ☐

I don't believe the results would justify the expense ☐

I have paid for advice in the past but I don't think it is worth continuing ☐

Other (please state) ☐

This question is for all taxpayers

12 Please add, in the space below, any suggestions for improving the administration of income tax and capital gains tax which you would like to make

0311

Thank you for completing this questionnaire

Please return it to Professor Sandford, University of Bath, in the enclosed reply-paid envelope.

APPENDIX C

Technical Aspects of the PAYE Study

(i) The PAYE Survey

The main method of survey was pre-piloted mail questionnaire surveys, supplemented by some follow-up interviews with respondents who chose to identify themselves.

Sampling

In the PAYE survey, a sample of 3,039 employers was drawn by Inland Revenue, using a fixed sampling fraction of 3 in 1,000. The sample was drawn from the two Inland Revenue national computerised PAYE files. These were categorised into eight types of scheme of which the first five (which are ranges of PAYE and NI payments) cover the majority of employers. The other three schemes were for quarterly paid employees; annually paid employees; and direct collection arrangements. Of the 3,039 employers, 303 received a pilot questionnaire in September 1981, and the remainder received a slightly modified questionnaire in June 1982. The pilot and main samples were drawn simultaneously to save on programming costs, which would otherwise have been virtually doubled. In both cases, two reminders were sent out at fortnightly intervals, with the final mailing including a further copy of the questionnaire.

The PAYE questionnaires were mailed by Inland Revenue: in this survey the research team had no access to the names and addresses of sample members unless they voluntarily identified themselves on the returned questionnaires. On the other hand, the questionnaires were returned in confidence to Bath University; neither Inland Revenue nor anyone else outside the research team had access to the completed responses.

In the PAYE survey, the overall response rate was 30 per cent, which, while low in absolute terms, is about normal for surveys of business compliance costs. Larger businesses responded better than smaller ones — response ranged from 57 per cent from the group of

245

businesses making the highest income tax and NI payments (£180,000 p.a. and above) — which also contribute the bulk of revenue — down to 21 per cent for the firms making the lowest payments (£1,200 or less).

(ii) The Calculation of Employers' Cash Flow Benefits

While the employer incurs costs in complying with PAYE and NI regulations, he also gains a cash flow benefit. The extent of the cash flow benefit depends on the length of time elapsing between the payment of wages and the payment of PAYE and NI. Thus the benefit differs between monthly and weekly paid employees. In the case of monthly paid employees, tax payments are due on the 19th of the month following the payment of the wage. If it is assumed that employees are paid on the last day of each calendar month, 18 days elapse between payment of wages and tax becoming due, so for an average month, the benefit is 1/12 of T (the annual tax and NI bill) x 18/365; this occurs in every month, so the total annual amount by which cash flow is improved is T/12 x 12 x 18/365 = 0.049T, or in round terms, 5 per cent of payments.

But if employees are paid earlier in the month than the last day, the gap between the pay day and the date when tax is due widens, and the cash flow benefit increases by T/365 for each additional day. Thus, if salaries are normally paid on the last Friday of the month, one month in seven will end on a Friday, giving no additional benefit; one month will end on a Thursday, giving one extra day's benefit; one month will end on a Wednesday, giving two extra days' benefit, and so on. An 'average' month will yield an additional 3.5 days' benefit, so the benefit for such a firm will be T/12 x 12 x 21.5/365 = 0.059T. The inclusion in the survey of a question asking the date on which monthly paid staff were paid made it possible to calculate the appropriate proportions for each respondent employer.

In the case of weekly paid staff, the benefit is composed of two elements: (a) the grace period between the *end* of the tax month and the date on which tax is due, and (b) the collection period in which the tax accrues week by week *during* the tax month — thus tax withheld from the first week's pay is retained by the employer for seven days longer than tax withheld from the second week's pay, and so on.

As with monthly paid employees, tax is due on the 19th of the month following the payment of the wage, but Inland Revenue collection 'months' for weekly paid employees are divided into eight four-week 'months' and four five-week 'months'. Assuming that employers always pay tax on the last official day for payment, it was calculated that the total cash benefit from weekly paid staff averages out over the year to 0.087T. Similar calculations yielded the appropriate fractions for employees paid fortnightly, quarterly, four-monthly and annually.

On this basis, an estimate was made of the cash flow benefit of PAYE and NI to employers. It was necessary to make the additional assumption that where some of a firm's employees were paid weekly and others monthly, the wage bill was divided in direct proportion to the percentage of employees in each category. To the extent that monthly paid staff are more highly paid than weekly paid staff, this assumption will have the effect of over-estimating the benefit to some extent. On the other hand, the assumption that all businesses pay tax on the due date is unrealistic: in practice, many firms take longer to pay. Thus our figure may equally well be an under-estimate of the benefit.

(iii) Facsimile (half size) of PAYE Questionnaire

Confidential

University of Bath
Centre for Fiscal Studies
1982

Pay As You Earn
A Survey of Costs to Businesses

1

1 What is your main business activity? (Please indicate industry and type of business, eg retail food store, manufacturer of chemicals, garage, hardware store etc.)

2 On what date did your last accounting year end (the date to which you make up your annual accounts)?

DAY   MONTH   YEAR

3 How many people, on average, were employed in the business during your last accounting year?

(a) Partners or proprietors of unincorporated businesses (if your business is incorporated, please write N/A).

(b) Full-time employees (including executive directors of incorporated businesses, ie companies).

(c) Part-time employees (employed for less than 21 hours a week). If there were no part-time employees, Please write NONE.

4 What proportion of your employees are paid

(a) Weekly: per cent of all employees

(b) Monthly: per cent of all employees

(c) Any other (please describe)

          per cent of all employees

2

5 Please state the date in the month on which monthly paid staff received their salaries. (If there were no monthly paid staff, please write N/A).

Cols.

37–38

6 How many employees did you take on during your last accounting year?

39–43

7 And how many employees left the business during the last accounting year?

44–48

8 What was the turnover of your business in the last accounting year? (please tick appropriate box)

Punch lead zeros

49–52

Under £20,000 0001

£20,000 but under £50,000 0002

£50,000 but under £100,000 0003

£100,000 but under £500,000 0004

£500,000 but under £1 million 0005

£1 million but under £10 million 0006

If £10 million or over, please state approximate amount .... £ ⬚ m　　*Code*

3

9 (a) How much in PAYE and National Insurance contributions combined did you pay over to the Inland Revenue in the tax year ended 5 April 1982?

£ [   ]

Code [   ]   Cols.

53–64

(b) Of this total, how much was PAYE?

£ [   ]

Code [   ]

65–74

10 What were your arrangements for submitting details of tax deductions to the Inland Revenue at the end of the year? (If more than one arrangement was used, please indicate):

(a) Standard documents supplied by the Inland Revenue

[   ]   1   75

(b) Substitute documents approved by the Inland Revenue

[   ]   2

(c) Magnetic tape

[   ]   3

11 How is PAYE work done in your business? (please tick one)

(a) Entirely within the firm

| Please go to question 14 on page 5 |

1   76

(b) Wholly or partly by a professional accountant in private practice

| Please go to question 12 on page 4 |

2

(c) Wholly or partly by a specialist agency (eg a computer payroll service)

| Please go to question 12 on page 4 |

3

End of Card 1

4

ONLY for employers who normally employ a professional accountant in private practice or a specialist agency to do PAYE work

12 What was your accountant's or specialist agency's total fee for the last 12 months for which you have been invoiced?

£ ⬚

13 (a) Does this fee include other work (eg accounting or audit work) as well as PAYE?

YES ⬚

NO ⬚

(b) If "YES", can you give an estimate of the proportion of the fee arising solely from PAYE work?

⬚

For all employers

14 What is your estimate of the labour costs of operating PAYE and NI procedures *within the firm* in your last accounting year? Please *exclude* overhead costs.

	Total number of hours spent (if none, write 0)	Average hourly cost of this time	
(a) By the directors, partners or proprietors		£	14–17, 18–22
(b) By employees other than computer staff		£	23–27, 28–32
(c) By computer staff		£	33–37, 38–42

15 (a) Are there any additional costs (other than those referred to in questions 12–14) involved in operating PAYE and NI?

YES [ ]   1   43

NO [ ]   2

(b) If "YES", please specify and estimate the approximate annual cost.

Annual Cost   *Code*   44–48

£ [ ]   [ ]   49

16 Can you divide the total costs of operating PAYE into the following two categories:

(a) Costs incurred at the end of the year (preparing the employer's annual statement, declaration and certificate P35 and the end of year return for each employee P14/P60)   [ ] per cent of PAYE costs   50–51

(b) All other PAYE costs including issue of P45s   [ ] per cent of PAYE costs   52–53

6

17 (a) Have you experienced any special difficulties with operating
PAYE in the last accounting year?

YES ☐

NO ☐

(b) If "YES", please describe them briefly, and if possible estimate
any extra costs incurred.

....

....   £ ☐

(c) Did you include these costs in your answers to questions 12—15
on pages 4 and 5?

YES ☐

NO ☐

18 In the light of your experience, do you think the PAYE system
(including the associated forms, instructions etc.) could be
improved? If so, how?

7

19 The suggestion has been made that the employer's NI contribution should be replaced by a monthly percentage tax on total payroll. Assuming that the amount paid would remain about the same as at present, do you think such a change would reduce your costs in administering the system?

NO ☐ 1   62

YES, MARGINALLY ☐ 2

YES, A LOT ☐ 3

20 If you are willing to answer any queries that arise from this questionnaire, or would like a summary of the results, please state your name, address, and telephone number, and tick the box(es):

Name ....

Address ....

....

....

....

Telephone ....

I would be willing to answer further questions ☐ 1   63

I would like a summary of the results ☐ 1   64

End of Card 2

THANK YOU AGAIN FOR COMPLETING THIS QUESTIONNAIRE. I HOPE YOU HAVE NOT FOUND IT TOO TIME-CONSUMING. PLEASE POST IT IN THE REPLY PAID ENVELOPE AS SOON AS POSSIBLE.

APPENDIX D

Technical Details of the VAT 2 Study

(i) The VAT 2 Survey

The VAT 2 survey was aimed primarily at updating the results of the earlier VAT survey. However, the opportunity was also taken to update the PAYE study, and to gather some data on corporation tax compliance costs. Because VAT was the principal focus of interest, the sample was drawn from the VAT register, with the co-operation of Customs and Excise. In consequence, all sample members were VAT registered traders; some (i.e. firms with employees) were also registered for PAYE; and some (i.e. companies) were also registered for corporation tax.

Reasons for Updating the VAT study

Out-of-date figures: the previous study related to the late 1970s, when there were fewer registered traders, and the structure of the tax was different: e.g. the two positive rates at the time of the earlier study had been amalgamated into one; and the standard rate of tax had been increased substantially. Several previously zero-rated activities had been brought into the VAT net, notably in the building industry, and in 1984 partial exemption regulations had been tightened up.

Under Keith recommendations (1983) an automatic penalty system for late returns and payments had been brought in.

There was a general impression that the business community was making increased use of computers, computer bureaux and other external advisers for VAT purposes.

Sample and Response to the Survey, by Size and Sector

The sample was selected as follows:

$$\frac{\text{Number in trade group(s)}}{\text{Total number of traders registered at 30/9/87}} \quad \text{x3,000}$$

to produce a random sample of 3,000 VAT registered traders. The questionnaire was mailed in mid-October 1987, with two reminders at fortnightly intervals, the second of which contained a further copy of the questionnaire. To safeguard confidentiality, Customs and Excise mailed the questionnaires, which were only known to the research team by code numbers (unless the respondents chose to identify themselves). However, the code number did include the sectoral classification of the respondent according to Customs and Excise records.

Overall positive usable response to the survey was low, at 680 questionnaires completed adequately for analysis. A further 11 questionnaires were returned partly completed, but without sufficient information for meaningful analysis. At least 65 sample members were ineligible for inclusion in the survey, having ceased trading or gone away from the registered premises. Thus, excluding the out of frame respondents from the sample, the positive response was 24 per cent. However, because the size and sector characteristics of the out of frame respondents were unknown, the (gross) response rate in the following tables appears as 23 per cent.

The self-classified response rates for financial services and professional services look odd compared with the Customs and Excise classifications. It may be that many respondents have divergent views from Customs and Excise on the borderline between financial and professional services. This factor may also explain the discrepancies between wholesale distribution and dealing. Otherwise the two types of response rate yield approximately similar results.

The response rates by size of firm show no consistent pattern. In previous surveys, differential response has been usual, with large firms yielding higher response rates than small firms. This survey is thus unusual in that the lowest response rate is shown by the firms with turnover in excess of £10m. However, this category is quite small, and we have no means of checking whether the real sample was exactly equivalent to the expected sample of 17.

Response to VAT 2 by Sector

Table D1

	Expected sample structure	Response	Response rate *a*	*b*
Primary sector	354	114	31	31
Manufacturing	295	52	18	21
Construction	462	111	24	24
Garage/motor trade	149	22	15	18*
Transport & communication	131	23	18	16
Wholesale distribution	165	31	19	22
Retail distribution	519	135	26	23
Dealers	60	19	32	13
Insurance, banking & finance	193	10	5	22
Prof/scientific services	201	75	37	27
Misc and public services	469	83	18	18*
Total	2,998	675#	23	23

a) Response rate according to respondents' sectoral classification.
b) Response rate according to C & E classification of respondents' trades.
* These two groups not separated in the C & E classification.
\# 5 respondents gave no information on business sector.

Response to VAT 2 by Size of Firm

Table D2

Turnover (£000s)		Population	Expected sample	Response	Response rate
Up to 20*		191,842	377	92	24.40
20-	50*	512,299	1,007	200	19.86
50-	100	319,128	627	114	18.18
100-	500	372,541	732	193	26.37
500-	1000	59,881	118	27	22.88
1,000-	10,000	61,652	121	34	28.10
10,000 or more		8,819	17	3	17.65
Total		1,526,162	2999	663#	22.11

* Note that the questionnaire asked for slightly different size bands —
(1) Up to £20,500 and (2) £20,500 to £50,000.
17 respondents provided no information on turnover.

(ii) The Calculation of Cash Flow Benefits

Payment traders benefit from holding net VAT until such time as it is paid to Customs and Excise. The value of this benefit can be considered as equal either to the interest they could gain by lending the money or alternatively (to traders in overdraft) the cost of borrowing the equivalent amount from a bank or other financial institution. Bank base rates have been used throughout this volume. Repayment traders, on the other hand, face a loss or disbenefit on money they have paid out but not yet recovered from Customs and Excise.

A particular trader's cash flow benefit (or disbenefit) from VAT has two elements: money held by the trader, owed to (or from) Customs and Excise and representing the difference between tax collected on outputs and tax paid on inputs; and the VAT component of any net credit arising from normal commercial transactions. It is convenient, initially, to examine these two elements separately.

Let us first examine the benefit to payment traders from holding VAT payable to Customs and Excise. The regulations state that VAT is payable within one month after the end of the quarter in which it becomes due. If all traders paid on the last day of the month the average credit would amount to half of the net tax due to be paid over to Customs and Excise during the quarter plus a quarter's tax due to Customs and Excise held for one month in four (the equivalent of one month's tax held throughout the year). Thus if T is the annual tax take, then the average credit is $T/8 + T/12 — 5T/24$ held throughout the year. Thus, in 1986-87 the benefit to the private sector was £7,103m., which had a value of £746m. at the bank base rate of 10.5 per cent.

Repayment traders are in effect generally lending money to Customs and Excise and generally have a return period of one month. If repayment is assumed to take one month, and R is the annual repayment, then the loss of credit each month (or the 'loan' to Customs and Excise) is $R/24 + R/12 = R/8$. Thus, in 1986-87 the detriment to the private sector was £1,584m., which had a value of £166m. at the base rate of 10.5 per cent. The net benefit to the private sector, including both payment and repayment traders, was £5,519m., which had a value of £580m. at the same rate of interest.

The presence of VAT on top of the value of goods and services bought and sold means that the value of normal commercial credit arrangements allowed by the trader is increased by the amount of the tax. A trader who orders and receives goods to the value of £10,000 plus (at 15 per cent) £1,500 VAT, but does not pay for them for 30 days is receiving a loan of £11,500 for that time. On the other hand, the vendor is making an interest-free loan of the same amount. He would, of course, be making the loan of £10,000 in any case, but the extra £1,500 is not insignificant. The cash flow benefit received will be modified by the commercial credit position of the individual firm.

(iii) Facsimile (half size) of VAT 2 Questionnaire

CONFIDENTIAL

October 1987

**Bath University
Centre for
Fiscal Studies**

University of Bath
Claverton Down
Bath BA2 7AY
Telephone Bath 826826
(STD code 0225)

Dear Sir/Madam

SURVEY OF COSTS TO BUSINESSES IN OPERATING THE TAX SYSTEM, 1987

Much concern has been expressed about the burden imposed on business by government regulations. But if the burden is to be lightened, it is necessary to find where, and on whom, it falls.

I am writing to ask you to give some of your time to complete the attached questionnaire on the cost of complying with tax regulations. Your business has been selected as part of a representative sample of VAT-registered traders, and every reply I receive will improve the reliability of the results.

Findings from this survey could influence government policy, but only if enough replies are received to carry weight. So please reply even if you think your business may not be typical of all firms. Most questions can be answered by a simple tick and very few businesses will need to answer all sections.

This is an independent study by the University of Bath. Although I have been helped in preparing the survey by the tax departments, no information has been given to me about your business; I will only know what you choose to tell me. All replies will be treated *in strict confidence,* and will not be seen by any tax official.

I would be very grateful if you would fill in the questionnaire and return it in the enclosed reply-paid envelope as soon as possible. Thanking you in advance for your help.

Yours faithfully,

Professor Cedric Sandford,
Project Director

Q1 What is your main business activity? *(Please tick one)*

Agriculture, fishing, mining or quarrying . . . . ☐

Manufacturing . . . . ☐

Construction . . . . ☐

Gas, electric or water corporation . . . . ☐

Garage/motor trade . . . . ☐

Transport or communication . . . . ☐

Wholesaling . . . . ☐

Retailing . . . . ☐

Other dealers . . . . ☐

Insurance, banking and finance . . . . ☐

Professional and scientific services . . . . ☐

Other services (e.g. entertainment, laundry, catering) . . . . ☐

Q2 When was the business first registered for VAT?   19. . . . .

Q3 On what date did your last accounting year end?

(day/month/year). . . . . /. . . . . /. . . . .

Q4 Do you employ an adviser in private practice (such as an accountant) or a specialist agency to do tax work?

Yes ☐   No ☐

(If NO, please go straight to question 8)

Questions 5, 6 and 7 ARE ONLY FOR TRADERS WHO EMPLOY AN ADVISER IN PRIVATE PRACTICE OR SPECIALIST AGENCY TO DO TAX WORK

Q5 From whom do you obtain tax advice? (please tick)
If you do not employ an adviser for VAT, PAYE, or with Corporation Tax, write NA in the appropriate column

	For VAT	For PAYE	For Corporation Tax
Accountant	☐	☐	☐
Legal practitioner	☐	☐	☐
Banker	☐	☐	☐
Bookkeeper/bookkeeping agency	☐	☐	☐
Computer Bureau	☐	☐	☐
Friend/member of family	☐	☐	☐
Other (please describe)	☐	☐	☐

. . . .
. . . .

Q6 How much were you charged for each of the following types of work by your adviser(s) in your last accounting year? Where precise figures are not available, please give an *approximate* breakdown.

If you employed more than one tax adviser, please state the occupation of, and give separate charges for, each adviser.

1st adviser: . . . . 2nd adviser: . . . .
. . . .

	1st adviser	2nd adviser
Non-tax work (e.g. audit fee):	£_____	£_____
VAT work:	£_____	£_____
PAYE & NI work:	£_____	£_____
Corporation Tax work:	£_____	£_____
Schedule D income tax/Capital Gains Tax Work:	£_____	£_____
Other tax work (such as exceptional consultancy work—please describe):	£_____	£_____

. . . .
. . . .

Total fee paid:	£_____	£_____

Q7 If you employ an adviser to do VAT work, how long have you done so?

_____years   Not applicable_____

FOR ALL TRADERS

Q8 **Approximately what proportion of your business is classed in each of the following VAT categories?** (please tick)

	Sales				*Purchases*			
	None	Up to a half	A half or more	All	None	Up to half	A Half or more	All
Standard rated:	☐	☐	☐	☐	☐	☐	☐	☐
Exports:	☐	☐	☐	☐				
Zero rated (other than exports):	☐	☐	☐	☐	☐	☐	☐	☐
Exempt from VAT:	☐	☐	☐	☐	☐	☐	☐	☐

Q9 **If you make exempt supplies, are you restricted in your deduction of input tax (i.e. are you a "partly exempt trader")?**

Yes ☐   No ☐   Not applicable ☐

Q10 **How often do you submit VAT returns?**   Monthly ☐   Quarterly ☐

Q11a **What were your VAT payments for your last year (i.e. for the last four quarterly returns)?**

Total tax due, i.e. Output Tax (total of box 3 on the year's
VAT returns):   £_____

Total tax deductible, i.e. Input Tax (total of box 6 on the year's
VAT returns):   £_____

Net VAT payment made (total of box 7 on the year's
VAT returns):   £_____

OR net VAT repayment received: £_____

Q11b **Are you a regular repayment trader?**   Yes ☐   No ☐

Q12 **Please tick the appropriate taxable turnover band for your business in your last financial year:**

Under the registration threshold (£20,500): . . . . ☐

£20,500-£50,000: . . . . ☐

£50,001-£100,000: . . . . ☐

£100,001-£250,000: . . . . ☐

£250,001-£500,000: . . . . ☐

£500,001 up to 1 million: . . . . ☐

£1 million up to £5 million: . . . . ☐

£5 million up to £10 million: . . . . ☐

If £10 million or more, ... ☐

please state approximate taxable turnover: £_____ million

Q13 Excluding bad debts, *approximately* what percentage of your purchases and sales (by value) are settled within each of the following periods after invoicing?

Settlement made   % of value of purchases   % of value of sales

For cash:

Within 1 week:

Between 1 week and 1 month:

During the second month:

During the third month:

During the fourth month:

More than 4 months
after invoicing:

Q14 Does record-keeping for VAT give you any benefits, e.g. saving money by doing more of your own accounts and giving less work to outside advisers?

Yes ☐   No ☐

If YES, please describe:

Q15 About how much time within the business was spent entirely on additional work for VAT purposes in your last year? Please *exclude* overhead costs.

Number of hours   **Hourly value of this time**

a) By the proprietor and family, or
    by partners in the business: _____ hours   £ _____ per hour

b) By directors of the company: _____ hours   £ _____ per hour

c) By qualified accounting staff
    employed in the business: _____ hours   £ _____ per hour

d) By other staff: _____ hours   £ _____ per hour

Q16a Did you incur any other costs in operating the VAT system during your last year not previously mentioned?

Yes ☐   No ☐

Q16b If YES, please describe them briefly:

Q16c And give an estimate of the costs: £_____

Q17a   Have any of the following major changes in VAT had an important effect on your business? (please tick)

Rating Changes:	Yes	No
Standard rating of building alterations	☐	☐
Standard rating of hot take-away food	☐	☐
Standard rating of newspaper advertisements	☐	☐

Other Changes:	Yes	No
Changes in official VAT notices	☐	☐
The new VAT penalty system	☐	☐
The new retail schemes	☐	☐
The cash accounting scheme	☐	☐

Changes in Exemptions and Reliefs:

	Yes	No
Withdrawal of postponed accounting for VAT on imports	☐	☐
Changes in partial exemption regulations	☐	☐
Exemption of credit card companies' transactions with their outlets	☐	☐
Extension of bad debt relief	☐	☐

Q17b   If you have ticked any YES boxes, please describe briefly:

Q18   Please indicate, by ticking the appropriate boxes, whether you have used the following sources of advice on VAT, and how helpful you found them:

	Have you used this source?		How helpful was it?				
	YES	NO	Very helpful	Helpful	Neither helpful nor unhelpful	Unhelpful	Very unhelpful
Your accountant	☐	☐					
Official VAT booklets	☐	☐					
Local VAT Office	☐	☐					
Visiting VAT Officer	☐	☐					
Other (please describe)	☐	☐					
....							

Q19   Please indicate, by ticking the appropriate boxes, your attitude to the following statements:

	Agree Strongly	Agree	Disagree	Disagree Strongly
I do not mind doing VAT work				
As it stands, VAT is unreasonably complicated				

Please add comments to your answer if you wish:

Q20 **Are you an employer with employees on PAYE?** Yes ☐ No ☐
(If NO, please go straight to Q30)

QUESTIONS 21-29 ARE ONLY FOR EMPLOYERS WITH EMPLOYEES ON PAYE

Q21 **How many people, on average, worked in the business during your last accounting year?**

(a) Partners/proprietors of an unincorporated business: ☐

(b) Full-time employees (including executive directors of a company) ☐

(c) Part-time employees (employed less than 21 hours/week): ☐

Q22 **Approximately what percentage of your wage bill is paid to**

(a) Weekly paid employees: ☐ per cent of wage bill

(b) Monthly paid employees: ☐ per cent of wage bill

(c) Other (please describe): ☐ per cent of wage bill

. . . .

Q23 **Please state the date in the month on which monthly paid staff receive their salaries:** ☐

Q24a **How much in PAYE income tax and National Insurance contributions did you pay over to the Inland Revenue in the tax year ended 5 April 1987 (before netting out Statutory Sick Pay)?**
£_____

Q24b **Of this total, how much was PAYE income tax?** £_____

Q25 **What arrangements did you have for submitting details of tax deductions to the Inland Revenue at the end of the year (please indicate if more than one arrangement was used)?**

(a) Standard documents supplied by the Inland Revenue: ☐

(b) Substitute documents approved by the Inland Revenue: ☐

(c) Magnetic tape (or other computer return) prepared within the business: ☐

(d) Magnetic tape (or other computer return) prepared by a computer bureau: ☐

Q26 **About how much time within the business was spent entirely on PAYE and NI work (over and above normal time spent on wages and payroll) in your last financial year?** Please *exclude* overhead costs.

	Number of hours	Hourly value of this time
a) By the proprietor and family, or by partners in the business:	_____ hours	£ _____ per hour
b) By directors of the company:	_____ hours	£ _____ per hour
c) By qualified accounting staff employed in the business:	_____ hours	£ _____ per hour
d) By other staff:	_____ hours	£ _____ per hour

Q27a **Did you incur any other costs in operating the PAYE system during your last financial year not previously mentioned?**　Yes ☐　　No ☐

Q27b **If YES, please describe them briefly:**

Q27c **And give an estimate of the costs:**　£_____

Q28 **The suggestion has been made that the employer's NI contribution should be replaced by a monthly percentage tax on total payroll. Assuming the amount paid would remain about the same as at present, do you think such a change would reduce your costs in administering the system?**

No ☐

Yes, marginally ☐

Yes, a lot ☐

Q29 **If you did not have to apply different rules to NI and to PAYE income tax, do you think such a change would reduce your costs in administering the system?**

No ☐

Yes, marginally ☐

Yes, a lot ☐

Q30 Is your business incorporated?   Yes ☐   No ☐
(If NO, please go straight to Q37a)

QUESTIONS 31-36 ARE ONLY FOR COMPANIES

Q31a Are you a member of a group of companies or do you have associated companies?

Yes ☐   No ☐

Q31b If YES, how much were you charged for tax administration by other companies in the group or association?   £_____

If you are a member of a group of companies, it would be helpful if you could supply figures in Q32 from both the company accounts and (on a separate sheet of paper) the consolidated accounts.

Q32 What were your last two years' figures for:

	Last year	Year before
(a) profit on ordinary activities before taxation:	£_____	£_____
(b) depreciation:	£_____	£_____
(c) corporation tax due:	£_____	£_____

Q33 About how much time within the business was spent entirely on additional work for Corporation Tax purposes in your last financial year? Please *exclude* overhead costs.

	Number of hours	Hourly value of this time
a) By directors of the company:	_____ hours	£_____ per hour
b) By qualified accounting staff employed in the business:	_____ hours	£_____ per hour
c) By other staff:	_____ hours	£_____ per hour

Q34 Please give an estimate of any *additional* costs incurred by the company in deducting basic rate income tax from interest payments (such as debenture interest) to individuals:

	Number of hours	Hourly value of this time
a) By directors of the company:	_____ hours	£ _____ per hour
b) By qualified accounting staff employed in the business:	_____ hours	£ _____ per hour
c) By other staff:	_____ hours	£ _____ per hour

Q35 Time spent on Corporation Tax may be divided into:

a) administration (such as maintaining additional ACT records)

b) planning activities (such as tax planning and other decision-making).

Of the time spent by staff on Corporation Tax work, *approximately* what percentage was devoted to *planning work*?

Company directors spent: _____ per cent of their Corporation Tax time on planning work

Qualified accountants in the firm spent: _____ per cent of their Corporation Tax time on planning work

Other office staff spent: _____ per cent of their Corporation Tax time on planning work

Q36a Did you incur any other costs in operating the Corporation Tax system during your last financial year not previously mentioned?

Yes ☐   No ☐

Q36b If YES, please describe them briefly:

Q36c And give an estimate of the costs: £_____

THIS FINAL SECTION IS FOR ALL TRADERS

Q37a How are your tax figures within the firm produced? (please tick)

If you are not involved with PAYE, or with Corporation Tax, write NA in the appropriate column

	VAT	PAYE and NI	Corporation Tax
Simple single entry hand written system with no ledgers:	☐	☐	☐
Double entry hand written system including ledgers, journals, etc.:	☐	☐	☐
Proprietary system, e.g. Simplex or Kalamazoo:	☐	☐	☐
Mechanised double entry system:	☐	☐	☐
Own computerised system:	☐	☐	☐
Data sent to computer bureau:	☐	☐	☐
Other (please describe):	☐	☐	☐

Q37b How long have you kept your records in this form?

_____years for VAT   _____years for PAYE   _____years for Corporation Tax

Q38 In the last year did you incur any costs not included above in storing records solely to meet the requirements of the tax authorities:

(a) For VAT: YES, Costs of about £_____   NO ☐

(b) For PAYE: YES, Costs of about £_____   NO ☐

(c) For Corporation Tax: YES, Costs of about £_____   NO ☐

Q39a Have you experienced any special difficulties in the last year with operating VAT, PAYE, NI, Statutory Sick Pay or Corporation Tax?

Yes ☐   No ☐

Q39b If YES, please describe them briefly:

Q40 Please add in the space below any suggestions which you would like to make for improving the administration of VAT, PAYE, NI, Statutory Sick Pay or Corporation Tax:

If you are willing to answer any queries that arise from this questionnaire, or would like a summary of the results, please state your name, address, and telephone number, and tick the appropriate boxes:

Name:

Post held:

Address:

Telephone:

I would be willing to answer some further questions ☐

I would like a summary of the results ☐

THANK YOU AGAIN FOR COMPLETING THIS QUESTIONNAIRE. WE HOPE YOU HAVE NOT FOUND IT TOO TIME—CONSUMING. PLEASE POST IT IN THE REPLY PAID ENVELOPE AS SOON AS POSSIBLE.

APPENDIX E

Compliance Costs and Efficiency Costs of Taxation

David Collard

Introduction

Though compliance costs have been researched for some time (see, for example, Sandford *et al*, 1981 and the present volume) they are relatively neglected in discussions of tax policy. For economists the efficiency cost of taxation essentially means 'deadweight loss' or 'excess burden'.

Excess burden arises because taxes cause economic agents (firms and households) to change the pattern of their economic activity even if compensated for their loss of purchasing power. Thus: if the tax on spirits is increased people will switch to wine or beer; if income tax is increased they will switch to leisure or untaxed activities; if taxes on saving are increased they will switch to current consumption. These substitutions constitute real losses over and above the tax itself and much of the economic literature, starting with Ramsey (1927), has sought for rules which minimise them.

There has been much less concern with compliance costs, i.e. the real resources used by taxpayers in complying with tax legislation. Thus firms which collect VAT or administer PAYE will have to set up office systems and accounting procedures (from scratch in the case of new taxes); similarly with individual taxpayers (e.g. under Schedule D). All such costs should be included, whether internal to the firm or external (accountants, consultants). Though they present difficult issues of definition and measurement (see Part I of this volume) they are much more tangible and direct than excess burden which is, after all, something of a theoretical construct.

This short appendix is concerned not with the details either of deadweight loss or of compliance costs but with their relative importance and with the relationship between them. A warning note: deadweight loss and compliance costs are important but should not be allowed to dominate discussions of tax policy: there are other equally important considerations such as progressivity and fairness which are, however, peripheral to the present discussion.

Average compliance costs are smaller than average excess burden.

Both compliance costs and excess burden may be measured as average costs or marginal costs with respect to output (or turnover or sales). To form a rough idea of their relative importance it is sufficient to compare average (gross) compliance costs with average excess burden as a proportion of revenue.

Following Harberger (1964) the total excess burden of a tax may be approximated by

$$1/2 \text{ x (tax rate squared) x (price elasticity)}$$

where the price elasticity is that of the compensated demand curve. The average excess burden is then given by

$$(1/2)\text{x(tax rate)x(price elasticity)}$$

and marginal excess burden by

$$(\text{tax rate})\text{x(price elasticity)}.$$

The average excess burden of a rather general tax, like a sales tax or income tax, is likely to be of the order of 8 per cent to 25 per cent (see Browning 1976, 1987). Some writers have suggested much higher figures both for average and marginal rates — see Stuart (1984) and Ballard *et al* (1985 and 1985a). The higher figures result from an upward technical adjustment, from embedding tax changes in a general equilibrium model and from using higher assumed values of the compensated elasticities. On the other hand the excess burden of taxes such as excise duties, where the compensated price elasticities tend to be rather low, will themselves be rather low. The range of elasticities now on offer has therefore become something of an embarrassment! Provisionally let us carry forward a figure of 16 per cent as typical of the estimates at the moderate end.

How does this compare with compliance costs? Most of our evidence on this comes from Sandford and his team whose earlier work, e.g. Sandford *et al* (1981, 1986) and Godwin *et al* (1983) is up-dated by and, to a large extent, replaced by the present volume. Its main results are summarised in Table 12.1 which reports compliance costs for 'broad' taxes, such as VAT and income tax, of between 3 per cent and 4 per cent of revenue and compliance costs of 2.8 per cent for central government taxes as a whole. If administrative costs (i.e. costs to the authorities) are added, the total for the system as a whole comes to about 3.9 per cent. For purposes of broad comparison, it is of interest that Browning (1976) put in a figure of 2.5 per cent for 'administrative and finance costs'.

Taking excess burden as 16 per cent and compliance costs and administrative costs between them as 4 per cent, the overall 'efficiency cost' of the system may be taken to be of the order of 20 per cent. But it should be emphasised that the figure for compliance costs and administrative costs is very much firmer than that for excess burden which remains sensitive to the theoretical assumptions made.

Marginal compliance costs may be non-trivial

The comparison so far has been between average compliance costs and average excess burden. Marginal compliance costs (i.e. those that vary with sales) are likely to be rather small because the principal compliance costs are of an 'overhead' nature. That is why they are so regressive. In considering changes in tax rates economists are normally concerned with marginal, rather than average, excess burden so we would expect the marginal burden of compliance costs also to be small. Ignoring the excess burden of taxes for the moment, in the spirit of our previous formulae marginal compliance cost would simply be

(tax rate) x (compliance cost rate) x (price elasticity)

(The tax rate appears in the formula even though we are ignoring tax because compliance costs are measured as a proportion of tax). Our average compliance cost rate was of the order of 4 per cent. The marginal rate is very much smaller than this and may in many situations be very near to zero. The marginal excess burden of compliance costs would therefore appear to be very small.

However, we do need to take into account interactions between tax rates and compliance costs. The interaction has the effect of increasing marginal excess burden over and above what it would have been with either compliance costs or excess burden alone. It turns out that the marginal excess burden of compliance costs has to be weighted by a term depending on the square of the tax rate. This will be small but not trivial. Similarly the marginal excess burden of the tax rate has to be weighted by a term depending on the square of the compliance cost rate. This latter will in general be trivial and may be disregarded.

To summarise this section, the marginal excess burden of compliance costs may be non-trivial simply because existing tax rates are non-trivial. To illustrate, if the tax rate is 0.3, the price elasticity unity and the compliance cost rate 0.02, the marginal excess burden may be of the order of 9 per cent.

Marginal compliance costs (slightly) affect the Ramsey type rule

The usual Ramsey type rule is that taxes should be inversely proportional to compensated price elasticities. If marginal compliance costs are to be treated as pseudo-taxes then the modified rule has to be written

$$\frac{t(1+c)}{p} \propto \frac{1}{e}$$

where t is the marginal tax rate, c the marginal compliance cost rate, p price and e the price elasticity. Thus, other things being equal, high marginal compliance costs in any one product should be offset by a lower rate of tax. *(NB. This rule only takes into account the excess burden aspect of compliance costs).* It is probably a coincidence that the principal excise duties, which carry very high rates of tax, have very low compliance costs relative to revenue. This is precisely what one might have expected if the authorities had been following a modified Ramsey rule.

Compliance costs reinforce the case for simple structures

So far it appears that both average and marginal compliance costs are smaller than the corresponding excess burdens. But compliance costs are much more relevant to the structure of taxation than they are to changes in tax rates.

It is interesting that Sandford's results reinforce the case against complex structures. Ballard *et al* (1957), using a computable general equilibrium model, attempted to estimate the efficiency gains of a U.S. adoption of VAT. They considered three types of VAT: a differentiated rate VAT, a flat rate VAT and a progressive expenditure tax. Each 'reform' was accompanied by a reduction in the marginal income tax rate so as to maintain revenue neutrality. For what they call the 'multiplicative' case (all marginal tax rates scaled down proportionally) and with 'Cobb-Douglas' commodity demands, the efficiency gains were calculated to be 0.3 per cent, 0.7 per cent and 0.6 per cent respectively. Thus the biggest efficiency gains came from the flat rate VAT: 'we find that rate differentiation leads to substantive reductions (of the order of 25-40 per cent) in the welfare gains from adoption of a VAT'.

So the compliance cost and deadweight loss considerations point in the same direction, away from complexity towards more simple structures. One has to remember, however, that complexity may be justified on other grounds — for example, vertical equity. Ballard *et al* incorporate a specific social welfare function into their model so that the greater our preference for equality, the more progressive — and hence more complex — will be the structure of VAT.

It is quite possible therefore that while Ramsey type rules point in the direction of complex tax structures, with rates of tax being very different depending upon elasticities, the presence of compliance costs point in the direction of simplification.

A principle for structural reform

Setting the important questions of equity and merit goods to one side, Sandford's work, together with the admittedly not very satisfactory literature on the size of the excess burden, suggests a rather simple rule for structural tax reform. The rule would be to minimise total efficiency losses (including compliance costs, administrative costs and excess burden) subject to a revenue constraint. If adopted it would accomplish much of what is sought in the policy section of Chapter XIII (though without actual compensation taking place: this is a distributional matter). A further attraction of the rule is that it could take into account the costs of disruption and learning as emphasised in Sandford's VAT studies.

Conclusion

Compliance costs may no longer be treated as the Cinderella of the costs of taxation. Marginal compliance costs are probably small in relation to taxes but their marginal excess burden is non-trivial. More importantly, average compliance costs should play a very important part in determining the structure of taxation.

BIBLIOGRAPHY

Ballard, C. L., J. B. Shoven and J. Whalley, 'General Equilibrium Computations of the Marginal Welfare Costs of Taxes in the United States', *American Economic Review*, Vol. 75, No. 128-138, March 1985.

Ballard, C. L., D. Fullerton, J. B. Shoven and J. Whalley, *A General Equilibrium Model for Tax Policy Evaluation, NBER*, Chicago, 1985.

Ballard, C. L., J. K. Scholz and J. B. Shoven, 'The Value-Added Tax: A General Equilibrium Look at its Efficiency and Incidence', in M. Feldstein (ed) *The Effects of Taxation on Capital Accumulation, NBER*, Chicago, 1987, pp.445-480.

Bannock, G. and H. Albach, *The Compliance Costs of VAT for Smaller Firms in Britain and Germany*, Graham Bannock and Partners, London, 1987.

Barker, P. A., 'Value Added Tax, the cost to the businessman', *Journal of Accountancy*, September 1972, pp.75-9.

Bond Stephen, Michael Devereux and Michael Saunders, *North Sea Taxation for the 1990s*, Institute for Fiscal Studies, December 1987.

Browning, E. K., 'The Marginal Cost of Public Funds', *JPE*, Vol. 84, No. 2, April 1976.

Browning, E. K., 'On the Marginal Welfare Cost of Taxation', *American Economic Review*, Vol. 77, No. 1, March 1987, pp.11-23.

Bryden, M. H., *The Cost of Tax Compliance*, Canadian Tax Foundation Paper, No. 25, 1961.

Commission of the European Communities, *Completion of the Internal Market: Approximation of Indirect Tax Rates and Harmonisation of Indirect Tax Structure. Global Communication from the Commission*, Cm.(87) 320, 1987.

Consultative Committee of Accountancy Bodies, *Annual Accounting for VAT*, London, 1977.

Dean, P. N. *Some Aspects of Tax Operating Costs with Particular Reference to Personal Taxation in the United Kingdom*, unpublished Ph.D. thesis, p.198, University of Bath, 1975.

Department of the Environment, *Papers and Proceedings of a Conference on Research into the Value of Time - Time Research Note 16*, July 1970.

Department of Trade and Industry, *Burdens on Business*, HMSO, 1985.

Earp, J. H., J. H. Ebden and R. D. Hall, *The Solent Travel Study: Research into the Value of Time*, Transportation Research Group, University of Southampton, 1974.

Gammie, M., *The Enactment of Tax Legislation: An Analysis of the Consultative Process and the Finance Acts 1979 to 1987*.

Godwin, M. R., 'VAT - Compliance Costs to the Independent Retailer', *Accountancy*, September 1976, pp.48-60.

Godwin, M. R., P. J. W. Hardwick and C. T. Sandford, 'PAYE: Costs v Benefits', *Accountancy*, November 1983.

Godwin, M. R. and C. T. Sandford, 'Simplifying VAT for Small Traders', *Accounting and Business Research*, No. 52, Autumn, 1983.

Goode, R. 'Some Economic Aspects of Tax Administration', International Monetary Fund, *Staff Papers*, 28 (June 1981), pp.249-74.

Haig, R. M., 'The Cost to Business Concerns of Compliance with Tax Laws', *Management Review*, 1935, pp.232-333.

Harberger, A. L., 'Taxation, Resource Allocation and Welfare', in *The Role of Direct and Indirect Taxes in the Federal Revenue System*, *NBER*, 1964.

Hensher, D. A. and T. P. Troung, 'Valuation of Travel Time Savings', *Journal of Transport Economics and Policy*, September 1985.

IFA (International Fiscal Association), *Cahiers de droit fiscal international*, administrative and compliance costs of taxation, Kluwer, The Netherlands, 1989.

Institute for Fiscal Studies, *Reforming Capital Gains Tax*, an Interim Report of the Capital Taxes Group, I.F.S., 1988.

Internal Revenue Service, Annual Report 1985, Washington.

James, S, A. Lewis and F. Allison, *The Comprehensibility of Taxation*, Avebury, 1987.

Johnston, K. S., *Corporations' Federal Income Tax Compliance Costs*, Ohio State University Bureau of Business Research, Monograph No. 10, 1961.

Keith Report, *Report of the Committee on Enforcement Powers of the Revenue Departments*, Vol. 2, 27.5.1., 1983.

Kempton, P. A., *The Control of Tax Evasion - Questions for Practising Accountants*, unpublished Ph.D. thesis, University of Bath, 1988.

Leonard, R. J., *PAYE/PSRI and Operating Costs*, unpublished M.Litt thesis, Trinity College, University of Dublin, 1986.

Little, Arthur D., Corporation, *Development of Methodology for Estimating Taxpayer Paperwork Burden. Final Report to Department of Treasury*, IRS, Washington, D.C., 1988.

Martin, J. W., 'Costs of Tax Administration, Examples of Compliance Expenses', *Bulletin of National Tax Association*, April 1944, pp.194-205.

Mathes, S. M. and G. C. Thompson, 'The high cost of compliance', *Business Record*, August 1959, pp.383-8.

Matthews, M. P., *A measurement of the cost of collecting sales tax monies in selected retail stores*, Bureau of Economic & Business Research, University of Utah, 1956.

May, J. B. and G. C. Thompson, 'The tax on taxes', *Conference Board Business Record*, April 1950, pp.130-3.

Meade, J. E., *The Structure and Reform of Direct Taxation*, Report of a Committee chaired by Professor J. E. Meade, Institute for Fiscal Studies, George Allen and Unwin, 1978.

Mill, J. S. (1948), *Principles of Political Economy*, Book V, Chapter 2, University of Toronto Press/Routledge and Kegan Paul, edition, 1965, p.805.

Muller, F. J., *The Burden of Compliance*, Seattle Bureau of Business Research, 1963.

National Economic Development Office, *Distilling - Scotch Whisky*, 1978.

Neeld, A. K., *Report of the Committee on Cost of Taxpayer Compliance and Administration*, Proceedings of the 55th Annual Meeting of the National Tax Association (USA), 1962, pp.286-312.

Niehus, R. J., 'German Added Value Tax - 2 Years After', *Taxes*, September 1969, pp.554-55.

O'Brien, D. P., Editorial Introduction to J. R. McCulloch, *Treatise on Taxation*, Scottish Academic Press, Edinburgh, 1975.

OECD, *Income Tax Collection Lags*, OECD, Paris, 1983.

OECD, *Taxing Consumption*, Paris, 1988.

Oster, C. V., *State Retail Sales Taxation*, Ohio State University Bureau of Business Research, 1957.

Oster, C. V. and A. D. Lynn, 'Compliance Costs and the Ohio Axle Mile Tax', *National Tax Journal*, Vol. 8, No. 2, 1953, pp.209-214.

Parker, S. K., 'Compliance costs of the Value Added Tax', *Taxes*, June 1976, pp.369-80.

Peat Marwick, *A Comparative Analysis of Sales Tax Compliance Costs for Retail Businesses*, mimeo, Small Business Administration, Washington, 1985.

Pitt, M. M. and J. R. Slemrod, *The Compliance Cost of Itemising Deductions: Evidence from Individual Tax Returns*, mimeo, 1988.

Ramsey, F. P., 'A Contribution to the Theory of Taxation', *Economic Journal*, 37, March 1927.

Report by the Commissioners of H. M. Customs and Excise, *Review of Value Added Tax*, Cmnd. 7415, 1978.

Robinson, A. and C. T. Sandford, *Tax Policy-Making in the United Kingdom*, Heinemann Educational Books, 1983.

Robinson, A. and C. T. Sandford, 'Financial Management Initiative: Has it a Future?', *Accountancy*, October 1987.

Robson, M. H. and R. K. Timmins, *Discretionary Trusts - A Research Study*, Inland Revenue, 1988.

Sandford, C. T., *Hidden Costs of Taxation*, Institute for Fiscal Studies, publication No. 6, July 1973.

Sandford, C. T., 'The Costs of Paying Tax', *Accountancy*, June 1986.

Sandford, C. T. and P. N. Dean, 'Accountants and the Tax System', *Accounting and Business Research*, No. 5, Winter 1971/2, pp.3-37.

Sandford, C. T., M. R. Godwin, P. J. W. Hardwick and M. I. Butterworth, *Costs and Benefits of VAT*, Heinemann Educational Books, 1981.

Sandford, C. T. and A. Lewis, 'The Poor Have Tax Problems Too' *Accountancy*, April 1986.

Sandford, C. T., and O. Morrissey, *The Irish Wealth Tax: A Case Study in Economics and Politics*, The Economic and Social Research Institute, Dublin, 1985.

Slemrod, J. R. and N. Sorum, 'The Compliance Cost of U.S. Individual Income Tax System', *National Tax Journal*, Vol. 37, No. 4, 1984, pp.461-474.

Smith, Adam (1776), *Inquiry into the Nature and Causes of the Wealth of Nations*, Book 5, Chapter 2, Part 2 'Of Taxes', Everyman Edition, pp.307-309, 1977.

Snijder, M. A., *De Invloed van de Fiscus op het Midden-En Kleinbedrijf*, Fed-Oeventer, Amsterdam, 1981.

Strümpel, B., 'The Disguised Tax Burden', *National Tax Journal*, Vol. 19, No. 1, 1966, pp.70-77.

Stuart, C., 'Welfare Costs per Dollar of Additional Tax Revenue in the United States', *American Economic Review*, Vol. 74, No. 3, June 1984, pp.352-362.

Tipping, D. G., 'Time Savings in Transport Studies', *Economic Journal*, December 1968.

Vaillancourt, F., 'The Compliance Costs of Taxes on Businesses and Individuals: a Review of the Evidence', *Public Finance*, No.3, 1987, pp.395-417.

Vaillancourt, F., *The Administrative and Compliance Costs of Personal Income Taxes and Payroll Taxes, Canada, 1986*, Canadian Tax Foundation, 1989.

Wabe, J. A., 'A Study of House Prices as a Means of Establishing the Value of Journey Time, The Rate of Time Preference and the Valuation of Some Aspects of Environment in the London Metropolitan Region', *Applied Economics*, Vol. 3, 1971.

White Paper, *Lifting the Burden*, Cmnd. 9571, HMSO, 1985.

White Paper, *Building Business Not Barriers*, Cmnd. 9794, 1986.

White Paper, *Releasing Enterprise*, Cmnd. 512, 1988.

Wicks, J. H., 'Taxpayer Compliance Costs from the Montana Personal Income Tax', *Montana Business Quarterly*, Fall, 1965, pp.36-42, 1965.

Wicks, J. H., 'Taxpayer Compliance Costs from Personal Income Taxation', *Iowa Business Digest*, 1966, pp.16-21.

Wicks, J. H. and N. M. Killworth, 'Administrative and Compliance Costs of State and Local Taxes', *National Tax Journal*, Vol. 20, No. 33, 1967, pp.309-315.

Yocum, J. C., *Retailers' Costs of Sales Tax Collection in Ohio*, Ohio State University Bureau of Business Research, 1961.

129th Report of the Board of Inland Revenue, Cm. 230, HMSO, December 1987.

78th Report of the Commissioners of Customs and Excise, Cm. 234, HMSO, November 1987.

INDEX